C-4919   CAREER EXAMINATION SERIES

This is your
PASSBOOK for...

Electrical Craft Helper

Test Preparation Study Guide
Questions & Answers

COPYRIGHT NOTICE

This book is SOLELY intended for, is sold ONLY to, and its use is RESTRICTED to individual, bona fide applicants or candidates who qualify by virtue of having seriously filed applications for appropriate license, certificate, professional and/or promotional advancement, higher school matriculation, scholarship, or other legitimate requirements of education and/or governmental authorities.

This book is NOT intended for use, class instruction, tutoring, training, duplication, copying, reprinting, excerption, or adaptation, etc., by:

1) Other publishers
2) Proprietors and/or Instructors of "Coaching" and/or Preparatory Courses
3) Personnel and/or Training Divisions of commercial, industrial, and governmental organizations
4) Schools, colleges, or universities and/or their departments and staffs, including teachers and other personnel
5) Testing Agencies or Bureaus
6) Study groups which seek by the purchase of a single volume to copy and/or duplicate and/or adapt this material for use by the group as a whole without having purchased individual volumes for each of the members of the group
7) Et al.

Such persons would be in violation of appropriate Federal and State statutes.

PROVISION OF LICENSING AGREEMENTS – Recognized educational, commercial, industrial, and governmental institutions and organizations, and others legitimately engaged in educational pursuits, including training, testing, and measurement activities, may address request for a licensing agreement to the copyright owners, who will determine whether, and under what conditions, including fees and charges, the materials in this book may be used them. In other words, a licensing facility exists for the legitimate use of the material in this book on other than an individual basis. However, it is asseverated and affirmed here that the material in this book CANNOT be used without the receipt of the express permission of such a licensing agreement from the Publishers. Inquiries re licensing should be addressed to the company, attention rights and permissions department.

All rights reserved, including the right of reproduction in whole or in part, in any form or by any means, electronic or mechanical, including photocopying, recording, or by any information storage and retrieval system, without permission in writing from the Publisher.

Copyright © 2024 by
National Learning Corporation

212 Michael Drive, Syosset, NY 11791
(516) 921-8888 • www.passbooks.com
E-mail: info@passbooks.com

PUBLISHED IN THE UNITED STATES OF AMERICA

PASSBOOK® SERIES

THE *PASSBOOK® SERIES* has been created to prepare applicants and candidates for the ultimate academic battlefield – the examination room.

At some time in our lives, each and every one of us may be required to take an examination – for validation, matriculation, admission, qualification, registration, certification, or licensure.

Based on the assumption that every applicant or candidate has met the basic formal educational standards, has taken the required number of courses, and read the necessary texts, the *PASSBOOK® SERIES* furnishes the one special preparation which may assure passing with confidence, instead of failing with insecurity. Examination questions – together with answers – are furnished as the basic vehicle for study so that the mysteries of the examination and its compounding difficulties may be eliminated or diminished by a sure method.

This book is meant to help you pass your examination provided that you qualify and are serious in your objective.

The entire field is reviewed through the huge store of content information which is succinctly presented through a provocative and challenging approach – the question-and-answer method.

A climate of success is established by furnishing the correct answers at the end of each test.

You soon learn to recognize types of questions, forms of questions, and patterns of questioning. You may even begin to anticipate expected outcomes.

You perceive that many questions are repeated or adapted so that you can gain acute insights, which may enable you to score many sure points.

You learn how to confront new questions, or types of questions, and to attack them confidently and work out the correct answers.

You note objectives and emphases, and recognize pitfalls and dangers, so that you may make positive educational adjustments.

Moreover, you are kept fully informed in relation to new concepts, methods, practices, and directions in the field.

You discover that you are actually taking the examination all the time: you are preparing for the examination by "taking" an examination, not by reading extraneous and/or supererogatory textbooks.

In short, this PASSBOOK®, used directedly, should be an important factor in helping you to pass your test.

ELECTRICAL CRAFT HELPER

DUTIES:
An Electrical Craft Helper assists a skilled journey-level worker engaged in one of the electrical trades. Typical assignments involve the maintenance and construction of electrical systems for buildings and facilities; installation and maintenance of overhead or underground power distribution systems; or shop repair activities. Apprentice training opportunities leading to craft positions are available in some departments.

SUBJECT OF EXAMINATION:
The written test will consist of multiple-choice questions by which the candidates may be examined for knowledge of: basic safety principles and procedures, including proper lifting techniques and procedures for working safely in confined spaces; specialized safety equipment to be used for various jobs; common types of knots sufficient to secure items to the hand line used in underground and overhead work; types and uses of conducting and insulating materials; basic arithmetic, including addition, subtraction, multiplication, and division; motor vehicle rules for operation of vehicles; mechanical theory and applications sufficient to perform basic and semi-skilled assembly and reassembly work of electrical and lighting equipment; basic physics principles as they apply to mechanical devices and tools sufficient to operate these devices efficiently; and the ability to perform vehicle safety inspections, including checking fuel levels, brake operation, and vehicle lights; use and care for hand and power tools; measure materials such as cables and wires; read, comprehend, and interpret test equipment, and written work instructions and documents, including plates on transformers and cables, safety precaution labels and street maps; alphabetize materials for filing sufficient to organize documents and materials; deal cooperatively, tactfully, and effectively with co-workers, supervisors and others; and other necessary skills, knowledge and abilities.

HOW TO TAKE A TEST

I. YOU MUST PASS AN EXAMINATION

A. WHAT EVERY CANDIDATE SHOULD KNOW

Examination applicants often ask us for help in preparing for the written test. What can I study in advance? What kinds of questions will be asked? How will the test be given? How will the papers be graded?

As an applicant for a civil service examination, you may be wondering about some of these things. Our purpose here is to suggest effective methods of advance study and to describe civil service examinations.

Your chances for success on this examination can be increased if you know how to prepare. Those "pre-examination jitters" can be reduced if you know what to expect. You can even experience an adventure in good citizenship if you know why civil service exams are given.

B. WHY ARE CIVIL SERVICE EXAMINATIONS GIVEN?

Civil service examinations are important to you in two ways. As a citizen, you want public jobs filled by employees who know how to do their work. As a job seeker, you want a fair chance to compete for that job on an equal footing with other candidates. The best-known means of accomplishing this two-fold goal is the competitive examination.

Exams are widely publicized throughout the nation. They may be administered for jobs in federal, state, city, municipal, town or village governments or agencies.

Any citizen may apply, with some limitations, such as the age or residence of applicants. Your experience and education may be reviewed to see whether you meet the requirements for the particular examination. When these requirements exist, they are reasonable and applied consistently to all applicants. Thus, a competitive examination may cause you some uneasiness now, but it is your privilege and safeguard.

C. HOW ARE CIVIL SERVICE EXAMS DEVELOPED?

Examinations are carefully written by trained technicians who are specialists in the field known as "psychological measurement," in consultation with recognized authorities in the field of work that the test will cover. These experts recommend the subject matter areas or skills to be tested; only those knowledges or skills important to your success on the job are included. The most reliable books and source materials available are used as references. Together, the experts and technicians judge the difficulty level of the questions.

Test technicians know how to phrase questions so that the problem is clearly stated. Their ethics do not permit "trick" or "catch" questions. Questions may have been tried out on sample groups, or subjected to statistical analysis, to determine their usefulness.

Written tests are often used in combination with performance tests, ratings of training and experience, and oral interviews. All of these measures combine to form the best-known means of finding the right person for the right job.

II. HOW TO PASS THE WRITTEN TEST

A. NATURE OF THE EXAMINATION

To prepare intelligently for civil service examinations, you should know how they differ from school examinations you have taken. In school you were assigned certain definite pages to read or subjects to cover. The examination questions were quite detailed and usually emphasized memory. Civil service exams, on the other hand, try to discover your present ability to perform the duties of a position, plus your potentiality to learn these duties. In other words, a civil service exam attempts to predict how successful you will be. Questions cover such a broad area that they cannot be as minute and detailed as school exam questions.

In the public service similar kinds of work, or positions, are grouped together in one "class." This process is known as *position-classification*. All the positions in a class are paid according to the salary range for that class. One class title covers all of these positions, and they are all tested by the same examination.

B. FOUR BASIC STEPS

1) Study the announcement

How, then, can you know what subjects to study? Our best answer is: "Learn as much as possible about the class of positions for which you've applied." The exam will test the knowledge, skills and abilities needed to do the work.

Your most valuable source of information about the position you want is the official exam announcement. This announcement lists the training and experience qualifications. Check these standards and apply only if you come reasonably close to meeting them.

The brief description of the position in the examination announcement offers some clues to the subjects which will be tested. Think about the job itself. Review the duties in your mind. Can you perform them, or are there some in which you are rusty? Fill in the blank spots in your preparation.

Many jurisdictions preview the written test in the exam announcement by including a section called "Knowledge and Abilities Required," "Scope of the Examination," or some similar heading. Here you will find out specifically what fields will be tested.

2) Review your own background

Once you learn in general what the position is all about, and what you need to know to do the work, ask yourself which subjects you already know fairly well and which need improvement. You may wonder whether to concentrate on improving your strong areas or on building some background in your fields of weakness. When the announcement has specified "some knowledge" or "considerable knowledge," or has used adjectives like "beginning principles of…" or "advanced … methods," you can get a clue as to the number and difficulty of questions to be asked in any given field. More questions, and hence broader coverage, would be included for those subjects which are more important in the work. Now weigh your strengths and weaknesses against the job requirements and prepare accordingly.

3) Determine the level of the position

Another way to tell how intensively you should prepare is to understand the level of the job for which you are applying. Is it the entering level? In other words, is this the position in which beginners in a field of work are hired? Or is it an intermediate or advanced level? Sometimes this is indicated by such words as "Junior" or "Senior" in the class title. Other jurisdictions use Roman numerals to designate the level – Clerk I, Clerk II, for example. The word "Supervisor" sometimes appears in the title. If the level is not indicated by the title, check the description of duties. Will you be working under very close supervision, or will you have responsibility for independent decisions in this work?

4) Choose appropriate study materials

Now that you know the subjects to be examined and the relative amount of each subject to be covered, you can choose suitable study materials. For beginning level jobs, or even advanced ones, if you have a pronounced weakness in some aspect of your training, read a modern, standard textbook in that field. Be sure it is up to date and has general coverage. Such books are normally available at your library, and the librarian will be glad to help you locate one. For entry-level positions, questions of appropriate difficulty are chosen – neither highly advanced questions, nor those too simple. Such questions require careful thought but not advanced training.

If the position for which you are applying is technical or advanced, you will read more advanced, specialized material. If you are already familiar with the basic principles of your field, elementary textbooks would waste your time. Concentrate on advanced textbooks and technical periodicals. Think through the concepts and review difficult problems in your field.

These are all general sources. You can get more ideas on your own initiative, following these leads. For example, training manuals and publications of the government agency which employs workers in your field can be useful, particularly for technical and professional positions. A letter or visit to the government department involved may result in more specific study suggestions, and certainly will provide you with a more definite idea of the exact nature of the position you are seeking.

III. KINDS OF TESTS

Tests are used for purposes other than measuring knowledge and ability to perform specified duties. For some positions, it is equally important to test ability to make adjustments to new situations or to profit from training. In others, basic mental abilities not dependent on information are essential. Questions which test these things may not appear as pertinent to the duties of the position as those which test for knowledge and information. Yet they are often highly important parts of a fair examination. For very general questions, it is almost impossible to help you direct your study efforts. What we can do is to point out some of the more common of these general abilities needed in public service positions and describe some typical questions.

1) General information

Broad, general information has been found useful for predicting job success in some kinds of work. This is tested in a variety of ways, from vocabulary lists to questions about current events. Basic background in some field of work, such as sociology or economics, may be sampled in a group of questions. Often these are principles which have become familiar to most persons through exposure rather than through formal training. It is difficult to advise you how to study for these questions; being alert to the world around you is our best suggestion.

2) Verbal ability

An example of an ability needed in many positions is verbal or language ability. Verbal ability is, in brief, the ability to use and understand words. Vocabulary and grammar tests are typical measures of this ability. Reading comprehension or paragraph interpretation questions are common in many kinds of civil service tests. You are given a paragraph of written material and asked to find its central meaning.

3) Numerical ability

Number skills can be tested by the familiar arithmetic problem, by checking paired lists of numbers to see which are alike and which are different, or by interpreting charts and graphs. In the latter test, a graph may be printed in the test booklet which you are asked to use as the basis for answering questions.

4) Observation

A popular test for law-enforcement positions is the observation test. A picture is shown to you for several minutes, then taken away. Questions about the picture test your ability to observe both details and larger elements.

5) Following directions

In many positions in the public service, the employee must be able to carry out written instructions dependably and accurately. You may be given a chart with several columns, each column listing a variety of information. The questions require you to carry out directions involving the information given in the chart.

6) Skills and aptitudes

Performance tests effectively measure some manual skills and aptitudes. When the skill is one in which you are trained, such as typing or shorthand, you can practice. These tests are often very much like those given in business school or high school courses. For many of the other skills and aptitudes, however, no short-time preparation can be made. Skills and abilities natural to you or that you have developed throughout your lifetime are being tested.

Many of the general questions just described provide all the data needed to answer the questions and ask you to use your reasoning ability to find the answers. Your best preparation for these tests, as well as for tests of facts and ideas, is to be at your physical and mental best. You, no doubt, have your own methods of getting into an exam-taking mood and keeping "in shape." The next section lists some ideas on this subject.

IV. KINDS OF QUESTIONS

Only rarely is the "essay" question, which you answer in narrative form, used in civil service tests. Civil service tests are usually of the short-answer type. Full instructions for answering these questions will be given to you at the examination. But in case this is your first experience with short-answer questions and separate answer sheets, here is what you need to know:

1) Multiple-choice Questions

Most popular of the short-answer questions is the "multiple choice" or "best answer" question. It can be used, for example, to test for factual knowledge, ability to solve problems or judgment in meeting situations found at work.

A multiple-choice question is normally one of three types—
- It can begin with an incomplete statement followed by several possible endings. You are to find the one ending which *best* completes the statement, although some of the others may not be entirely wrong.
- It can also be a complete statement in the form of a question which is answered by choosing one of the statements listed.

- It can be in the form of a problem – again you select the best answer.

Here is an example of a multiple-choice question with a discussion which should give you some clues as to the method for choosing the right answer:

When an employee has a complaint about his assignment, the action which will *best* help him overcome his difficulty is to
  A. discuss his difficulty with his coworkers
  B. take the problem to the head of the organization
  C. take the problem to the person who gave him the assignment
  D. say nothing to anyone about his complaint

In answering this question, you should study each of the choices to find which is best. Consider choice "A" – Certainly an employee may discuss his complaint with fellow employees, but no change or improvement can result, and the complaint remains unresolved. Choice "B" is a poor choice since the head of the organization probably does not know what assignment you have been given, and taking your problem to him is known as "going over the head" of the supervisor. The supervisor, or person who made the assignment, is the person who can clarify it or correct any injustice. Choice "C" is, therefore, correct. To say nothing, as in choice "D," is unwise. Supervisors have and interest in knowing the problems employees are facing, and the employee is seeking a solution to his problem.

2) True/False Questions

The "true/false" or "right/wrong" form of question is sometimes used. Here a complete statement is given. Your job is to decide whether the statement is right or wrong.

SAMPLE: A roaming cell-phone call to a nearby city costs less than a non-roaming call to a distant city.

This statement is wrong, or false, since roaming calls are more expensive.

This is not a complete list of all possible question forms, although most of the others are variations of these common types. You will always get complete directions for answering questions. Be sure you understand *how* to mark your answers – ask questions until you do.

V. RECORDING YOUR ANSWERS

Computer terminals are used more and more today for many different kinds of exams.

For an examination with very few applicants, you may be told to record your answers in the test booklet itself. Separate answer sheets are much more common. If this separate answer sheet is to be scored by machine – and this is often the case – it is highly important that you mark your answers correctly in order to get credit.

An electronic scoring machine is often used in civil service offices because of the speed with which papers can be scored. Machine-scored answer sheets must be marked with a pencil, which will be given to you. This pencil has a high graphite content which responds to the electronic scoring machine. As a matter of fact, stray dots may register as answers, so do not let your pencil rest on the answer sheet while you are pondering the correct answer. Also, if your pencil lead breaks or is otherwise defective, ask for another.

Since the answer sheet will be dropped in a slot in the scoring machine, be careful not to bend the corners or get the paper crumpled.

The answer sheet normally has five vertical columns of numbers, with 30 numbers to a column. These numbers correspond to the question numbers in your test booklet. After each number, going across the page are four or five pairs of dotted lines. These short dotted lines have small letters or numbers above them. The first two pairs may also have a "T" or "F" above the letters. This indicates that the first two pairs only are to be used if the questions are of the true-false type. If the questions are multiple choice, disregard the "T" and "F" and pay attention only to the small letters or numbers.

Answer your questions in the manner of the sample that follows:

32. The largest city in the United States is
    A. Washington, D.C.
    B. New York City
    C. Chicago
    D. Detroit
    E. San Francisco

1) Choose the answer you think is best. (New York City is the largest, so "B" is correct.)
2) Find the row of dotted lines numbered the same as the question you are answering. (Find row number 32)
3) Find the pair of dotted lines corresponding to the answer. (Find the pair of lines under the mark "B.")
4) Make a solid black mark between the dotted lines.

VI. BEFORE THE TEST

Common sense will help you find procedures to follow to get ready for an examination. Too many of us, however, overlook these sensible measures. Indeed, nervousness and fatigue have been found to be the most serious reasons why applicants fail to do their best on civil service tests. Here is a list of reminders:

- Begin your preparation early – Don't wait until the last minute to go scurrying around for books and materials or to find out what the position is all about.
- Prepare continuously – An hour a night for a week is better than an all-night cram session. This has been definitely established. What is more, a night a week for a month will return better dividends than crowding your study into a shorter period of time.
- Locate the place of the exam – You have been sent a notice telling you when and where to report for the examination. If the location is in a different town or otherwise unfamiliar to you, it would be well to inquire the best route and learn something about the building.
- Relax the night before the test – Allow your mind to rest. Do not study at all that night. Plan some mild recreation or diversion; then go to bed early and get a good night's sleep.
- Get up early enough to make a leisurely trip to the place for the test – This way unforeseen events, traffic snarls, unfamiliar buildings, etc. will not upset you.
- Dress comfortably – A written test is not a fashion show. You will be known by number and not by name, so wear something comfortable.

- Leave excess paraphernalia at home – Shopping bags and odd bundles will get in your way. You need bring only the items mentioned in the official notice you received; usually everything you need is provided. Do not bring reference books to the exam. They will only confuse those last minutes and be taken away from you when in the test room.
- Arrive somewhat ahead of time – If because of transportation schedules you must get there very early, bring a newspaper or magazine to take your mind off yourself while waiting.
- Locate the examination room – When you have found the proper room, you will be directed to the seat or part of the room where you will sit. Sometimes you are given a sheet of instructions to read while you are waiting. Do not fill out any forms until you are told to do so; just read them and be prepared.
- Relax and prepare to listen to the instructions
- If you have any physical problem that may keep you from doing your best, be sure to tell the test administrator. If you are sick or in poor health, you really cannot do your best on the exam. You can come back and take the test some other time.

VII. AT THE TEST

The day of the test is here and you have the test booklet in your hand. The temptation to get going is very strong. Caution! There is more to success than knowing the right answers. You must know how to identify your papers and understand variations in the type of short-answer question used in this particular examination. Follow these suggestions for maximum results from your efforts:

1) Cooperate with the monitor

The test administrator has a duty to create a situation in which you can be as much at ease as possible. He will give instructions, tell you when to begin, check to see that you are marking your answer sheet correctly, and so on. He is not there to guard you, although he will see that your competitors do not take unfair advantage. He wants to help you do your best.

2) Listen to all instructions

Don't jump the gun! Wait until you understand all directions. In most civil service tests you get more time than you need to answer the questions. So don't be in a hurry. Read each word of instructions until you clearly understand the meaning. Study the examples, listen to all announcements and follow directions. Ask questions if you do not understand what to do.

3) Identify your papers

Civil service exams are usually identified by number only. You will be assigned a number; you must not put your name on your test papers. Be sure to copy your number correctly. Since more than one exam may be given, copy your exact examination title.

4) Plan your time

Unless you are told that a test is a "speed" or "rate of work" test, speed itself is usually not important. Time enough to answer all the questions will be provided, but this does not mean that you have all day. An overall time limit has been set. Divide the total time (in minutes) by the number of questions to determine the approximate time you have for each question.

5) Do not linger over difficult questions

If you come across a difficult question, mark it with a paper clip (useful to have along) and come back to it when you have been through the booklet. One caution if you do this – be sure to skip a number on your answer sheet as well. Check often to be sure that you have not lost your place and that you are marking in the row numbered the same as the question you are answering.

6) Read the questions

Be sure you know what the question asks! Many capable people are unsuccessful because they failed to *read* the questions correctly.

7) Answer all questions

Unless you have been instructed that a penalty will be deducted for incorrect answers, it is better to guess than to omit a question.

8) Speed tests

It is often better NOT to guess on speed tests. It has been found that on timed tests people are tempted to spend the last few seconds before time is called in marking answers at random – without even reading them – in the hope of picking up a few extra points. To discourage this practice, the instructions may warn you that your score will be "corrected" for guessing. That is, a penalty will be applied. The incorrect answers will be deducted from the correct ones, or some other penalty formula will be used.

9) Review your answers

If you finish before time is called, go back to the questions you guessed or omitted to give them further thought. Review other answers if you have time.

10) Return your test materials

If you are ready to leave before others have finished or time is called, take ALL your materials to the monitor and leave quietly. Never take any test material with you. The monitor can discover whose papers are not complete, and taking a test booklet may be grounds for disqualification.

VIII. EXAMINATION TECHNIQUES

1) Read the general instructions carefully. These are usually printed on the first page of the exam booklet. As a rule, these instructions refer to the timing of the examination; the fact that you should not start work until the signal and must stop work at a signal, etc. If there are any *special* instructions, such as a choice of questions to be answered, make sure that you note this instruction carefully.

2) When you are ready to start work on the examination, that is as soon as the signal has been given, read the instructions to each question booklet, underline any key words or phrases, such as *least, best, outline, describe* and the like. In this way you will tend to answer as requested rather than discover on reviewing your paper that you *listed without describing*, that you selected the *worst* choice rather than the *best* choice, etc.

3) If the examination is of the objective or multiple-choice type – that is, each question will also give a series of possible answers: A, B, C or D, and you are called upon to select the best answer and write the letter next to that answer on your answer paper – it is advisable to start answering each question in turn. There may be anywhere from 50 to 100 such questions in the three or four hours allotted and you can see how much time would be taken if you read through all the questions before beginning to answer any. Furthermore, if you come across a question or group of questions which you know would be difficult to answer, it would undoubtedly affect your handling of all the other questions.

4) If the examination is of the essay type and contains but a few questions, it is a moot point as to whether you should read all the questions before starting to answer any one. Of course, if you are given a choice – say five out of seven and the like – then it is essential to read all the questions so you can eliminate the two that are most difficult. If, however, you are asked to answer all the questions, there may be danger in trying to answer the easiest one first because you may find that you will spend too much time on it. The best technique is to answer the first question, then proceed to the second, etc.

5) Time your answers. Before the exam begins, write down the time it started, then add the time allowed for the examination and write down the time it must be completed, then divide the time available somewhat as follows:
    - If 3-1/2 hours are allowed, that would be 210 minutes. If you have 80 objective-type questions, that would be an average of 2-1/2 minutes per question. Allow yourself no more than 2 minutes per question, or a total of 160 minutes, which will permit about 50 minutes to review.
    - If for the time allotment of 210 minutes there are 7 essay questions to answer, that would average about 30 minutes a question. Give yourself only 25 minutes per question so that you have about 35 minutes to review.

6) The most important instruction is to *read each question* and make sure you know what is wanted. The second most important instruction is to *time yourself properly* so that you answer every question. The third most important instruction is to *answer every question*. Guess if you have to but include something for each question. Remember that you will receive no credit for a blank and will probably receive some credit if you write something in answer to an essay question. If you guess a letter – say "B" for a multiple-choice question – you may have guessed right. If you leave a blank as an answer to a multiple-choice question, the examiners may respect your feelings but it will not add a point to your score. Some exams may penalize you for wrong answers, so in such cases *only*, you may not want to guess unless you have some basis for your answer.

7) Suggestions
    a. Objective-type questions
        1. Examine the question booklet for proper sequence of pages and questions
        2. Read all instructions carefully
        3. Skip any question which seems too difficult; return to it after all other questions have been answered
        4. Apportion your time properly; do not spend too much time on any single question or group of questions

5. Note and underline key words – *all, most, fewest, least, best, worst, same, opposite,* etc.
6. Pay particular attention to negatives
7. Note unusual option, e.g., unduly long, short, complex, different or similar in content to the body of the question
8. Observe the use of "hedging" words – *probably, may, most likely,* etc.
9. Make sure that your answer is put next to the same number as the question
10. Do not second-guess unless you have good reason to believe the second answer is definitely more correct
11. Cross out original answer if you decide another answer is more accurate; do not erase until you are ready to hand your paper in
12. Answer all questions; guess unless instructed otherwise
13. Leave time for review

  b. Essay questions
1. Read each question carefully
2. Determine exactly what is wanted. Underline key words or phrases.
3. Decide on outline or paragraph answer
4. Include many different points and elements unless asked to develop any one or two points or elements
5. Show impartiality by giving pros and cons unless directed to select one side only
6. Make and write down any assumptions you find necessary to answer the questions
7. Watch your English, grammar, punctuation and choice of words
8. Time your answers; don't crowd material

8) Answering the essay question

Most essay questions can be answered by framing the specific response around several key words or ideas. Here are a few such key words or ideas:

M's: manpower, materials, methods, money, management
P's: purpose, program, policy, plan, procedure, practice, problems, pitfalls, personnel, public relations

  a. Six basic steps in handling problems:
1. Preliminary plan and background development
2. Collect information, data and facts
3. Analyze and interpret information, data and facts
4. Analyze and develop solutions as well as make recommendations
5. Prepare report and sell recommendations
6. Install recommendations and follow up effectiveness

  b. Pitfalls to avoid
1. *Taking things for granted* – A statement of the situation does not necessarily imply that each of the elements is necessarily true; for example, a complaint may be invalid and biased so that all that can be taken for granted is that a complaint has been registered

2. *Considering only one side of a situation* – Wherever possible, indicate several alternatives and then point out the reasons you selected the best one
3. *Failing to indicate follow up* – Whenever your answer indicates action on your part, make certain that you will take proper follow-up action to see how successful your recommendations, procedures or actions turn out to be
4. *Taking too long in answering any single question* – Remember to time your answers properly

IX. AFTER THE TEST

Scoring procedures differ in detail among civil service jurisdictions although the general principles are the same. Whether the papers are hand-scored or graded by machine we have described, they are nearly always graded by number. That is, the person who marks the paper knows only the number – never the name – of the applicant. Not until all the papers have been graded will they be matched with names. If other tests, such as training and experience or oral interview ratings have been given, scores will be combined. Different parts of the examination usually have different weights. For example, the written test might count 60 percent of the final grade, and a rating of training and experience 40 percent. In many jurisdictions, veterans will have a certain number of points added to their grades.

After the final grade has been determined, the names are placed in grade order and an eligible list is established. There are various methods for resolving ties between those who get the same final grade – probably the most common is to place first the name of the person whose application was received first. Job offers are made from the eligible list in the order the names appear on it. You will be notified of your grade and your rank as soon as all these computations have been made. This will be done as rapidly as possible.

People who are found to meet the requirements in the announcement are called "eligibles." Their names are put on a list of eligible candidates. An eligible's chances of getting a job depend on how high he stands on this list and how fast agencies are filling jobs from the list.

When a job is to be filled from a list of eligibles, the agency asks for the names of people on the list of eligibles for that job. When the civil service commission receives this request, it sends to the agency the names of the three people highest on this list. Or, if the job to be filled has specialized requirements, the office sends the agency the names of the top three persons who meet these requirements from the general list.

The appointing officer makes a choice from among the three people whose names were sent to him. If the selected person accepts the appointment, the names of the others are put back on the list to be considered for future openings.

That is the rule in hiring from all kinds of eligible lists, whether they are for typist, carpenter, chemist, or something else. For every vacancy, the appointing officer has his choice of any one of the top three eligibles on the list. This explains why the person whose name is on top of the list sometimes does not get an appointment when some of the persons lower on the list do. If the appointing officer chooses the second or third eligible, the No. 1 eligible does not get a job at once, but stays on the list until he is appointed or the list is terminated.

X. HOW TO PASS THE INTERVIEW TEST

The examination for which you applied requires an oral interview test. You have already taken the written test and you are now being called for the interview test – the final part of the formal examination.

You may think that it is not possible to prepare for an interview test and that there are no procedures to follow during an interview. Our purpose is to point out some things you can do in advance that will help you and some good rules to follow and pitfalls to avoid while you are being interviewed.

What is an interview supposed to test?

The written examination is designed to test the technical knowledge and competence of the candidate; the oral is designed to evaluate intangible qualities, not readily measured otherwise, and to establish a list showing the relative fitness of each candidate – as measured against his competitors – for the position sought. Scoring is not on the basis of "right" and "wrong," but on a sliding scale of values ranging from "not passable" to "outstanding." As a matter of fact, it is possible to achieve a relatively low score without a single "incorrect" answer because of evident weakness in the qualities being measured.

Occasionally, an examination may consist entirely of an oral test – either an individual or a group oral. In such cases, information is sought concerning the technical knowledges and abilities of the candidate, since there has been no written examination for this purpose. More commonly, however, an oral test is used to supplement a written examination.

Who conducts interviews?

The composition of oral boards varies among different jurisdictions. In nearly all, a representative of the personnel department serves as chairman. One of the members of the board may be a representative of the department in which the candidate would work. In some cases, "outside experts" are used, and, frequently, a businessman or some other representative of the general public is asked to serve. Labor and management or other special groups may be represented. The aim is to secure the services of experts in the appropriate field.

However the board is composed, it is a good idea (and not at all improper or unethical) to ascertain in advance of the interview who the members are and what groups they represent. When you are introduced to them, you will have some idea of their backgrounds and interests, and at least you will not stutter and stammer over their names.

What should be done before the interview?

While knowledge about the board members is useful and takes some of the surprise element out of the interview, there is other preparation which is more substantive. It *is* possible to prepare for an oral interview – in several ways:

1) Keep a copy of your application and review it carefully before the interview

This may be the only document before the oral board, and the starting point of the interview. Know what education and experience you have listed there, and the sequence and dates of all of it. Sometimes the board will ask you to review the highlights of your experience for them; you should not have to hem and haw doing it.

2) Study the class specification and the examination announcement

Usually, the oral board has one or both of these to guide them. The qualities, characteristics or knowledges required by the position sought are stated in these documents. They offer valuable clues as to the nature of the oral interview. For example, if the job involves supervisory responsibilities, the announcement will usually indicate that knowledge of modern supervisory methods and the qualifications of the candidate as a supervisor will be tested. If so, you can expect such questions, frequently in the form of a hypothetical situation which you are expected to solve. NEVER go into an oral without knowledge of the duties and responsibilities of the job you seek.

3) Think through each qualification required

Try to visualize the kind of questions you would ask if you were a board member. How well could you answer them? Try especially to appraise your own knowledge and background in each area, *measured against the job sought*, and identify any areas in which you are weak. Be critical and realistic – do not flatter yourself.

4) Do some general reading in areas in which you feel you may be weak

For example, if the job involves supervision and your past experience has NOT, some general reading in supervisory methods and practices, particularly in the field of human relations, might be useful. Do NOT study agency procedures or detailed manuals. The oral board will be testing your understanding and capacity, not your memory.

5) Get a good night's sleep and watch your general health and mental attitude

You will want a clear head at the interview. Take care of a cold or any other minor ailment, and of course, no hangovers.

What should be done on the day of the interview?

Now comes the day of the interview itself. Give yourself plenty of time to get there. Plan to arrive somewhat ahead of the scheduled time, particularly if your appointment is in the fore part of the day. If a previous candidate fails to appear, the board might be ready for you a bit early. By early afternoon an oral board is almost invariably behind schedule if there are many candidates, and you may have to wait. Take along a book or magazine to read, or your application to review, but leave any extraneous material in the waiting room when you go in for your interview. In any event, relax and compose yourself.

The matter of dress is important. The board is forming impressions about you – from your experience, your manners, your attitude, and your appearance. Give your personal appearance careful attention. Dress your best, but not your flashiest. Choose conservative, appropriate clothing, and be sure it is immaculate. This is a business interview, and your appearance should indicate that you regard it as such. Besides, being well groomed and properly dressed will help boost your confidence.

Sooner or later, someone will call your name and escort you into the interview room. *This is it.* From here on you are on your own. It is too late for any more preparation. But remember, you asked for this opportunity to prove your fitness, and you are here because your request was granted.

What happens when you go in?

The usual sequence of events will be as follows: The clerk (who is often the board stenographer) will introduce you to the chairman of the oral board, who will introduce you to the other members of the board. Acknowledge the introductions before you sit down. Do not be surprised if you find a microphone facing you or a stenotypist sitting by. Oral interviews are usually recorded in the event of an appeal or other review.

Usually the chairman of the board will open the interview by reviewing the highlights of your education and work experience from your application – primarily for the benefit of the other members of the board, as well as to get the material into the record. Do not interrupt or comment unless there is an error or significant misinterpretation; if that is the case, do not hesitate. But do not quibble about insignificant matters. Also, he will usually ask you some question about your education, experience or your present job – partly to get you to start talking and to establish the interviewing "rapport." He may start the actual questioning, or turn it over to one of the other members. Frequently, each member undertakes the questioning on a particular area, one in which he is perhaps most competent, so you can expect each member to participate in the examination. Because time is limited, you may also expect some rather abrupt switches in the direction the questioning takes, so do not be upset by it. Normally, a board member will not pursue a single line of questioning unless he discovers a particular strength or weakness.

After each member has participated, the chairman will usually ask whether any member has any further questions, then will ask you if you have anything you wish to add. Unless you are expecting this question, it may floor you. Worse, it may start you off on an extended, extemporaneous speech. The board is not usually seeking more information. The question is principally to offer you a last opportunity to present further qualifications or to indicate that you have nothing to add. So, if you feel that a significant qualification or characteristic has been overlooked, it is proper to point it out in a sentence or so. Do not compliment the board on the thoroughness of their examination – they have been sketchy, and you know it. If you wish, merely say, "No thank you, I have nothing further to add." This is a point where you can "talk yourself out" of a good impression or fail to present an important bit of information. Remember, *you close the interview yourself*.

The chairman will then say, "That is all, Mr. _____, thank you." Do not be startled; the interview is over, and quicker than you think. Thank him, gather your belongings and take your leave. Save your sigh of relief for the other side of the door.

How to put your best foot forward

Throughout this entire process, you may feel that the board individually and collectively is trying to pierce your defenses, seek out your hidden weaknesses and embarrass and confuse you. Actually, this is not true. They are obliged to make an appraisal of your qualifications for the job you are seeking, and they want to see you in your best light. Remember, they must interview all candidates and a non-cooperative candidate may become a failure in spite of their best efforts to bring out his qualifications. Here are 15 suggestions that will help you:

1) **Be natural – Keep your attitude confident, not cocky**

If you are not confident that you can do the job, do not expect the board to be. Do not apologize for your weaknesses, try to bring out your strong points. The board is interested in a positive, not negative, presentation. Cockiness will antagonize any board member and make him wonder if you are covering up a weakness by a false show of strength.

2) **Get comfortable, but don't lounge or sprawl**

Sit erectly but not stiffly. A careless posture may lead the board to conclude that you are careless in other things, or at least that you are not impressed by the importance of the occasion. Either conclusion is natural, even if incorrect. Do not fuss with your clothing, a pencil or an ashtray. Your hands may occasionally be useful to emphasize a point; do not let them become a point of distraction.

3) **Do not wisecrack or make small talk**

This is a serious situation, and your attitude should show that you consider it as such. Further, the time of the board is limited – they do not want to waste it, and neither should you.

4) Do not exaggerate your experience or abilities

In the first place, from information in the application or other interviews and sources, the board may know more about you than you think. Secondly, you probably will not get away with it. An experienced board is rather adept at spotting such a situation, so do not take the chance.

5) If you know a board member, do not make a point of it, yet do not hide it

Certainly you are not fooling him, and probably not the other members of the board. Do not try to take advantage of your acquaintanceship – it will probably do you little good.

6) Do not dominate the interview

Let the board do that. They will give you the clues – do not assume that you have to do all the talking. Realize that the board has a number of questions to ask you, and do not try to take up all the interview time by showing off your extensive knowledge of the answer to the first one.

7) Be attentive

You only have 20 minutes or so, and you should keep your attention at its sharpest throughout. When a member is addressing a problem or question to you, give him your undivided attention. Address your reply principally to him, but do not exclude the other board members.

8) Do not interrupt

A board member may be stating a problem for you to analyze. He will ask you a question when the time comes. Let him state the problem, and wait for the question.

9) Make sure you understand the question

Do not try to answer until you are sure what the question is. If it is not clear, restate it in your own words or ask the board member to clarify it for you. However, do not haggle about minor elements.

10) Reply promptly but not hastily

A common entry on oral board rating sheets is "candidate responded readily," or "candidate hesitated in replies." Respond as promptly and quickly as you can, but do not jump to a hasty, ill-considered answer.

11) Do not be peremptory in your answers

A brief answer is proper – but do not fire your answer back. That is a losing game from your point of view. The board member can probably ask questions much faster than you can answer them.

12) Do not try to create the answer you think the board member wants

He is interested in what kind of mind you have and how it works – not in playing games. Furthermore, he can usually spot this practice and will actually grade you down on it.

13) Do not switch sides in your reply merely to agree with a board member

Frequently, a member will take a contrary position merely to draw you out and to see if you are willing and able to defend your point of view. Do not start a debate, yet do not surrender a good position. If a position is worth taking, it is worth defending.

14) Do not be afraid to admit an error in judgment if you are shown to be wrong

The board knows that you are forced to reply without any opportunity for careful consideration. Your answer may be demonstrably wrong. If so, admit it and get on with the interview.

15) Do not dwell at length on your present job

The opening question may relate to your present assignment. Answer the question but do not go into an extended discussion. You are being examined for a *new* job, not your present one. As a matter of fact, try to phrase ALL your answers in terms of the job for which you are being examined.

Basis of Rating

Probably you will forget most of these "do's" and "don'ts" when you walk into the oral interview room. Even remembering them all will not ensure you a passing grade. Perhaps you did not have the qualifications in the first place. But remembering them will help you to put your best foot forward, without treading on the toes of the board members.

Rumor and popular opinion to the contrary notwithstanding, an oral board wants you to make the best appearance possible. They know you are under pressure – but they also want to see how you respond to it as a guide to what your reaction would be under the pressures of the job you seek. They will be influenced by the degree of poise you display, the personal traits you show and the manner in which you respond.

ABOUT THIS BOOK

This book contains tests divided into Examination Sections. Go through each test, answering every question in the margin. We have also attached a sample answer sheet at the back of the book that can be removed and used. At the end of each test look at the answer key and check your answers. On the ones you got wrong, look at the right answer choice and learn. Do not fill in the answers first. Do not memorize the questions and answers, but understand the answer and principles involved. On your test, the questions will likely be different from the samples. Questions are changed and new ones added. If you understand these past questions you should have success with any changes that arise. Tests may consist of several types of questions. We have additional books on each subject should more study be advisable or necessary for you. Finally, the more you study, the better prepared you will be. This book is intended to be the last thing you study before you walk into the examination room. Prior study of relevant texts is also recommended. NLC publishes some of these in our Fundamental Series. Knowledge and good sense are important factors in passing your exam. Good luck also helps. So now study this Passbook, absorb the material contained within and take that knowledge into the examination. Then do your best to pass that exam.

EXAMINATION SECTION

EXAMINATION SECTION
TEST 1

DIRECTIONS: Each question or incomplete statement is followed by several suggested answers or completions. Select the one that BEST answers the question or completes the statement. *PRINT THE LETTER OF THE CORRECT ANSWER IN THE SPACE AT THE RIGHT.*

1. Soft iron is MOST suitable for use in a 1.____

    A. permanent magnet
    B. natural magnet
    C. temporary magnet
    D. magneto

2. Static electricity is MOST often produced by 2.____

    A. pressure   B. magnetism   C. heat   D. friction

3. A fundamental law of electricity is that the current in a circuit is 3.____

    A. inversely proportional to the voltage
    B. equal to the voltage
    C. directly proportional to the resistance
    D. directly proportional to the voltage

4. A substance is classed as a magnet if it has 4.____

    A. the ability to conduct lines of force
    B. the property of high permeability
    C. the property of magnetism
    D. a high percentage of iron in its composition

5. If a compass is placed at the center of a bar magnet, the compass needle 5.____

    A. *points* to the geographic south pole
    B. *points* to the geographic north pole
    C. *alines* itself parallel to the bar
    D. *alines* itself perpendicular to the bar

6. When electricity is produced by heat in an iron-and-copper thermocouple, electrons move from 6.____

    A. north to south
    B. the hot junction, through the copper, across the cold junction to the iron, and then to the hot junction
    C. the hot junction, through the iron, across the cold junction to the copper, and then return through the copper to the hot junction
    D. east to west

7. The four factors affecting the resistance of a wire are its 7.____

    A. length, material, diameter, and temperature
    B. size, length, material, and insulation
    C. length, size, relative resistance, and material
    D. size, insulation, relative resistance, and material

8. Electricity in a battery is produced by

   A. chemical action
   B. chemical reaction
   C. a chemical acting upon metallic plates
   D. all of the above

9. Resistance is ALWAYS measured in

   A. coulombs   B. henrys   C. ohms   D. megohms

10. The magnetic pole that points northward on a compass

    A. is called the north pole
    B. is actually a south magnetic pole
    C. points to the north magnetic pole of the earth
    D. indicates the direction of the north geographic pole

11. Of the six methods of producing a voltage, which is the LEAST used?

    A. Chemical action   B. Heat
    C. Friction   D. Pressure

12. As the temperature of carbon is increased, its resistance will

    A. increase   B. decrease
    C. remain constant   D. double

13. Around a magnet, the external lines of force

    A. leave the magnet from the north pole and enter the south pole
    B. often cross one another
    C. leave the magnet from the south pole and enter the north pole
    D. may be broken by a piece of iron shielding

14. When a voltage is applied to a conductor, free electrons

    A. are forced into the nucleus of their atom
    B. are impelled along the conductor
    C. unite with protons
    D. cease their movement

15. When the molecules of a substance are altered, the action is referred to as

    A. thermal   B. photoelectric
    C. electrical   D. chemical

16. When matter is separated into individual atoms, it

    A. has undergone a physical change only
    B. has been reduced to its basic chemicals
    C. retains its original characteristics
    D. has been reduced to its basic elements

17. MOST permanent magnets and all electro-magnets are 17.____

    A. classed as natural magnets
    B. manufactured in various shapes from lodestone
    C. classed as artificial magnets
    D. manufactured in various shapes from magnetite

18. When a conductor moves across a magnetic field, 18.____

    A. a voltage is induced in the conductor
    B. a current is induced in the conductor
    C. both current and voltage are induced in the conductor
    D. neither a voltage nor a current is induced

19. The nucleus of an atom contains 19.____

    A. electrons and neutrons
    B. protons and neutrons
    C. protons and electrons
    D. protons, electrons, and neutrons

20. An alnico artificial magnet is composed of 20.____

    A. magnetite, steel, and nickel
    B. cobalt, nickel, and varnish
    C. aluminum, copper, and cobalt
    D. aluminum, nickel, and cobalt

21. A material that acts as an insulator for magnetic flux is 21.____

    A. glass   B. aluminum
    C. soft iron   D. unknown today

22. The force acting through the distance between two dissimilarly-charged bodies 22.____

    A. is a chemical force
    B. is referred to as a magnetic field
    C. constitutes a flow of ions
    D. is referred to as an electrostatic field

23. An atom that has lost or gained electrons 23.____

    A. is negatively charged   B. has a positive charge
    C. is said to be ionized   D. becomes electrically neutral

24. Which of the following is considered to be the BEST conductor? 24.____

    A. Zinc   B. Copper   C. Aluminum   D. Silver

25. As the temperature increases, the resistance of most conductors also increases. 25.____
    A conductor that is an EXCEPTION to this is

    A. aluminum   B. carbon   C. copper   D. brass

KEY (CORRECT ANSWERS)

1. C
2. D
3. D
4. C
5. C

6. B
7. A
8. D
9. C
10. A

11. C
12. B
13. A
14. B
15. D

16. D
17. C
18. A
19. B
20. D

21. D
22. D
23. C
24. D
25. B

TEST 2

DIRECTIONS: Each question or incomplete statement is followed by several suggested answers or completions. Select the one that BEST answers the question or completes the statement. *PRINT THE LETTER OF THE CORRECT ANSWER IN THE SPACE AT THE RIGHT.*

1. The dry cell battery is a _____ cell.   1.____
   A. secondary   B. polarized   C. primary   D. voltaic

2. The electrolyte of a lead-acid wet cell is   2.____
   A. sal ammoniac   B. manganese dioxide
   C. sulfuric acid   D. distilled water

3. A battery which can be restored after discharge is a _____ cell.   3.____
   A. primary   B. galvanic   C. dry   D. secondary

4. Lead-acid battery plates are held together by a   4.____
   A. glass wool mat   B. wood separator
   C. grid work   D. hard rubber tube

5. When mixing electrolyte, ALWAYS pour   5.____
   A. water into acid
   B. acid into water
   C. both acid and water into vat simultaneously
   D. first acid, then water into vat

6. When charging a battery, the electrolyte should NEVER exceed a temperature of   6.____
   A. 125° F.   B. 113° F.   C. 80° F.   D. 40° F.

7. The plates of a lead-acid battery are made of   7.____
   A. lead and lead dioxide   B. lead and lead oxide
   C. silver and peroxide   D. lead and lead peroxide

8. A battery is receiving a normal charge. It begins to gas freely.
   The charging current should   8.____
   A. be increased
   B. be decreased
   C. be cut off and the battery allowed to cool
   D. remain the same

9. A hydrometer reading is 1.265 at 92° F.
   The CORRECTED reading is   9.____
   A. 1.229   B. 1.261   C. 1.269   D. 1.301

10. In the nickel-cadmium battery, KOH is   10.____
    A. the positive plate   B. the negative plate
    C. the electrolyte   D. none of the above

11. When sulfuric acid, H_2SO_4, and water, H_2O, are mixed together, they form a

    A. gas
    B. compound
    C. mixture
    D. hydrogen solution

12. How many No. 6 dry cells are required to supply power to a load requiring 6 volts if the cells are connected in series?

    A. Two　　B. Four　　C. Five　　D. Six

13. The ordinary 6-volt lead-acid storage battery consists of how many cells?

    A. Two　　B. Three　　C. Four　　D. Six

14. A fully-charged aircraft battery has a specific gravity reading of

    A. 1.210 to 1.220
    B. 1.250 to 1.265
    C. 1.285 to 1.300
    D. 1.300 to 1.320

15. What is the ampere-hour rating of a storage battery that can deliver 20 amperes continuously for 10 hours?
    _____ ampere-hour.

    A. 20　　B. 40　　C. 200　　D. 400

16. The normal cell voltage of a fully-charged nickel-cadmium battery is _____ volts.

    A. 2.0　　B. 1.5　　C. 1.4　　D. 1.0

17. The electrolyte in a mercury cell is

    A. sulfuric acid
    B. KOH
    C. potassium hydroxide, zincate, and mercury
    D. potassium hydroxide, water, and zincate

18. Concentrated sulfuric acid has a specific gravity of

    A. 1.285　　B. 1.300　　C. 1.830　　D. 2.400

19. The number of negative plates in a lead-acid cell is ALWAYS _____ of positive plates.

    A. one greater than the number
    B. equal to the number
    C. one less than the number
    D. double the number

20. A lead-acid battery is considered fully charged when the specific gravity readings of all cells taken at half-hour intervals show no change for _____ hour(s).

    A. four　　B. three　　C. two　　D. one

KEY (CORRECT ANSWERS)

1.	C	11.	C
2.	C	12.	B
3.	D	13.	B
4.	C	14.	C
5.	B	15.	C
6.	A	16.	C
7.	D	17.	D
8.	B	18.	C
9.	C	19.	A
10.	C	20.	A

TEST 3

DIRECTIONS: Each question or incomplete statement is followed by several suggested answers or completions. Select the one that BEST answers the question or completes the statement. *PRINT THE LETTER OF THE CORRECT ANSWER IN THE SPACE AT THE RIGHT.*

1. In which direction does current flow in an electrical circuit?

    A. - to + externally, + to - internally
    B. + to - externally, + to - internally
    C. - to + externally, - to + internally
    D. + to - externally, - to + internally

2. Given the formula $P = E^2/R$, solve for E.

    A. $E = \sqrt{ER}$ B. $E = \sqrt{PR}$ C. $E = IR$ D. $E = \sqrt{P/R}$

3. Resistance in the power formula equals

    A. $R = \sqrt{I/P}$ B. $R = E/I$ C. $R = \sqrt{P \times I}$ D. $R = E^2/P$

4. One joule is equal to

    A. 1 watt second
    B. 10 watt seconds
    C. 1 watt minute
    D. 10 watt minutes

5. A lamp has a source voltage of 110 v. and a current of 0.9 amps. What is the resistance of the lamp?

    A. 12.22 Ω B. 122.2 Ω C. 0.008 Ω D. 0.08 Ω

6. In accordance with Ohm's law, the relationship between current and voltage in a simple circuit is that the

    A. current varies inversely with the resistance if the voltage is held constant
    B. voltage varies as the square of the applied e.m.f.
    C. current varies directly with the applied voltage if the resistance is held constant
    D. voltage varies inversely as the current if the resistance is held constant

7. The current needed to operate a soldering iron which has a rating of 600 watts at 110 volts is

    A. 0.182 a. B. 5.455 a. C. 18.200 a. D. 66.000 a.

8. In electrical circuits, the time rate of doing work is expressed in

    A. volts B. amperes C. watts D. ohms

9. If the resistance is held constant, what is the relationship between power and voltage in a simple circuit?

    A. Resistance must be varied to show a true relationship.
    B. Power will vary as the square of the applied voltage.
    C. Voltage will vary inversely proportional to power.
    D. Power will vary directly with voltage.

10. How many watts are there in 1 horsepower?

    A. 500   B. 640   C. 746   D. 1,000

11. What formula is used to find watt-hours?

    A. E x T   B. E x I x T   C. E x I x $\sqrt{\theta}$ D. E x I²

12. What is the resistance of the circuit shown at the right?

    A. 4.8 Ω
    B. 12.0 Ω
    C. 48 Ω
    D. 120 Ω

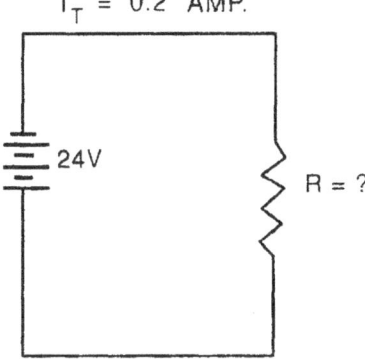

13. In the figure at the right, solve for I_T.

    A. 0.5 a.
    B. 1 a.
    C. 13 a.
    D. 169 a.

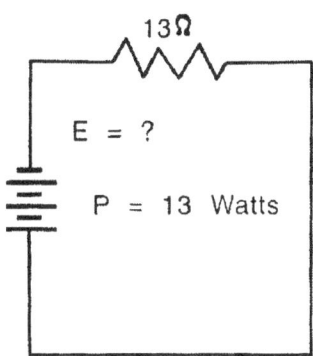

14. A simple circuit consists of one power source,

    A. and one power consuming device
    B. one power consuming device, and connecting wiring
    C. protective device, and control device
    D. one power consuming device, and protective device

15. The device used in circuits to prevent damage from overloads is called a

    A. fuse   B. switch   C. resistor   D. connector

16. What happens in a series circuit when the voltage remains constant and the resistance increases?
Current

    A. increases   B. decreases
    C. remains the same   D. increases by the square

17. Other factors remaining constant, what would be the effect on the current flow in a given circuit if the applied potential were doubled?
It would

   A. double
   B. remain the same
   C. be divided by two
   D. be divided by four

18. Which of the following procedures can be used to calculate the resistance of a load?

   A. *Multiply* the voltage across the load by the square of the current through the load
   B. *Divide* the current through the load by the voltage across the load
   C. *Multiply* the voltage across the load by the current through the load
   D. *Divide* the voltage across the load by the current through the load

19. A cockpit light operates from a 24-volt d-c supply and uses 72 watts of power. The current flowing through the bulb is _____ amps.

   A. 0.33   B. 3   C. 600   D. 1,728

20. If the resistance is held constant, what happens to power if the current is doubled?
Power is

   A. doubled
   B. multiplied by 4
   C. halved
   D. divided by 4

KEY (CORRECT ANSWERS)

1. A
2. B
3. D
4. A
5. B

6. C
7. B
8. C
9. B
10. C

11. B
12. D
13. B
14. B
15. A

16. B
17. A
18. D
19. B
20. B

TEST 4

DIRECTIONS: Each question or incomplete statement is followed by several suggested answers or completions. Select the one that BEST answers the question or completes the statement. *PRINT THE LETTER OF THE CORRECT ANSWER IN THE SPACE AT THE RIGHT.*

1. If a circuit is constructed so as to allow the electrons to follow only one possible path, the circuit is called a(n) _____ circuit.

    A. series-parallel
    B. incomplete
    C. series
    D. parallel

    1._____

2. According to Kirchhoff's Law of Voltages, the algebraic sum of all the voltages in a series circuit is equal to

    A. zero
    B. source voltage
    C. total voltage drop
    D. the sum of the IR drop of the circuit

    2._____

3. In a series circuit, the total current is

    A. always equal to the source voltage
    B. determined by the load only
    C. the same through all parts of the circuit
    D. equal to zero at the positive side of the source

    3._____

4.

    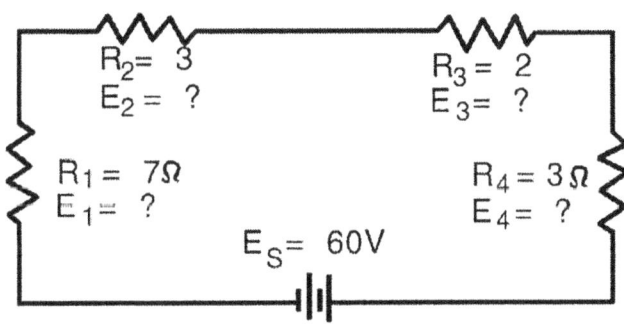

    The CORRECT voltage equation for the circuit above is

    A. $E_S + E_1 + E_2 + E_3 + E_4 = 0$
    B. $E_S - E_1 - E_2 - E_3 - E_4 = 0$
    C. $E_S = -E_1 - E_2 - E_3 - E_4$
    D. $-E_S = E_1 + E_2 + E_3 + E_4$

    4._____

5. Referring to the circuit shown in Question 4 above, after expressing the voltage drops around the circuit in terms of current and resistance and the given values of source voltage, the equation becomes

    A. $-60 - 7I - 3I - 2I - 3I = 0$
    B. $-60 + 7I + 3I + 2I + 3I = 0$
    C. $60 - 7I - 3I - 2I - 3I = 0$
    D. $60 + 7I + 3I + 2I + 3I = 0$

    5._____

11

6. By the use of the correct equation, it is found that the current (I) in the circuit shown in Question 4 is of positive value. This indicates that the

    A. assumed direction of current flow is correct
    B. assumed direction of current flow is incorrect
    C. problem is not solvable
    D. battery polarity should be reversed

6._____

7.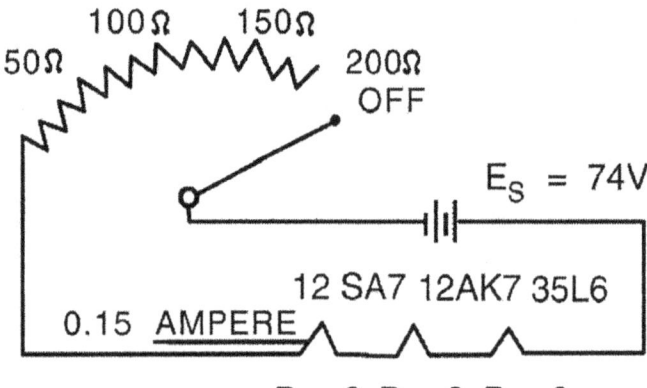

$R_1 = ?$ $R_2 = ?$ $R_3 = ?$

In what position would the variable rheostat in the circuit above be placed in order that the filaments of the tubes operate properly with a current flow of 0.15 ampere?
_____ position.

    A. 50 Ω   B. 100 Ω   C. 150 Ω   D. 200 Ω

7._____

8. The power absorbed by the variable rheostat in the circuit used in Question 7 above, when placed in its proper operating position, would be _____ watts.

    A. 112.50   B. 2.25   C. 337.50   D. 450.00

8._____

9.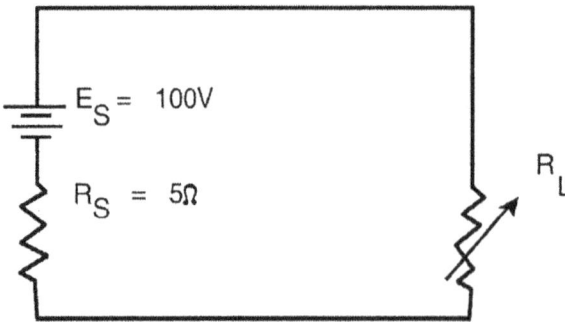

In the circuit above, maximum power would be transferred from the source to the load (R_L) if R_L were set at _____ ohms.

    A. 2   B. 5   C. 12   D. 24

9._____

10.

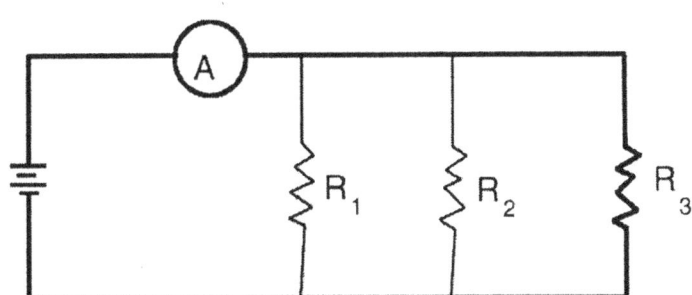

In the circuit above, if an additional resistor were placed in parallel to R_3, the ammeter reading would

- A. increase
- B. decrease
- C. remain the same
- D. drop to zero

11. In a parallel circuit containing a 4-ohm, 5-ohm, and 6-ohm resistor, the current flow is

- A. *highest* through the 4-ohm resistor
- B. *lowest* through the 4-ohm resistor
- C. *highest* through the 6-ohm resistor
- D. *equal* through all three resistors

12. Three resistors of 2, 4, and 6 ohms, respectively, are connected in parallel. Which resistor would absorb the GREATEST power?

- A. The 2-ohm resistor
- B. The 4-ohm resistor
- C. The 6-ohm resistor
- D. It will be the same for all resistors

13. If three lamps are connected in parallel with a power source, connecting a fourth lamp in parallel will

- A. decrease E_T
- B. decrease I_T
- C. increase E_T
- D. increase I_T

14.

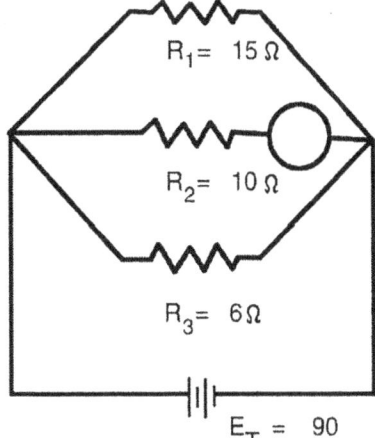

What is the current flow through the ammeter in the circuit shown above?
_____ amps.

- A. 4
- B. 9
- C. 15
- D. 28

15.

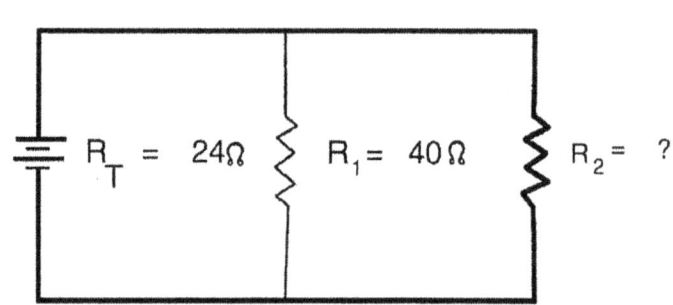

In the circuit shown above, the TOTAL resistance is 24 ohms. What is the value of R_2?
_____ ohms.

A. 16   B. 40   C. 60   D. 64

16.

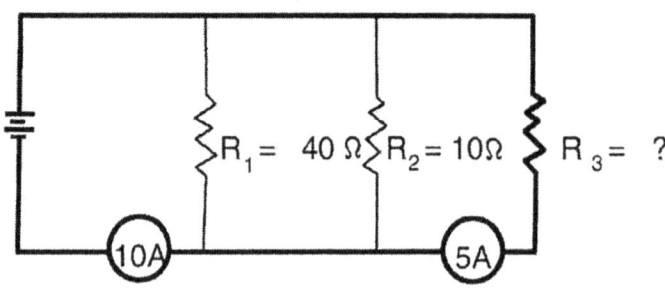

What is the source voltage of the circuit shown above?
_____ volts.

A. 40   B. 50   C. 100   D. 500

17. What is the value of R_3 in the circuit shown in Question 16 above?
_____ ohms.

A. 8   B. 10   C. 20   D. 100

18.

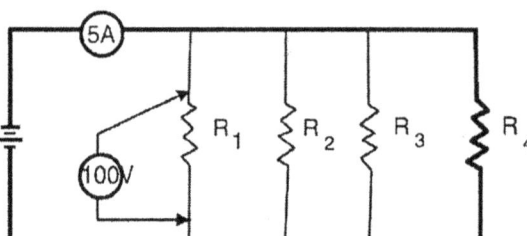

If all 4 resistors in the circuit above are of equal ohmic resistances, what is the value of R_3?
_____ ohms.

A. 5   B. 20   C. 60   D. 80

19.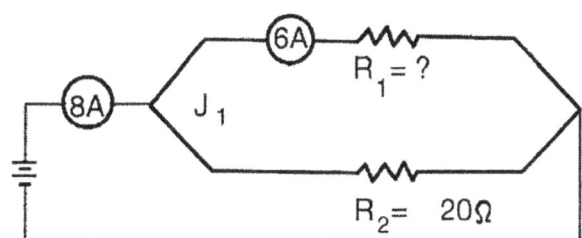

What is the value of the source voltage in the circuit above?
_____ volts

A. 20 B. 40 C. 120 D. 160

20.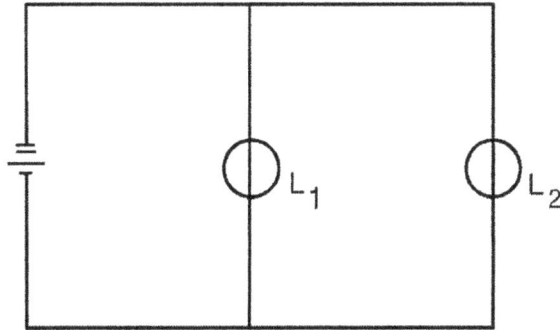

If Lamp L_2 in the circuit above should suddenly burn out, which of the statements below is CORRECT?

A. More current would flow through lamp L_1.
B. Source voltage would decrease.
C. The filament resistance of lamp L_1 would decrease.
D. Lamp L_1 would still burn normal.

21. When referring to a circuit's conductance, you visualize the degree to which the circuit

A. *permits* or conducts voltage
B. *opposes* the rate of voltage changes
C. *permits* or conducts current flow
D. *opposes* the rate of current flow

22.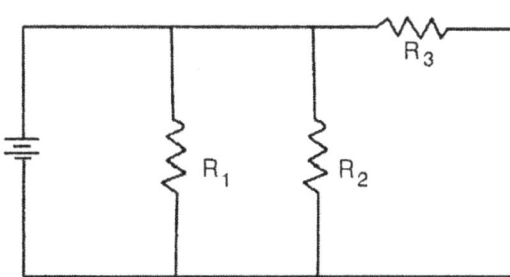

The TOTAL conductance of the circuit above would be solved by which of the equations?

A. $G_T - G_1 - G_2 - G_3 = 0$
B. $G_T + G_1 + G_2 + G_3 = 0$
C. $G_T = G_1 - G_2 - G_3$
D. $G_T = G_1 + G_2 + G_3$

23.

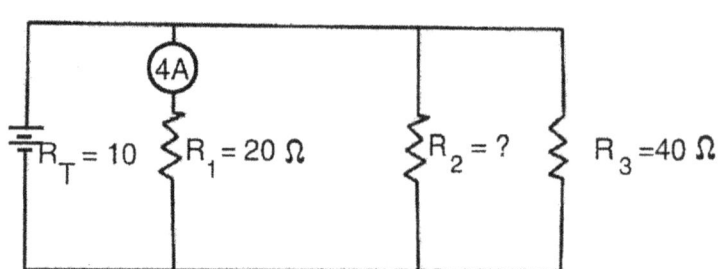

If the resistors in the circuit above are all rated at 250 watts, which resistor or resistors would overheat?

A. R_1 B. R_2 C. R_3 D. All

24.

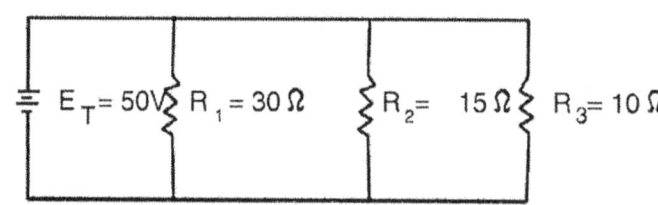

The TOTAL conductance of the circuit above is

A. 0.15G   B. 0.20G   C. 0.50G   D. 0.75G

KEY (CORRECT ANSWERS)

1. C
2. A
3. C
4. B
5. C

6. A
7. B
8. B
9. B
10. A

11. A
12. A
13. D
14. B
15. C

16. A
17. A
18. D
19. B
20. D

21. C
22. D
23. A
24. B

TEST 5

DIRECTIONS: Each question or incomplete statement is followed by several suggested answers or completions. Select the one that BEST answers the question or completes the statement. *PRINT THE LETTER OF THE CORRECT ANSWER IN THE SPACE AT THE RIGHT.*

1. The MINIMUM number of resistors in a compound circuit is (are)

   A. four B. three C. two D. one

   1.____

2.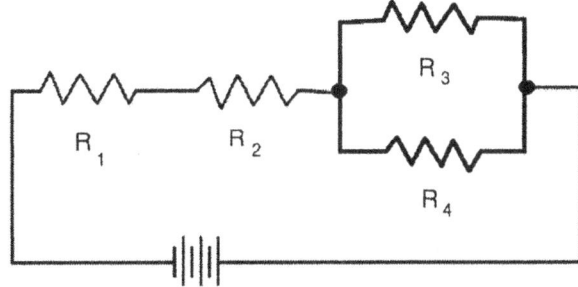

   Total resistance of the circuit shown is determined by the formula

   A. $R_1R_2 + \dfrac{R_3R_4}{R_4+R_3}$
   B. $R_1+R_2 + \dfrac{R_3+R_4}{R_3R_4}$
   C. $R_1+R_2 + \dfrac{R_3R_4}{R_3+R_4}$
   D. $R_1+R_2 + (\dfrac{R_3R_4}{R_3+R_4})$

   2.____

3.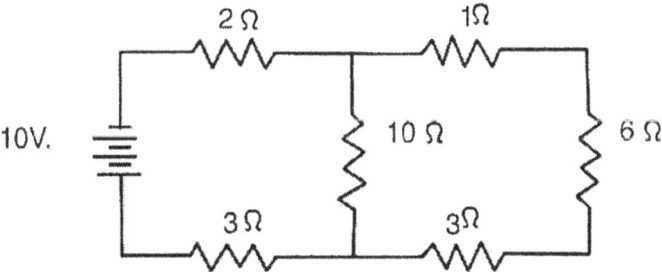

   In the circuit above, what is the value of I_t?
   $I_t = $ _____ amp.

   A. 1.14 B. 0.4 C. 0.667 D. 1

   3.____

4. In the circuit in Question 3 above, how much power is consumed by the 6-ohm resistor? _____ watts.

   A. 15 B. 1.5 C. 60 D. 6

   4.____

5. A voltage divider is used to

   A. provide different voltage values for multiple loads from a single source
   B. provide several voltage drops in parallel
   C. increase the voltage to the load at several taps
   D. provide tap points to alter power supplied

   5.____

6. The total power supplied to the entire circuit by a voltage divider and 4 loads is the

   A. sum of the 4 loads
   B. voltage divider minus 4 loads
   C. voltage divider plus the 4 loads
   D. voltage divider only

7. The total voltage of a voltage divider is the

   A. input voltage minus the load's voltages
   B. the load's voltages only
   C. sum of the input and load voltage
   D. sum of the voltages across the divider

8. An attenuator is

   A. a network of resistors used to reduce power, voltage, or current
   B. a network of resistors to change the input voltage
   C. also called a pad
   D. used in every power circuit

9. In an attenuator, the resistors are

   A. adjusted separately
   B. connected in parallel with the load
   C. connected in series with the load
   D. ganged

10. What two conditions may be observed in a bridge circuit?

    A. T and L network characteristics
    B. No-load and full-load bridge current
    C. Unequal potential and unequal current
    D. Balance and unbalance

11.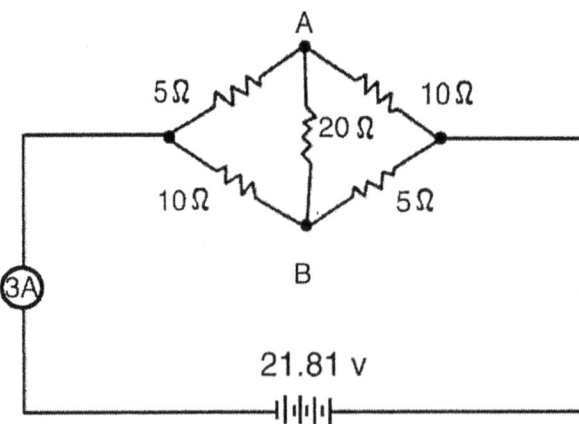

In the circuit above, how much current flows in the resistor and what is its direction?

A. 26 a.; B to A
C. 0.273 a.; A to B
B. 1a.; A to B
D. 1a.; B to A

12. In a three-wire distribution system, an unbalanced situation is indicated by the

    A. potential of the positive wire being equal to the negative wire
    B. positive wire carrying more amperage than the negative wire
    C. current in the neutral wire
    D. neutral wire carrying the total current

12._____

13.

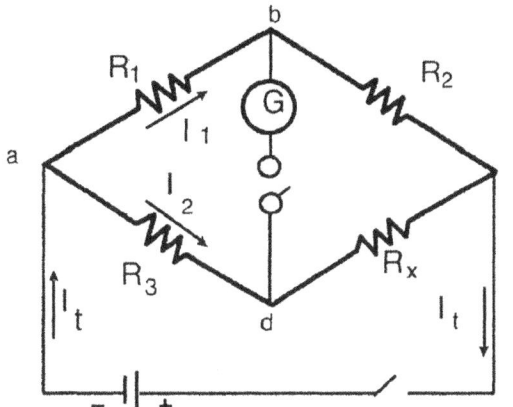

SCHEMATIC WHEATSTONE-BRIDGE CIRCUIT

In the figure above, the galvanometer will show zero deflection when

A. $\dfrac{R_1}{R_2} + \dfrac{R_3}{R_x}$

B. $R_x = \dfrac{R_1 R_3}{R_2}$

C. $\dfrac{I_1 R_1}{I_2 R_x} = \dfrac{I_2 R_3}{I_1 R_2}$

D. $R_x = \dfrac{R_1 R_2}{R_3}$

13._____

14. In the Wheatstone Bridge type circuit shown at the right, the bridge current is toward Point A.
    The resistance of R_X is

    A. $30\,\Omega$
    B. greater than $45\,\Omega$
    C. $20\,\Omega$
    D. less than $15\,\Omega$

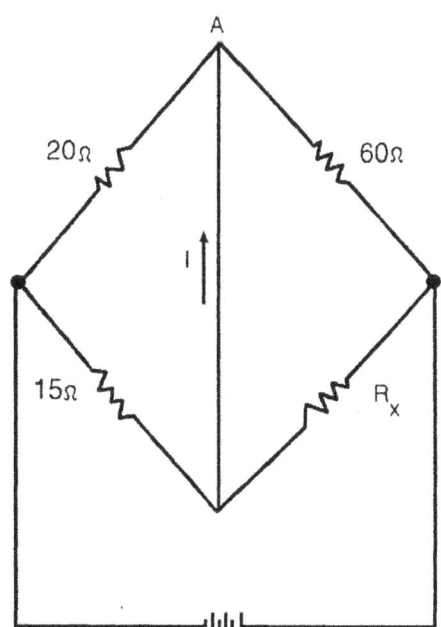

14._____

15.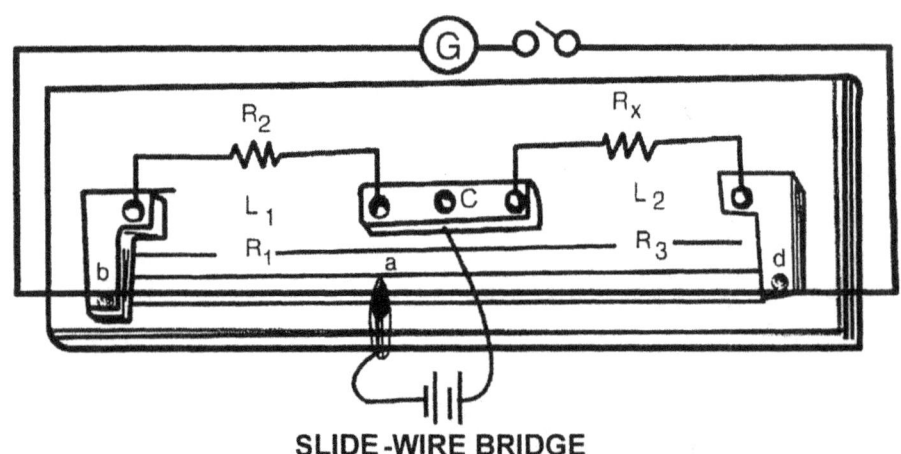

SLIDE-WIRE BRIDGE

In the slide-wire bridge shown above, L_1 is equal to

A. $L_1 = \dfrac{R_2 L_2}{R_1}$

B. $L_1 = \dfrac{R_1 + L_2}{R_2}$

C. $\dfrac{R_2}{R_1 L_2} = L_1$

D. $\dfrac{R_2 L_2}{R_x} = L_1$

16.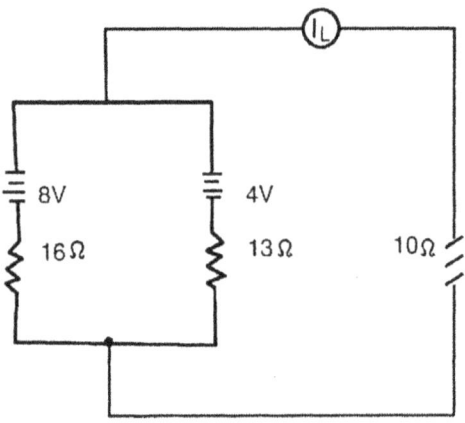

In the circuit above, I line is

A. 4.44 a.   B. 0.444 a.   C. 0.337 a.   D. 5.22 a.

17. When checking a 3-wire distribution circuit going against the direction of current flow, the IR drop is ALWAYS

A. negative
B. positive
C. not used
D. always in direction of current flow

18.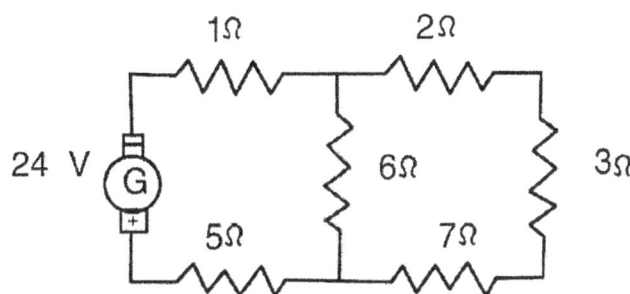

In the circuit above, the voltage drop across the 3-ohm resistor is _____ volts.

A. 2.4 B. 24 C. 9.6 D. 0.96

19. The resistance of the wire is taken into consideration in the 2- and 3-wire distribution systems because the

A. source and load are very close
B. resistance of the wire is the same throughout
C. load and source are at a considerable distance from each other
D. load must be decreased in order to determine accurate circuit values

20. What is Kirchhoff's second law as applied to 3-wire distribution circuits?

A. Sum of all the voltages is zero.
B. Algebraic sum of all the voltages about closed path is zero.
C. Algebraic sum of all voltage is zero.
D. All IR drops in the circuit are negative.

KEY (CORRECT ANSWERS)

1. B
2. C
3. D
4. B
5. A

6. C
7. D
8. A
9. D
10. D

11. C
12. C
13. A
14. B
15. D

16. C
17. B
18. A
19. C
20. B

TEST 6

DIRECTIONS: Each question or incomplete statement is followed by several suggested answers or completions. Select the one that BEST answers the question or completes the statement. *PRINT THE LETTER OF THE CORRECT ANSWER IN THE SPACE AT THE RIGHT.*

1. A mil is what part of an inch?

   A. 1/10
   B. 1/100
   C. 1/1000
   D. 1/1,000,000

2. The discharge (electrical leakage) that MIGHT occur from a wire carrying a high potential is called

   A. arcing
   B. sparking
   C. static discharge
   D. corona

3. Bare wire ends are spliced by the

   A. western union method
   B. rat-tail joint method
   C. fixture joint method
   D. all of the above

4. What is a unit conductor called that has a length of one foot and a cross-sectional area of one circular mil?

   A. Square mil
   B. Circular mil
   C. Circular mil foot
   D. Square mil foot

5. The induction-type soldering iron is commonly known as the

   A. soldering copper
   B. pencil iron
   C. soldering gun
   D. resistance gun

6. All good quality soldering irons operate at what temperature?

   A. 400 - 500° F.
   B. 500 - 600° F.
   C. 600 - 700° F.
   D. 300 - 600° F.

7. A No. 12 wire has a diameter of 80.81 mils. What is the area in circular mils? _____ cm.

   A. 6,530   B. 5,630   C. 4,530   D. 3,560

8. Dielectric strength is the

   A. opposite of potential difference
   B. ability of a conductor to carry large amounts of current
   C. ability of an insulator to withstand a potential difference
   D. strength of a magnetic field

9. To readily transfer the heat from the soldering iron tip, it FIRST should be

   A. tinned with solder
   B. allowed to form an oxide film
   C. cleaned with carbon tetrachloride
   D. allowed to heat for 25 minutes

10. A No. 12 wire has a diameter of 80.81 mils. 10.____
    What is the area in square mils?
    _____ square mils.

    A. 2,516.8   B. 5,128.6   C. 6,530   D. 8,512.6

11. Varnished cambric insulation is used to cover conductors carrying voltages above 11.____
    _____ volts.

    A. 1,000   B. 1,500   C. 15,000   D. 5,000

12. The solder splicer is used to 12.____

    A. prevent the waste of rosin core solder
    B. connect together small lengths of solder
    C. connect two conductors together
    D. none of the above

13. The conductance of a conductor is the ease with which current will flow through it. 13.____
    It is measured in

    A. ohms   B. mhos   C. henrys   D. amperes

14. Asbestos insulation loses its insulating properties when it becomes 14.____

    A. overaged
    B. overheated
    C. used over a long period of time
    D. wet

15. How are solderless connectors installed on conductors? 15.____

    A. Bolted on   B. Chemical compound
    C. Crimped on   D. All of the above

16. The factor(s) governing the selection of wire size is (are) 16.____

    A. (I^2R loss) in the line
    B. (IR drop) in the line
    C. current-carrying ability of the line
    D. all of the above

17. Enamel insulated conductors are USUALLY called 17.____

    A. magnet wire   B. high voltage wire
    C. low voltage wire   D. transmission lines

18. The advantage of solderless connectors over soldered-type connectors is that they are 18.____

    A. mechanically stronger B. easier to install
    C. free of corrosion   D. all of the above

19. The basic requirement of any splice is that it be   19.____

    A. soldered
    B. mechanically and electrically as strong as the conductor that is spliced
    C. made with a splicer
    D. taped

20. The type of tape that is used for electrical circuits having a temperature of 175° F. or   20.____
    above is

    A. glass cloth
    B. plastic
    C. synthetic rubber compound
    D. impregnated cloth

KEY (CORRECT ANSWERS)

1. C	11. C
2. D	12. C
3. D	13. B
4. C	14. D
5. A	15. C
6. B	16. D
7. A	17. A
8. C	18. B
9. A	19. B
10. B	20. A

EXAMINATION SECTION
TEST 1

DIRECTIONS: Each question or incomplete statement is followed by several suggested answers or completions. Select the one that BEST answers the question or completes the statement. *PRINT THE LETTER OF THE CORRECT ANSWER IN THE SPACE AT THE RIGHT.*

1. The cathode of a phototube is USUALLY coated with a thin layer of _____ oxide. 1._____

   A. magnesium   B. cesium   C. titanium   D. zinc

2. The capacitor on a capacitor motor is connected in _____ winding. 2._____

   A. parallel with the starting
   B. series with the running
   C. parallel with the running
   D. series with the starting

3. The refrigerant used in MOST modern home electric cooling appliances is 3._____

   A. neon   B. argon   C. zenon   D. freon

4. Splicing compound is USUALLY referred to as 4._____

   A. cable varnish   B. friction tape
   C. rubber tape   D. varnish cambric

5. The filament supports of an incandescent lamp are affixed to the 5._____

   A. button rod   B. lead-in wires
   C. steam seal   D. ceramic insulator

6. A non-tamperable fuse is known as a 6._____

   A. fusetron   B. fusetat
   C. circuit breaker   D. Kirkman tamp-lock

7. The wall plate used to cover two toggle switches mounted side by side in a wall box is known as a _____ plate. 7._____

   A. multiple toggle   B. duplex
   C. two gang   D. double

8. Building wire with a thermoplastic insulation is called type 8._____

   A. T.P.   B. R.H.   C. T.W.   D. RH-RW

9. A repulsion-start induction motor operates on 9._____

   A. 4 wire A.C.   B. single phase A.C.
   C. D.C. - 110V-220V   D. A.C. - D.C.

10. A *fish tape* is used to 10._____

    A. pull wires through a conduit   B. weatherproof a splice
    C. test a grounded circuit   D. support long cable runs

11. The color code of a 3 wire #12 cable is

    A. white black green
    B. blue black red
    C. white black red
    D. red white green

12. The motor that has no brushes or commutator is known as a _____ motor.

    A. split phase
    B. capacitor
    C. compound
    D. shunt

13. The temperature of a well-designed continuously run motor, delivering its full rated horsepower, should NOT increase by more than _____ Fahrenheit.

    A. 40° B. 52° C. 60° D. 72°

14. A floodlight operating at a point 500 feet from the meter, wired with #14 wire whose resistance is 2.575 ohms per 1000', has a voltage drop of *approximately* _____ volts.

    A. 5.7 B. 11.33 C. 12.74 D. 15.37

15. The grid in the vacuum tube was introduced by

    A. Fauere B. Oersted C. De Forest D. Le Lanche

16. In an element for an electric range, the material that insulates the wire from the tube is

    A. magnesium oxide
    B. asbestos
    C. high temperature fibre glass
    D. titanium oxide

17. Most thermostats and relays that are used to activate and control a home heating system operate on _____ volts.

    A. 6 B. 24 C. 32 D. 46

18. The revolutions per minute of an electric motor can be determined by using a(n)

    A. hydrometer
    B. tachometer
    C. pulse indicator
    D. prony brake

19. A record player pick-up arm, equipped with a phono cartridge that contains Rochelle-Salts, will produce a voltage known as

    A. phono-electric
    B. bio-electric
    C. piezoelectric
    D. pyrometric

20. The device that controls the flow of electrons in a solid is the

    A. electron tube
    B. transistor
    C. anode
    D. cathode

21. Fluorescent lamps are designed to operate on

    A. the rated voltage that appears on the lamp
    B. a rectifier controlled voltage
    C. a 115 volt or 230 volt circuit
    D. a circuit where the voltage fluctuation does not exceed 5%

22. The efficiency of a 3 horsepower motor that requires 2.4 kilowatts to drive it is

    A. 74% B. 82% C. 90% D. 94%

23. The magnetic resistance that opposes the flow of magnetic current is

    A. inductance B. reluctance
    C. reactance   D. impedance

24. The output in lumens per watt for an incandescent lamp (filament type) is _____ to _____ lumens.

    A. 14; 23 B. 30; 55 C. 50; 57 D. 58; 75

25. The voltage of a battery cell depends upon

    A. the number of lines cut per second
    B. the size of the plates and the distance they are set apart
    C. material that the plate is made of and the electrolyte used
    D. area of the zinc container

26. Most window-type air conditioners, such as used in the home, are equipped with a(n) _____ motor.

    A. synchronous B. R-I
    C. seal-vac   D. hermetically sealed

27. Light that contains only a single color and also a single wave length is known as the _____ light.

    A. spectrum B. laser
    C. aurora   D. sodium vapor

28. The *Edison effect* led to the development of the

    A. mercury vapor lamp B. radio tube
    C. phonograph   D. fluorescent lamp

29. A device for producing high tension induced current is the _____ coil.

    A. Ruhmkorff B. Solenoid C. Thury D. Choke

30. In a triode tube, the element placed between the cathode and the plate is called

    A. rectifier B. controlled grid
    C. S C C   D. D C C

KEY (CORRECT ANSWERS)

1.	B	11.	C	21.	C
2.	D	12.	A	22.	D
3.	D	13.	D	23.	B
4.	C	14.	C	24.	A
5.	A	15.	C	25.	C
6.	B	16.	A	26.	D
7.	C	17.	B	27.	B
8.	C	18.	B	28.	B
9.	B	19.	C	29.	A
10.	A	20.	B	30.	B

TEST 2

DIRECTIONS: Each question or incomplete statement is followed by several suggested answers or completions. Select the one that BEST answers the question or completes the statement. *PRINT THE LETTER OF THE CORRECT ANSWER IN THE SPACE AT THE RIGHT.*

1. A fixture hickey is used to

   A. bend pipe
   B. suspend a ceiling light
   C. make a 60° offset in BX
   D. ground a fixture

   1._____

2. Nichrome wire is used in electrical heating devices because it

   A. is non-magnetic
   B. has a low melting point
   C. is cheaper than copper wire
   D. has a high resistance

   2._____

3. The letters *E M T* in conduit work refer to

   A. underwriters approval   B. thin wall conduit
   C. A.C. use only   D. ready for first inspection

   3._____

4. A 120 volt three-way incandescent lamp bulb has

   A. one filament   B. two filaments
   C. three filaments   D. a variable resistor

   4._____

5. When an object to be copperplated is immersed in its electrolyte, it should be connected to the

   A. anode   B. cathode
   C. right terminal D. electrolyte

   5._____

6. A voltmeter consists of a milliammeter and a high resistance which are connected in

   A. multiple   B. parallel   C. series   D. shunt

   6._____

7. A device for producing electricity directly from heat is called a

   A. turbine   B. thermocouple
   C. transformer   D. rheostat

   7._____

8. The combined resistance of a circuit containing five 40 ohm resistances in parallel is _____ ohms.

   A. 8   B. 20   C. 40   D. 200

   8._____

9. An alternator differs from a D.C. generator because it has no

   A. brushes   B. commutator
   C. field poles   D. rotor

   9._____

10. The resistance of a wire 1/16 inch in diameter is one OHM. A wire of the same length, but twice the diameter, has a resistance of ohms.

    A. 1/4   B. 1/2   C. 1   D. 2

    10._____

29

11. A device that measures energy consumption of electricity is called a

   A. wattmeter
   B. kilowatthourmeter
   C. kilowatt meter
   D. ammeter

12. A *universal* motor is a(n) _____ motor.

   A. shunt   B. induction   C. series   D. synchronous

13. In a three phase, four wire, 208 volt distribution system, the voltage between any phase wire and the neutral is _____ volts.

   A. 0   B. 120   C. 208   D. 240

14. Of the following, the motor that does NOT have a commutator is

   A. universal
   B. series
   C. repulsion induction
   D. split phase

15. An incandescent lamp rated at 130 volts-100 watts, and operated at 115 volts will

   A. consume more wattage and impair the life of the filament
   B. increase lamp life and reduce wattage consumed
   C. produce fewer lumens per watt and increase lamp efficiency
   D. have no effect on the lamp

16. A 2 horsepower 75% efficient D.C. motor operating at full load draws *approximately* _____ watts.

   A. 1000   B. 1500   C. 2000   D. 3000

17. An insulating material that withstands heat better than wire with more ordinary insulation is

   A. rubber
   B. plastic
   C. rubber with cotton covering
   D. varnished cambric

18. Electrical resistance can be measured with a(n)

   A. voltmeter and an ammeter
   B. A.C. wattmeter
   C. thermocouple
   D. induction coil

19. The property of a circuit that enables it to store electrical energy in the form of an electrostatic field is called

   A. inductance
   B. reactance
   C. resistance
   D. capacitance

20. If a 50 ohm resistance draws two amperes from a circuit, the power it uses is

   A. 0.2 KW
   B. 25 watts
   C. 100 watts
   D. none of the above

21. The world's FIRST central light and power plant was developed by

   A. Samuel F.B. Morse
   B. Lee De Forest
   C. Edwin H. Armstrong
   D. Thomas A. Edison

22. A *tuner* circuit consists of a

   A. zener diode and tunnel transistor
   B. capacitor and inductance coil
   C. resistor and R.F. amplifier tube
   D. resistor and capacitor

23. A hotplate having a resistance of 30 ohms, connected to a 120 volt outlet, would draw a current of _____ amperes.

   A. 4   B. 90   C. 150   D. 3600

24. Of the following, the term that does NOT relate to magnetism is

   A. reluctance
   B. oersted
   C. coulomb
   D. magneto-motive force

25. A basic difference between radio waves and sound waves is that radio waves are

   A. of a different frequency
   B. electrical currents
   C. molecules of air in motion
   D. electromagnetic waves

26. An object that has a positive electrostatic charge would have an excess of

   A. electrons
   B. protons
   C. neutrons
   D. omega minus particles

27. Of the following, the statement that does NOT apply to a capacitor is that it can

   A. store electrons
   B. pass alternating current
   C. pass direct current
   D. be used to smooth out pulsating direct current

28. The section of a radio transmitter or receiver that causes a stream of electrons to vibrate back and forth at high frequencies is known as a(n)

   A. modulator   B. oscillator   C. amplifier   D. detector

29. The separation of speech or music from a radio wave carrying music or speech is referred to as

   A. audio filtration
   B. separation
   C. demodulation
   D. tracing

30. A circuit used to smooth out the surges of pulsating direct current from a rectifier is called a

   A. filter
   B. multiplexer
   C. demodulator
   D. local oscillator

KEY (CORRECT ANSWERS)

1.	B	11.	B	21.	D
2.	D	12.	C	22.	B
3.	B	13.	B	23.	A
4.	B	14.	D	24.	C
5.	B	15.	B	25.	D
6.	C	16.	C	26.	B
7.	B	17.	D	27.	C
8.	A	18.	A	28.	B
9.	B	19.	D	29.	C
10.	A	20.	A	30.	A

TEST 3

DIRECTIONS: Each question or incomplete statement is followed by several suggested answers or completions. Select the one that BEST answers the question or completes the statement. *PRINT THE LETTER OF THE CORRECT ANSWER IN THE SPACE AT THE RIGHT.*

1. The simple motor found in an electric clock is called a(n) _____ motor.   1.____
   - A. synchronous
   - B. induction
   - C. rotor
   - D. D.C.

2. The amperage of a fully charged car storage battery is USUALLY near _____ amps.   2.____
   - A. 10
   - B. 100
   - C. 1000
   - D. 10,000

3. To prevent the initial surge of current drawn by an electric motor from *burning out* the fuse in the circuit, one uses a   3.____
   - A. cartridge fuse
   - B. circuit breaker
   - C. plug fuse
   - D. fusetron

4. The many radio waves striking the antenna of a receiver are tuned-in with the   4.____
   - A. transformer
   - B. choke coil
   - C. variable condenser
   - D. diode detector

5. The starting motor of an automobile engine is shifted into mesh with the flywheel gear by a   5.____
   - A. vibrator
   - B. solenoid
   - C. bendix
   - D. starter button

6. The picture tube of a television set is also referred to as a _____ tube.   6.____
   - A. cathode-ray
   - B. power beam
   - C. oscilliscope
   - D. photo-electric

7. Generators that have two or more sets of field poles and require fewer revolutions to generate a 60-cycle-per second current are called   7.____
   - A. duo-dynamos
   - B. vibrators
   - C. poly-phase generators
   - D. alternators

8. A bar that has been artificially magnetized can be demagnetized by   8.____
   - A. quenching it in hot oil
   - B. pounding it with a heavy hammer
   - C. bending it into a *U* shape
   - D. wrapping it in insulating tape

9. The part of a generator which determines if it is a direct current generator is the   9.____
   - A. stator
   - B. field
   - C. commutator
   - D. brush

10. The term which refers to pressure or force in electric current is   10.____
    - A. amperage
    - B. voltage
    - C. ohms
    - D. electrons

11. Nichrome wire is MOST likely to be found in a(n)

    A. T.V. circuit
    B. electric motor
    C. electric clock
    D. electric heater

12. Electromagnetic waves are changed into pulses capable of producing sound waves in a radio by means of a

    A. transformer
    B. speaker
    C. detector
    D. oscillator

13. The SIMPLEST form of electronic tube is called

    A. cathode   B. diode   C. plate   D. triode

14. Of the following, the one that is NOT a part of a radio tube is the

    A. envelope   B. plate   C. condenser   D. filament

15. The speed of a simple electric motor can be controlled with the use of a

    A. variable resistor
    B. electrolytic condenser
    C. variable condenser
    D. prony-brake

16. A single wet cell can be made from a copper penny and a *zinc* penny attached to two copper leads immersed in

    A. mineral oil
    B. salt-water solution
    C. distilled water
    D. chromate of soda

17. The MINIMUM gauge wire for house circuits should be

    A. 10   B. 18   C. 14   D. 22

18. The safety device used in a house wiring circuit to protect against an overload is a

    A. circuit breaker
    B. knife switch
    C. cut-off
    D. mercury switch

19. To prevent the generator from burning out at high speeds, the battery circuit of the automobile employs a

    A. choke coil
    B. variable resistor
    C. voltage regulator
    D. current trap

20. An interrupted current of 6 volts flows in the primary circuit of an induction coil of 100 turns of wire. If the secondary coil has 1,000 turns, the theoretical voltage output is

    A. .6   B. 60   C. 600   D. .06

21. A 200 watt bulb in a 100 volt circuit uses _____ ampere(s).

    A. .2   B. .02   C. 2   D. 20

22. A 220 volt air conditioner drawing 15 amperes of current operates 10 hours a day. The total cost of operation for four weeks at the rate of 4 cents per kilowatt hour would be

    A. $18.48   B. $55.44   C. $26.40   D. $36.96

23. If a dry cell battery is capable of supplying a force of two volts and ten amperes of current, connecting five such batteries in parallel will result in a total capacity of _____ volts with _____ amperes.

    A. 2; 50   B. 20; 10   C. 10; 50   D. 10; 10

24. To calculate the number of turns of wire needed to make a step-up or step-down transformer when the voltages are known, and one set of windings is determined, we use the following formula:

    A. $\dfrac{\text{Primary turns}}{\text{Secondary turns}} = \dfrac{\text{Primary volts}}{\text{Secondary volts}}$

    B. $\dfrac{\text{Primary turns}}{\text{Primary volts}} = \dfrac{\text{Secondary volts}}{\text{Secondary turns}}$

    C. $\dfrac{\text{Primary turns}}{\text{Secondary volts}} = \dfrac{\text{Primary volts}}{\text{Secondary turns}}$

    D. $\dfrac{\text{Primary turns}}{\text{Secondary volts}} = \dfrac{\text{Primary volts}}{\text{Secondary turns}}$

25. To measure the specific gravity of the contents of a storage battery, one uses a

    A. hygrometer   B. galvanometer
    C. ammeter   D. hydrometer

26. Lightning is _____ electricity.

    A. induced   B. ionized   C. static   D. magnetic

27. A lodestone is related to

    A. magnetism   B. resistance
    C. conductivity D. reluctance

28. The term related to a storer of electricity is

    A. milliampere   B. microfarad
    C. megohm   D. microvolt

29. The thermostat as a switch employs the use of a

    A. diode tube   B. tungsten filament
    C. bimetallic strip D. thermocouple

30. In servicing electrical apparatus, it is necessary to know the values of amperage, voltage, and resistance. When two of the factors are known, the third may be found by applying *Ohm's Law*.
    Of the following formulas, the one that does NOT apply is

    A. I = R/E   B. R = E/I   C. E = IR   D. I = E/R

KEY (CORRECT ANSWERS)

1.	A	11.	D	21.	C
2.	B	12.	C	22.	D
3.	D	13.	B	23.	A
4.	C	14.	C	24.	A
5.	B	15.	A	25.	D
6.	A	16.	B	26.	C
7.	D	17.	C	27.	A
8.	B	18.	A	28.	B
9.	C	19.	C	29.	C
10.	B	20.	B	30.	A

TEST 4

DIRECTIONS: Each question or incomplete statement is followed by several suggested answers or completions. Select the one that BEST answers the question or completes the statement. *PRINT THE LETTER OF THE CORRECT ANSWER IN THE SPACE AT THE RIGHT.*

1. The effect of a capacitor on direct current is to _____ it.

    A. modulate
    B. block
    C. pass
    D. demodulate

    1._____

2. Factors which determine the resistance of a wire are:

    A. Diameter, insulating material, length, strands
    B. Length, diameter, material, temperature
    C. Material, light factor, pressure, circumference
    D. Pressure, magnetism, binding, length

    2._____

3. Current flow in a triode vacuum tube may be controlled by the

    A. plate and the grid
    B. filament and the plate
    C. grid and the heater
    D. cathode and the filament

    3._____

4. If the resistance in a parallel circuit is *increased,* the voltage drop across a resistor would

    A. *increase*
    B. vary proportionally
    C. *decrease*
    D. remain the same

    4._____

5. In parallel and series circuits, current is

    A. inversely proportional to resistance and directly proportional to voltage
    B. directly proportional to resistance and inversely proportional to voltage
    C. not affected by voltage
    D. not affected by resistance

    5._____

6. The process of mixing audio waves with radio waves is called

    A. rectification
    B. attenuation
    C. modulation
    D. superimposition

    6._____

7. Transistors are made of three parts: a base, a collector, and an emitter. When compared to a vacuum tube, the collector is comparable to the

    A. grid   B. plate   C. cathode   D. filament

    7._____

8. Resistance wire used in electrical appliances is *usually* an alloy of

    A. tungsten, chromium, brass
    B. nickel, chromium, iron
    C. copper, nickel, tungsten
    D. iron, copper, molybdenum

    8._____

9. A meter with terminals connected in series and across the line is a

    A. voltmeter   B. ammeter   C. ohmmeter   D. wattmeter

    9._____

10. One hundred volts will push _____ milliamperes through 20k ohms of resistance.

    A. 2   B. 5   C. 50   D. 2000

    10._____

11. A resistor having bands of orange, red, yellow, and silver would have a resistance value of _____ ohms.   11._____

    A. 32k   B. 320k   C. 2.3 meg   D. 43 meg

12. A flashbulb used for photographic purposes contains   12._____

    A. aluminum and oxygen
    B. tungsten and helium
    C. aluminum and hydrogen
    D. tungsten and argon

13. A generator having a cummutator produces _____ current.   13._____

    A. alternating   B. direct
    C. synchronous   D. modulating

14. A step-down transformer has 1,200 turns on the primary. 90 volts is applied to the primary, and the second is to produce 15 volts.   14._____
    How many turns should be wound on the secondary?

    A. 200   B. 600   C. 7,200   D. 108,000

15. In a radio circuit, a transformer CANNOT be used to   15._____

    A. step-up a-c voltage
    B. isolate part of a circuit
    C. step-down d-c voltage
    D. couple part of a circuit to another

16. A transformer has 200 turns of #14 wire wound on primary and 1,000 turns of #14 wire wound on the secondary.   16._____
    A voltmeter attached to the secondary terminals would indicate _____ volts if 50 volts were attached to the primary.

    A. 0   B. 10   C. 250   D. 600

17. Service entrance cable for the typical home is usually made up of three wires. The *hot* wires are usually No.   17._____

    A. 4 or No. 6   B. 8 or No. 10
    C. 12 or No. 14   D. 16 or No. 18

18. In the PNP type transistor, the collector is *normally*   18._____

    A. negative   B. positive
    C. shorted out   D. not needed

19. In a beam power tube, the screen grid is   19._____

    A. the plate   B. positive
    C. the suppressor   D. negative

20. A silicon controlled rectifier is   20._____

    A. a nuvistor   B. a CRT
    C. thermally operated   D. a semi-conductor

21. In copper plating a metallic object, it should be placed at the   21.____

    A. anode   B. switch   C. cathode   D. electrolyte

22. At five cents per kilowatt hour, a 100-watt lamp which is operated for one hundred (100)   22.____
    hours would use energy that would cost

    A. 5 cents   B. less than 10 cents
    C. 50 cents   D. 5 dollars

23. A galvanometer may be converted to a voltmeter by adding a   23.____

    A. shunt in series   B. multiplier in series
    C. multiplier in parallel   D. shunt in parallel

24. The counter emf of an inductance coil is measured in   24.____

    A. milliamperes   B. microfarads
    C. henrys   D. millivolts

25. A fluorescent lamp lights when the   25.____

    A. ballast coil produces a high-voltage charge
    B. starter switch is placed in parallel with the filament
    C. mercury forms minute droplets on the filament
    D. ballast changes the A.C. to D.C. in the tube

26. The electrolyte used in a dry cell is composed of   26.____

    A. carbon, magnesium oxide, ammonia, sodium chloride
    B. sodium, manganese dioxide, alumina, zinc sulphate
    C. carbon, manganese dioxide, sal ammoniac, zinc chloride
    D. sodium, magnesium sulphate, arsenic, zinc oxide

27. A variable capacitor has its capacitance *increased* when the   27.____

    A. plates are open
    B. rotor is attached to the stator
    C. plates are meshed
    D. dielectric is given a full charge

28. The gas mixture commonly used in incandescent lamps is   28.____

    A. nitrogen and argon   B. nitrogen and helium
    C. helium and argon   D. hydrogen and oxygen

29. A motor with a high-starting torque and rapid acceleration is a(n) _____ motor.   29.____

    A. D.C. shunt wound   B. D.C. series wound
    C. A.C. synchronous   D. A.C. split phase

30. Bry cells used for powering cordless electric razors are usually _____ cells.   30.____

    A. manganese alkaline   B. nickel cadmium
    C. nickel silver   D. zinc carbon

KEY (CORRECT ANSWERS)

1.	B	11.	B	21.	C
2.	B	12.	A	22.	C
3.	A	13.	B	23.	B
4.	D	14.	A	24.	C
5.	A	15.	C	25.	A
6.	C	16.	A	26.	C
7.	B	17.	A	27.	C
8.	B	18.	A	28.	A
9.	D	19.	B	29.	B
10.	B	20.	D	30.	B

EXAMINATION SECTION
TEST 1

DIRECTIONS: Each question or incomplete statement is followed by several suggested answers or completions. Select the one that BEST answers the question or completes the statement. *PRINT THE LETTER OF THE CORRECT ANSWER IN THE SPACE AT THE RIGHT.*

1. Which of the following capacitors could be damaged by a reversal in polarity? A(n) _____ capacitor.

    A. ceramic
    B. paper
    C. mica
    D. electrolytic
    E. vacuum

2. If the current through a resistor is 6 amperes and the voltage drop across it is 100 volts, what is the approximate value of the resistor in ohm(s)?

    A. 1660   B. 166   C. 16.6   D. 1.66   E. 0.0166

3. What is the CORRECT use for an arbor press?

    A. Bending sheet metal
    B. Driving self-tapping screws
    C. Removing screws
    D. Removing "C" rings
    E. Removing bearings from shafts

4. Which one of the following is a tensioning device in bulk-belt-type conveyor systems? _____ take-up.

    A. Spring
    B. Power
    C. Hydraulic
    D. Fluid coupled
    E. Flexible coupled

5. When $X_L = X_C$ in a series circuit, what condition exists?

    A. The circuit impedance is increasing
    B. The circuit is at resonant frequency
    C. The circuit current is minimum
    D. The circuit has no e.m.f. at this time
    E. None of the above

6. Which of the following pieces of information is NOT normally found on a schematic diagram?

    A. Functional stage name
    B. Supply voltages
    C. Part symbols
    D. Part values
    E. Physical location of parts

7. When a single-phase induction motor drawing 24 amps at 120 VAC is reconnected to 240 VAC, what will be the amperage at 240 VAC? _____ amps.

    A. 6   B. 8   C. 12   D. 24   E. 36

8. Which one of the following meters measures the SMALLEST current?

    A. Kilometer B. Milliammeter C. Microvoltmeter
    D. Millivoltmeter E. Kilovoltmeter

9. If the current through a 1000-ohm resistor is 3 milliamperes, the voltage drop across the resistor is _____ volt(s).

    A. 1 B. 2.5 C. 3 D. 30 E. 300

10. The normally closed contacts of a relay are open when its solenoid is energized with VDC. The voltage at which the contacts re-close will be

    A. dependent upon the current through the contacts
    B. dependent upon the voltage applied to the contacts
    C. 24 VDC through the coil
    D. more than 24 VDC through the contacts
    E. less than 24 VDC through the coil

11. Electrical energy is converted to mechanical rotation by what component in the electric motor?

    A. Armature B. Commutator C. Field
    D. Start windings E. Stator

12. Ohm's Law expresses the basic relationship of

    A. current, voltage, and resistance
    B. current, voltage, and power
    C. current, power, and resistance
    D. resistance, impedance, and voltage
    E. resistance, power, and impedance

13. In parallel circuits, the voltage is *always*

    A. variable B. constant C. alternating
    D. fluctuating E. sporadic

14. Which one of the following is used as a voltage divider?

    A. Rotary converter B. Potentiometer C. Relay
    D. Circuit breaker E. Voltmeter

Question 15.

Question 15 is based on the following diagram.

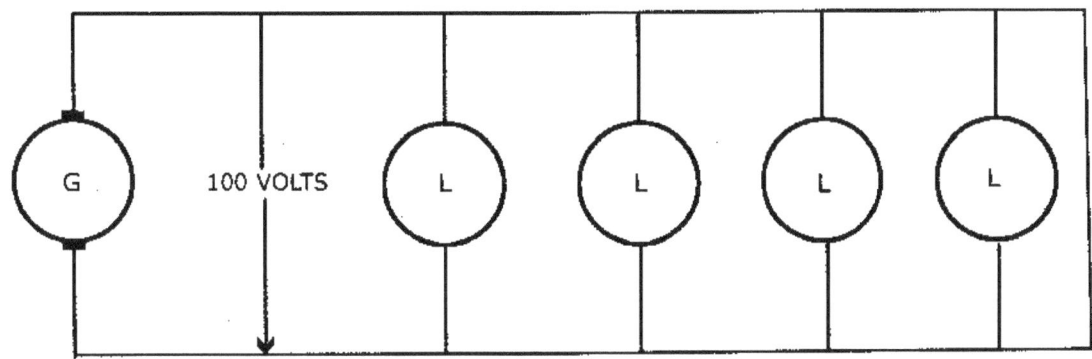

CURRENT IN EACH LAMP 1/2 AMPERE

15. What is the resistance of the entire circuit? _____ ohms. 15.____

    A. 15   B. 25   C. 35   D. 45   E. 50

16. Which one of the following tools is used to bring a bore to a specified tolerance? 16.____

    A. Tap
    D. Counterbore
    B. Reamer
    E. Center drill
    C. Countersink

17. The primary function of a take-up pulley in a belt conveyor is to 17.____

    A. carry the belt on the return trip
    B. track the belt
    C. maintain the proper belt tension
    D. change the direction of the belt
    E. regulate the speed of the belt

Question 18.

Question 18 is based on the following diagram.

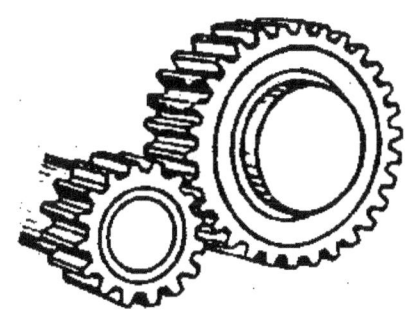

18. What is the name of the gears? 18.____

    A. Spur external
    D. Herringbone
    B. Spur internal
    D. Worm
    C. Helical

Question 19.

Question 19 is based on the following diagram.

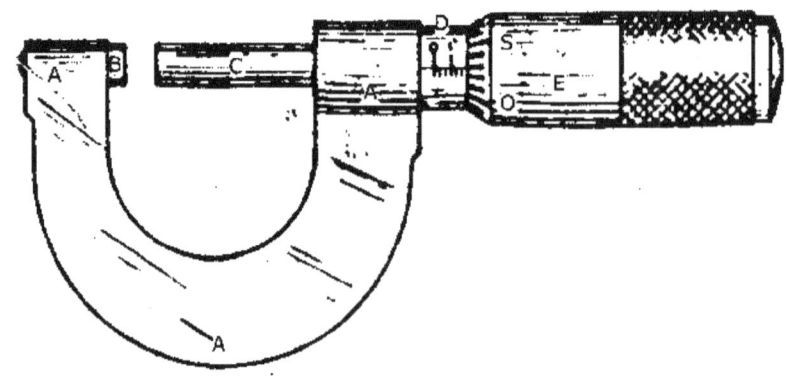

19. The part labeled D is the   19.____

    A. sleeve   B. thimble   C. frame
    D. anvil   E. pindle

Question 20.

Question 20 is based on the following symbol.

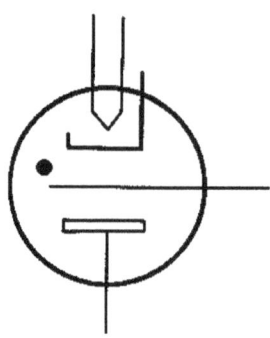

20. This symbol represents a _____ tube.   20.____

    A. thyratron vacuum   B. thyratron gas
    C. variable-mu vacuum   D. variable-mu gas
    E. vacuum photo

21. A diode can be substituted for which one of the following?   21.____

    A. Transformer   B. Relay   C. Rectifier
    D. Condenser   E. Rheostat

Question 22.

Question 22 is based on the following diagram.

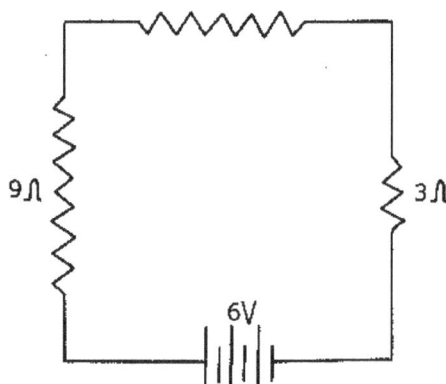

22. The rate of amperes flowing in the circuit is: 22.____

    A. .03 1/3   B. .18   C. .24
    D. .30 1/3   E. .33 1/3

23. The firing point in a thyratron tube is *most usually* controlled by the 23.____

    A. cathode   B. grid   C. plate
    D. heater   E. envelope

Questions 24-25.

Questions 24 and 25 shall be answered in accordance with the diagram below.

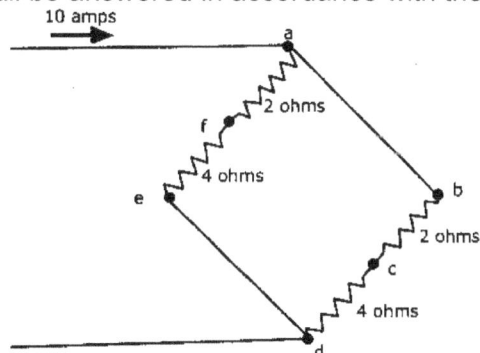

24. With reference to the above diagram, the voltage difference between 24.____
    points c and f is, *most nearly,* in volts,

    A. 40   B. 20   C. 10   D. 5   E. 0

25. With reference to the above diagram, the current flowing through the resistance 25.____
    c d is, *most nearly,* in amperes,

    A. 10   B. 5   C. 4   D. 2   E. 1

KEY (CORRECT ANSWERS)

1. D	6. E	11. A	16. B	21. C
2. C	7. C	12. A	17. C	22. E
3. E	8. B	13. B	18. A	23. B
4. A	9. C	14. B	19. A	24. E
5. B	10. E	15. E	20. B	25. B

EXAMINATION SECTION
TEST 1

DIRECTIONS: Each question or incomplete statement is followed by several suggested answers or completions. Select the one that BEST answers the question or completes the statement. *PRINT THE LETTER OF THE CORRECT ANSWER IN THE SPACE AT THE RIGHT.*

1. Two gears are meshed. The first gear has 20 teeth per inch and is rotating at 500 rpms. What is the speed of the second gear if it has 40 teeth per inch? _____ rpms.

    A. 500   B. 400   C. 250   D. 200

2. With two meshed gears, the first gear rotates at 100 rpms, the second gear rotates at 2000 rpms and has 10 teeth per inch.
The first gear has _____ number of teeth per inch.

    A. 200   B. 100   C. 50   D. 150

3. Two pulleys are connected. The first pulley has a diameter of 5 inches; the second pulley has a diameter of 15 inches and rotates at 25 rpms.
The speed of the first pulley is _____ rpms.

    A. 30   B. 75   C. 200   D. 400

4. Of two connected pulleys, the first has a radius of 10 inches and rotates at 50 rpms; the second rotates at 25 rpms.
The diameter of the second pulley is _____ inches.

    A. 40   B. 30   C. 20   D. 10

5. Two pulleys are connected. The first pulley rotates at 75 rpms; the second pulley rotates at 100 rpms and has a diameter of 9 inches.
The diameter of the first pulley is _____ inches.

    A. 10   B. 12   C. 15   D. 20

6. Of two connected pulleys, the first pulley has a radius of 12 inches and rotates at 60 rpms; the second pulley has a diameter of 16 inches.
The speed of the second pulley is _____ rpms.

    A. 1000   B. 1020   C. 1040   D. 1080

7. If 16_{10} were converted to base 2, 8, and 16, the results would be _____ base 2, _____ base 8, and _____ base 16, respectively.

    A. 10000; 20; 10
    B. 1000; 2000; 20
    C. 20000; 200; 20
    D. 2000; 100; 10

8. Converting CAF_{16} to base 10 and base 8, the results would be _____ base 10 and _____ base 8, respectively.

    A. 2437; 2567
    B. 3247; 6257
    C. 4327; 5267
    D. 3427; 2657

1.____
2.____
3.____
4.____
5.____
6.____
7.____
8.____

9. Converting 101011001_2 to base 8, 10, and 16, the results would be _____ base 8, _____ base 10, and _____ base 16, respectively.

   A. 135; 45; 59
   B. 567; 435; 259
   C. 315; 245; 135
   D. 531; 345; 159

10. If 136_8 were converted to base 2, 10, and 16, the results would be _____ base 2, _____ base 10, and _____ base 16, respectively.

    A. 001011110; 94, 5E
    B. 010100110; 92; 10E
    C. 00100000; 90; 15E
    D. 011001110; 96; 20E

11. It may be correctly stated that 1000 picofarads are equal to _____ microfarads.

    A. .0001   B. .001   C. .01   D. .1

12. If 5 megohms were converted to kohms, the result would be _____ kohms.

    A. 1000   B. 2000   C. 4000   D. 5000

13. 1 nanohenry would convert to _____ millihenries.

    A. .001   B. .0001   C. .00001   D. .0000001

14. If 7 milliamps were converted to microamps, the answer would be _____ microamps.

    A. 7000   B. 700   C. 70   D. 7

15. If two resistors are in parallel and are 100 ohms each, the total resistance is

    A. 100   B. 150   C. 50   D. 10

16. In reference to the circuit in Question 15, if the first resistor has 25 volts DC, (VDC) across it, the second resistor also has 25 VDC across it, and there are no other components in the circuit except for the power source, the total circuit voltage is _____ VDC.

    A. 25   B. 50   C. 250   D. 500

17. In reference to the circuit in Question 15, if the first resistor has 1 amp on it, and the second resistor also has 1 amp on it, the total circuit amperage is _____ amps.

    A. 1   B. 2   C. 3   D. 4

18. If two resistors are in series and are 100 ohms each, the total resistance is

    A. 50   B. 100   C. 150   D. 200

19. In reference to the circuit in Question 18, if the first resistor has 25 VDC across it and the second resistor also has 25 VDC across it, the total circuit voltage is

    A. 50   B. 100   C. 200   D. 500

20. In reference to the circuit in Question 18, if the first resistor has 1 amp across it and the second resistor also has 1 amp on it, the total circuit amperage is

    A. 1   B. 5   C. 10   D. 15

21. Where two resistors are in parallel, one is 100 ohms and the other is 300 ohms. 21.____
    The total resistance is _____ ohms.

    A. 25   B. 35   C. 55   D. 75

22. Three resistors in series are 25 ohms, 50 ohms, and 75 ohms, respectively. 22.____
    The total resistance is _____ ohms.

    A. 25   B. 50   C. 100   D. 150

23. Two inductors are in parallel; the first is 50 henries and the second is also 50 henries. 23.____
    The total inductance is _____ henries.

    A. 25   B. 50   C. 55   D. 60

24. Two inductors are in series and the first is 50 henries; the second is 50 henries. 24.____
    The total inductance is _____ henries.

    A. 25   B. 50   C. 75   D. 100

25. Where two inductors are in parallel, the first is 100 henries and the second is 200 henries. 25.____
    The total inductance is _____ henries.

    A. 50   B. 75   C. 65   D. 100

KEY (CORRECT ANSWERS)

1. C	6. D	11. B	16. A	21. D
2. A	7. A	12. D	17. B	22. D
3. B	8. B	13. D	18. D	23. A
4. A	9. D	14. A	19. A	24. D
5. B	10. A	15. C	20. A	25. B

TEST 2

DIRECTIONS: Each question or incomplete statement is followed by several suggested answers or completions. Select the one that BEST answers the question or completes the statement. *PRINT THE LETTER OF THE CORRECT ANSWER IN THE SPACE AT THE RIGHT.*

1. Two inductors are in series; the first inductor is 100 henries and the second is 200 henries.
   The total inductance is _____ henries.

   A. 200   B. 300   C. 400   D. 500

   1._____

2. Two capacitors are in parallel; each capacitor is 30 farads.
   The total capacitance is _____ farads.

   A. 60   B. 80   C. 100   D. 200

   2._____

3. Two capacitors are in series; each capacitor is 30 farads. The total capacitance is _____ farads.

   A. 10   B. 15   C. 20   D. 25

   3._____

4. Two capacitors are in parallel; the first is 50 farads and the second is 100 farads.
   The total capacitance is _____ farads.

   A. 50   B. 100   C. 125   D. 150

   4._____

5. Two capacitors are in series; the first is 50 farads and the second is 100 farads.
   The total capacitance is _____ farads.

   A. 33.333   B. 49.999   C. 13.333   D. 25.555

   5._____

6. A resistor's color codes are orange, blue, yellow, and gold, in that order.
   The value of the resistor is _____ kohms ± _____ %.

   A. 200; 2   B. 300; 4   C. 360; 5   D. 400; 7

   6._____

7. If a resistors color codes are red, black, and blue, the value of this resistor is _____ megohms ± _____ %.

   A. 20; 20   B. 40; 80   C. 30; 30   D. 50; 50

   7._____

8. If a resistor's color codes are gray, green, black, and silver, the resistor's value is _____ ohms ± _____ %.

   A. 55; 5   B. 75; 15   C. 85; 10   D. 100; 25

   8._____

9. One complete cycle of a sinewave takes 1000 microseconds. Its frequency is _____ hertz.

   A. 500   B. 1000   C. 2000   D. 5000

   9._____

10. If one complete cycle of a squarewave takes 5 microseconds, its frequency is _____ khertz.

    A. 200   B. 500   C. 700   D. 1000

    10._____

2 (#2)

11. What is the PRT (pulse repetition time) of a 50 hertz (hz) sinewave? _____ milliseconds.   11._____
    A. 10   B. 20   C. 40   D. 60

12. The PRT of a 20 khz sawtooth signal is _____ megahertz.   12._____
    A. 50   B. 100   C. 200   D. 500

13. If a resistor measures 10 volts and 2 amps across it, the resistance is _____ ohms.   13._____
    A. 0   B. 2   C. 5   D. 10

14. If a 30 ohm resistor measures 10 volts, the power consumed by the resistor is _____ watts.   14._____
    A. 3000   B. 5000   C. 6500   D. 7000

15. If a 50 ohm resistor measures 4 amps across, the power consumed by it is _____ watts.   15._____
    A. 200   B. 400   C. 600   D. 800

16. If a 100 ohm resistor measures 25 volts across, the current on it is _____ amps.   16._____
    A. .15   B. .25   C. .55   D. .65

Questions 17-23.

DIRECTIONS: Questions 17 through 23 are to be answered on the basis of the following diagram.

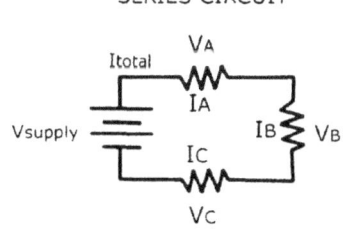
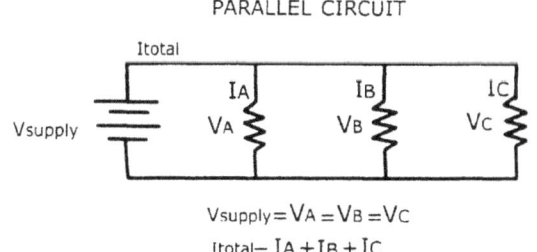

17. In the series circuit above, if Vsupply = 100 VDC, resistor A is 10 ohms, resistor B is 50 ohms, and resistor C is 5 ohms, the total circuit current is _____ amps.   17._____
    A. 1.538   B. 1.267   C. 1.358   D. 1.823

18. In the series circuit shown above, the current across each individual resistor is _____ amps.   18._____
    A. .5   B. 1.5   C. 2.5   D. 3.5

19. In the series circuit shown above, the total power drawn by the circuit is _____ watts.   19.____

    A. 140.25   B. 150.75   C. 153.38   D. 173.38

20. In the series circuit shown above, the power drawn from each individual resistor is   20.____
    _____ , _____ , and _____ watts, respectively.

    A. 23.65; 118.27; 11.827   B. 17.567; 123.27; 11.27
    C. 18.627; 145.27; 12.27   D. 21.735; 116.87; 11.83

21. In the parallel circuit shown above, if Vsupply = 100 VDC, resistor A is 10 ohms, resistor   21.____
    B is 50 ohms, and resistor C is 5 ohms, the total circuit current is _____ amps.

    A. 21   B. 27   C. 32   D. 45

22. In the parallel circuit shown above, the total power drawn by the circuit is _____ watts.   22.____

    A. 1200   B. 2300   C. 2700   D. 3200

23. In the parallel circuit above, the power drawn by each individual resistor is _____ watts,   23.____
    respectively.

    A. 100; 200; 2000   B. 200; 400; 5000
    C. 300; 500; 750   D. 450; 600; 1500

24. On an 0-scope display, one cycle of a signal takes up 4 1/2 divisions and the peak-to-   24.____
    peak amplitude of the signal takes up 3 3/4 divisions.
    With the volts/division knob set on 5 volts and the time/division knob set to 5 microsec-
    onds, the peak-to-peak amplitude and the frequency of the signal are _____ volts and
    _____ khz, respectively.

    A. 15.75; 100   B. 22.5; 200
    C. 37.5; 350   D. 45.75; 570

25. If a signal that has a peak-to-peak amplitude of 15 volts and a frequency of 5 megaherz   25.____
    is to be observed on an 0-scope with one complete cycle shown, the time/division knob
    and volts/division knob should be set on _____ microseconds and _____ volts per
    division, respectively.

    A. .02; 2   B. .05; 4   C. .07; 3.5   D. 10; 7.5

KEY (CORRECT ANSWERS)

1. B	6. C	11. B	16. B	21. C
2. A	7. A	12. A	17. A	22. D
3. B	8. C	13. C	18. B	23. A
4. D	9. B	14. A	19. C	24. B
5. A	10. A	15. D	20. A	25. A

EXAMINATION SECTION
TEST 1

DIRECTIONS: Each question or incomplete statement is followed by several suggested answers or completions. Select the one that BEST answers the question or completes the statement. *PRINT THE LETTER OF THE CORRECT ANSWER IN THE SPACE AT THE RIGHT.*

Questions 1-6.

DIRECTIONS: Questions 1 through 6 are to be answered on the basis of the circuit diagram below. All switches are initially open.

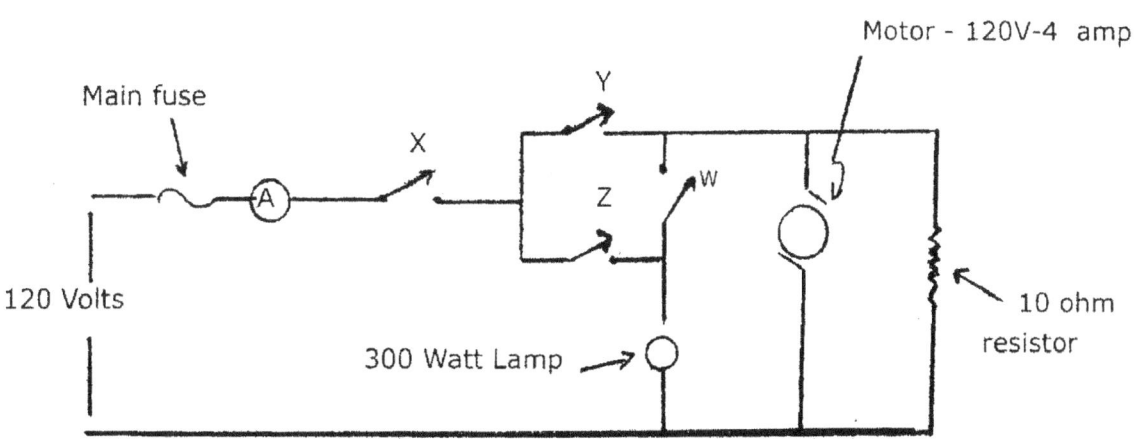

1. To light the 300 watt lamp, the following switches MUST be closed: 1.____

   A. X and Y   B. Y and Z   C. X and Z   D. X and W

2. If all of the switches W, X, Y, and Z are closed, the following will happen: 2.____

   A. The lamp will light and the motor will rotate
   B. The lamp will light and the motor will not rotate
   C. The lamp will not light and the motor will not rotate
   D. A short circuit will occur and the main fuse will blow

3. With 120 volts applied across the 10 ohm resistor, the current drawn by the resistor is _____ amp(s). 3.____

   A. 1/12   B. 1.2   C. 12   D. 1200

4. With 120 volts applied to the 10 ohm resistor, the power used by the resistor is _____ kw. 4.____

   A. 1.44   B. 1.2   C. .144   D. .12

5. The current drawn by the 300 watt lamp when lighted should be APPROXIMATELY _____ amps. 5.____

   A. 2.5   B. 3.6   C. 25   D. 36

6. In the circuit shown, the symbol A is used to indicate a (n)

   A. ammeter
   B. *and* circuit
   C. voltmeter
   D. wattmeter

7. Of the following materials, the BEST conductor of electricity is

   A. iron
   B. copper
   C. aluminum
   D. glass

8. The sum of 6'6", 5'9", and 2' 1 1/2" is

   A. 13'4 1/2"
   B. 13'6 1/2"
   C. 14'4 1/2"
   D. 14'6 1/2"

9.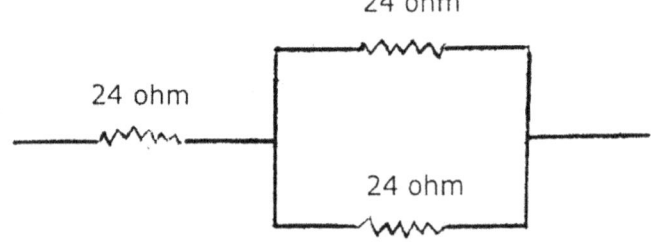

   The equivalent resistance of the three resistors shown in the sketch above is _____ ohms.

   A. 8
   B. 24
   C. 36
   D. 72

10.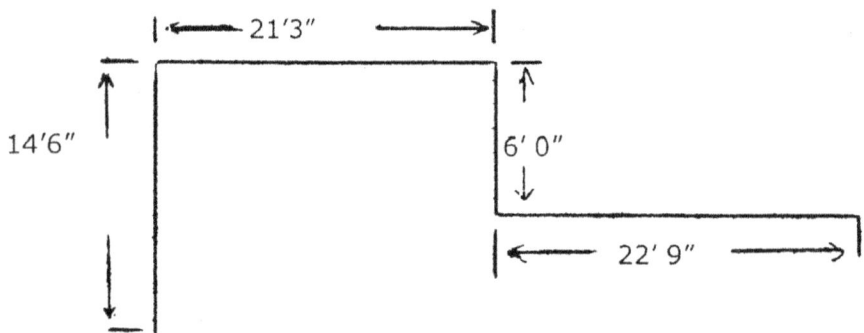

    The TOTAL length of electrical conduit that must be run along the path shown on the diagram above is

    A. 63'8"
    B. 64'6"
    C. 65'6"
    D. 66'8"

11. Of the following electrical devices, the one that is NOT normally used in direct current electrical circuits is a (n)

    A. circuit breaker
    B. double-pole switch
    C. transformer
    D. inverter

12. The number of 120-volt light bulbs that should NORMALLY be connected in series across a 600-volt electric line is

    A. 1
    B. 2
    C. 3
    D. 5

13. Of the following motors, the one that does NOT have any brushes is the _____ motor. 13.____

    A. d.c. shunt
    B. d.c. series
    C. squirrel cage induction
    D. compound

14. Of the following materials, the one that is COMMONLY used as an electric heating element in an electric heater is 14.____

    A. zinc
    B. brass
    C. terne plate
    D. nichrome

Questions 15-25.

DIRECTIONS: Questions 15 through 25 are to be answered on the basis of the instruments listed below. Each instrument is listed with an identifying number in front of it.

    1 - Hygrometer   9 - Vernier caliper
    2 - Ammeter   10 - Wire gage
    3 - Voltmeter   11 - 6-foot folding rule
    4 - Wattmeter   12 - Architect's scale
    5 - Megger   13 - Planimeter
    6 - Oscilloscope   14 - Engineer's scale
    7 - Frequency meter   15 - Ohmmeter
    8 - Micrometer

15. The instrument that should be used to accurately measure the resistance of a 4,700 ohm resistor is Number 15.____

    A. 3 B. 4 C. 7 D. 15

16. To measure the current in an electrical circuit, the instrument that should be used is Number 16.____

    A. 2 B. 7 C. 8 D. 15

17. To measure the insulation resistance of a rubber-covered electrical cable, the instrument that should be used is Number 17.____

    A. 4 B. 5 C. 8 D. 15

18. An AC motor is hooked up to a power distribution box. 18.____
    In order to check the voltage at the motor terminals, the instrument that should be used is Number

    A. 2 B. 3 C. 4 D. 7

19. To measure the shaft diameter of a motor accurately to one-thousandth of an inch, the instrument that should be used is Number 19.____

    A. 8 B. 10 C. 11 D. 14

20. The instrument that should be used to determine whether 25 Hz. or 60 Hz. is present in an electrical circuit is Number 20.____

    A. 4 B. 5 C. 7 D. 8

21. Of the following, the PROPER instrument to use to determine the diameter of the conductor of a piece of electrical hook-up wire is Number

    A. 10 B. 11 C. 12 D. 14

22. The amount of electrical power being used in a balanced three-phase circuit should be measured with Number

    A. 2 B. 3 C. 4 D. 5

23. The electrical wave form at a given point in an electronic circuit can be observed with Number

    A. 2 B. 3 C. 6 D. 7

24. The PROPER instrument to use for measuring the width of a door is Number

    A. 11 B. 12 C. 13 D. 14

25. A one-inch hole with a tolerance of plus or minus three-thousandths is reamed in a steel block.
    The PROPER instrument to use to accurately check the diameter of the hole is Number

    A. 8 B. 9 C. 11 D. 14

KEY (CORRECT ANSWERS)

1. C
2. A
3. C
4. A
5. A
6. A
7. B
8. C
9. C
10. B
11. C
12. D
13. C
14. D
15. D
16. A
17. B
18. B
19. A
20. C
21. A
22. C
23. C
24. A
25. B

TEST 2

DIRECTIONS: Each question or incomplete statement is followed by several suggested answers or completions. Select the one that BEST answers the question or completes the statement. *PRINT THE LETTER OF THE CORRECT ANSWER IN THE SPACE AT THE RIGHT.*

1. The number of conductors required to connect a 3-phase delta connected heater bank to an electric power panel board is   1._____

   A. 2   B. 3   C. 4   D. 5

2. Of the following, the wire size that is MOST commonly used for branch lighting circuits in homes is _____ A.W.G.   2._____

   A. #12   B. #8   C. #6   D. #4

3. When installing electrical circuits, the tool that should be used to pull wire through a conduit is a   3._____

   A. mandrel   B. snake
   C. rod   D. pulling iron

4. Of the following AC voltages, the LOWEST voltage that a neon test lamp can detect is _____ volts.   4._____

   A. 6   B. 12   C. 80   D. 120

5. Of the following, the BEST procedure to use when storing tools that are subject to rusting is to   5._____

   A. apply a thin coating of soap onto the tools
   B. apply a light coating of oil to the tools
   C. wrap the tools in clean cheesecloth
   D. place the tools in a covered container

6. If a 3 1/2 inch long nail is required to nail wood framing members together, the nail size to use should be   6._____

   A. 2d   B. 4d   C. 16d   D. 60d

7. Of the four motors listed below, the one that can operate only on alternating current is a(n) _____ motor.   7._____

   A. series   B. shunt
   C. compound   D. induction

8. The sum of 1/3 + 2/5 + 5/6 is   8._____

   A. 1 17/30   B. 1 3/5   C. 1 15/24   D. 1 5/6

9. Of the following instruments, the one that should be used to measure the state of charge of a lead-acid storage battery is a(n)   9._____

   A. ammeter   B. ohmmeter
   C. hydrometer   D. thermometer

59

10. If three 1 1/2 volt dry cell batteries are wired in series, the TOTAL voltage provided by the three batteries is _____ volts. 10._____

    A. 1.5   B. 3   C. 4.5   D. 6.0

11. Taking into account time and one-half payment for time over 40 hours of work, the gross pay of an employee who works 43 hours in a week at a rate of pay of $10.68 per hour is 11._____

    A. $427.20   B. $459.24   C. $475.26   D. $491.28

12. The sum of 0.365 + 3.941 + 10.676 + 0.784 is 12._____

    A. 13.766   B. 15.666   C. 15.756   D. 15.766

13. In order to transmit mechanical power between two rotating shafts at right angles to each other, two gears are used. Of the following, the type of gears that should be used are _____ gears. 13._____

    A. herringbone   B. spur
    C. bevel   D. rack and pinion

14. To properly ground the service electrical equipment in a building, a ground connection should be made to _____ the building. 14._____

    A. the waste or soil line leaving
    B. the vent line going to the exterior of
    C. any steel beam in
    D. the cold water line entering

15. The area of the triangle shown at the right is _____ square inches. 15._____
    A. 120
    B. 240
    C. 360
    D. 480

Questions 16-25.

DIRECTIONS: Questions 16 through 25 are to be answered on the basis of the tools shown on the next page. The tools are not shown to scale. Each tool is shown with an identifying number alongside it.

3 (#2)

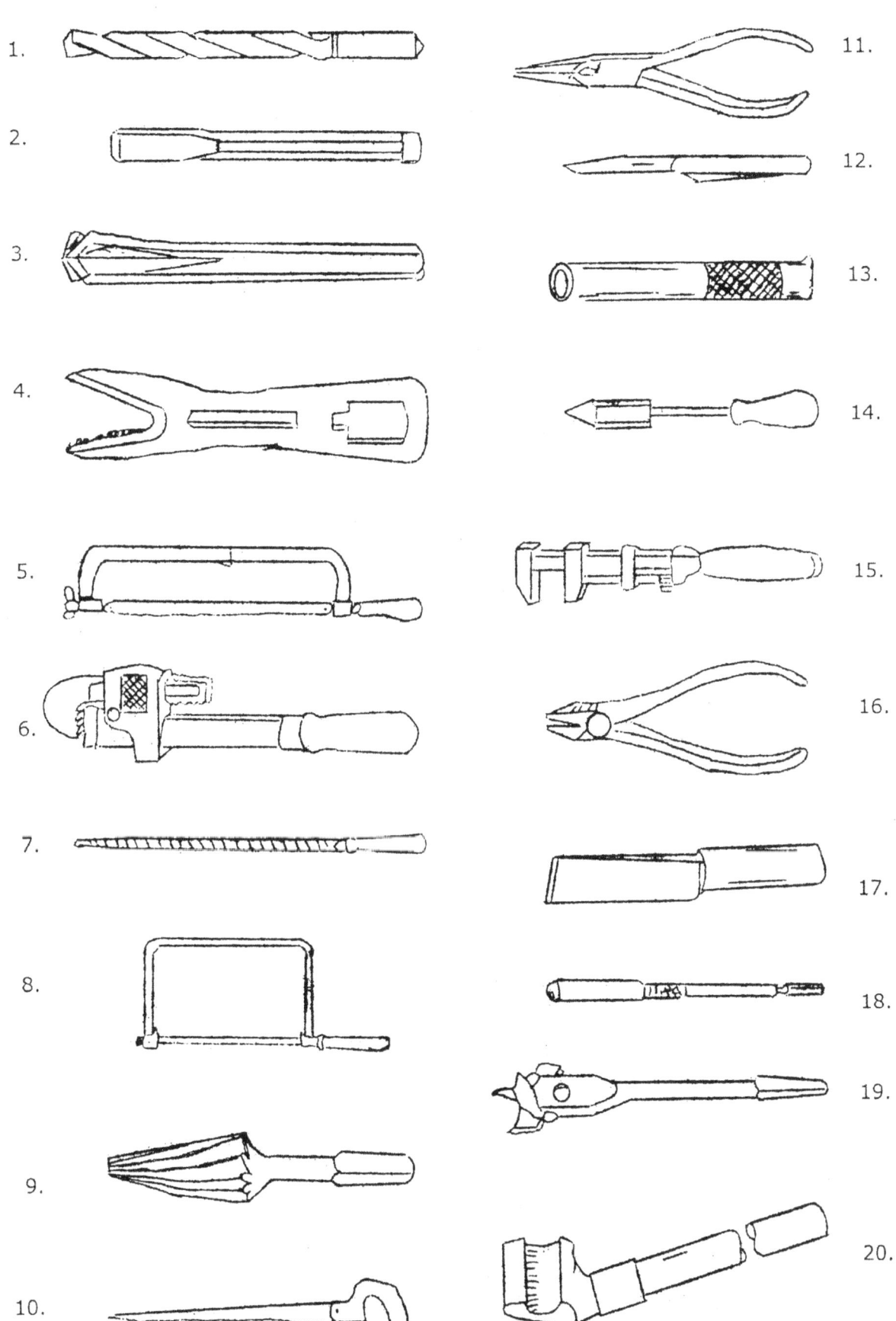

16. The tool that should be used for cutting thin wall steel conduit is Number   16._____
    A. 5   B. 8   C. 10   D. 16

17. The tool that should be used for cutting a 1 7/8 inch diameter hole in a wood joist is Number   17._____
    A. 3   B. 9   C. 14   D. 19

18. The tool that should be used for soldering splices in electrical wire is Number   18._____
    A. 3   B. 7   C. 13   D. 14

19. After cutting off a piece of 3/4 inch diameter electrical conduit, the tool that should be used for removing a burr from the inside of the conduit is Number   19._____
    A. 9   B. 11   C. 12   D. 14

20. The tool that should be used for turning a coupling onto a threaded conduit is Number   20._____
    A. 6   B. 11   C. 15   D. 16

21. The tool that should be used for cutting wood lathing in plaster walls is Number   21._____
    A. 5   B. 7   C. 10   D. 12

22. The tool that should be used for drilling a 3/8 inch diameter hole in a steel beam is Number   22._____
    A. 1   B. 2   C. 3   D. 9

23. Of the following, the BEST tool to use for stripping insulation from electrical hook-up wire is Number   23._____
    A. 11   B. 12   C. 15   D. 20

24. The tool that should be used for bending an electrical wire around a terminal post is Number   24._____
    A. 4   B. 11   C. 15   D. 16

25. The tool that should be used for cutting electrical hookup wire is Number   25._____
    A. 5   B. 12   C. 16   D. 17

KEY (CORRECT ANSWERS)

1.	B	11.	C
2.	A	12.	D
3.	B	13.	C
4.	C	14.	D
5.	B	15.	A
6.	C	16.	A
7.	D	17.	D
8.	A	18.	D
9.	C	19.	A
10.	C	20.	A

21. C
22. A
23. B
24. B
25. C

TEST 3

DIRECTIONS: Each question or incomplete statement is followed by several suggested answers or completions. Select the one that BEST answers the question or completes the statement. *PRINT THE LETTER OF THE CORRECT ANSWER IN THE SPACE AT THE RIGHT.*

1. An electric circuit has current flowing through it. The panel board switch feeding the circuit is opened, causing arcing across the switch contacts.
Generally, this arcing is caused by

   A. a lack of energy storage in the circuit
   B. electrical energy stored by a capacitor
   C. electrical energy stored by a resistor
   D. magnetic energy induced by an inductance

   1.____

2. MOST filter capacitors in radios have a capacity rating given in

   A. microvolts   B. milliamps
   C. millihenries   D. microfarads

   2.____

3. Of the following, the electrical wire size that is COMMONLY used for telephone circuits is _____ A.W.G.

   A. #6   B. #10   C. #12   D. #22

   3.____

Questions 4-9.

DIRECTIONS: Questions 4 through 9 are to be answered on the basis of the electrical circuit diagram shown below, where letters are used to identify various circuit components.

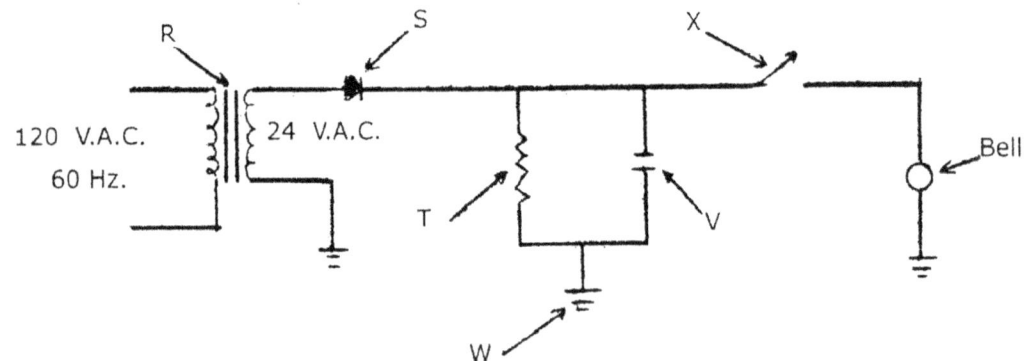

4. The device indicated by the letter R is a

   A. capacitor   B. converter
   C. resistor   D. transformer

   4.____

5. The device indicated by the letter S is a

   A. transistor   B. diode
   C. thermistor   D. directional relay

   5.____

64

6. The devices indicated by the letters T and V are used together to _____ components of the secondary current.

   A. reduce the AC
   B. reduce the DC
   C. transform the AC
   D. invert the AC

7. The letter W points to a standard electrical symbol for a

   A. wire
   B. ground
   C. terminal
   D. lightning arrestor

8. Closing switch X will apply the following type of voltage to the bell:

   A. 60 Hz. AC
   B. DC
   C. pulsating AC
   D. 120 Hz. AC

9. The circuit shown contains a _____ rectifier.

   A. mercury-arc
   B. full-wave
   C. bridge
   D. half-wave

10. A bolt specified as 1/4-28 means the following:
    The

    A. bolt is 1/4 inch in diameter and has 28 threads per inch
    B. bolt is 1/4 inch in diameter and is 2.8 inches long
    C. bolt is 1/4 inch long and has 28 threads
    D. threaded portion of the bolt is 1/4 inch long and has 28 threads per inch

11. When cutting 0.045-inch thickness sheet metal, it is BEST to use a hacksaw blade that has _____ teeth per inch.

    A. 7   B. 12   C. 18   D. 32

12. To accurately tighten a bolt to 28 foot-pounds, it is BEST to use a(n) _____ wrench.

    A. pipe   B. open end   C. box   D. torque

13. When bending a 2-inch diameter conduit, the CORRECT tool to use is a

    A. hickey
    B. pipe wrench
    C. hydraulic bender
    D. stock and die

14. When soldering two #20 A.W.G. copper wires together to form a splice, the solder that SHOULD be used is _____ solder.

    A. acid-core
    B. solid-core
    C. rosin-core
    D. liquid

15. A bathroom heating unit draws 10 amperes at 115 volts.
    The hot resistance of the heating unit should be _____ ohms.

    A. .08   B. 8   C. 11.5   D. 1150

16. Of the following materials, the one that is NOT suitable as an electrical insulator is

    A. glass   B. mica   C. rubber   D. platinum

17. An air conditioning unit is rated at 1000 watts. The unit is run for 10 hours per day, five days per week.
    If the cost for electrical energy is 5 cents per kilowatt-hour, the weekly cost for electricity should be

    A. 25¢   B. 50¢   C. $2.50   D. $25.00

18. If a fuse is protecting the circuit of a 15 ohm electric heater and it is designed to blow out at a current exceeding 10 amperes, the MAXIMUM voltage from among the following that should be applied across the terminals of the heater is _____ volts.

    A. 110   B. 120   C. 160   D. 600

19. Before opening a pneumatic hose connection, it is important to remove pressure from the hose line PRIMARILY to avoid

    A. losing air
    B. personal injury
    C. damage to the hose connection
    D. a build-up of pressure in the air compressor

20. If the scale on a shop drawing is 1/4 inch to the foot, then a part which measures 3 3/8 inches long on the drawing has an ACTUAL length of _____ feet _____ inches.

    A. 12; 6   B. 13; 6   C. 13; 9   D. 14; 9

21. The function that is USUALLY performed by a motor controller is to

    A. start and stop a motor
    B. protect a motor from a short circuit
    C. prevent bearing failure of a motor
    D. control the brush wear in a motor

22. Of the following galvanized sheet metal electrical outlet boxes, the one that is NOT a commonly used size is the _____ box.

    A. 4" square   B. 4" octagonal
    C. 4" x 2 1/8"   D. 4" x 1"

23. When soldering a transistor into a circuit, it is MOST important to protect the transistor from

    A. the application of an excess of rosin flux
    B. excessive heat
    C. the application of an excess of solder
    D. too much pressure

24. When installing BX type cable, it is important to protect the wires in the cable from the cut ends of the armored sheath.
    The APPROVED method of providing this protection is to

    A. use a fiber or plastic insulating bushing
    B. file the cut ends of the sheath smooth
    C. use a connector where the cable enters a junction box
    D. tie the wires into an Underwriter's knot

25. While lifting a heavy piece of equipment off the floor, a person should NOT   25._____

    A. twist his body
    B. grasp it firmly
    C. maintain a solid footing on the ground
    D. bend his knees

26. It is important that metal cabinets and panels that house electrical equipment should be grounded PRIMARILY in order to   26._____

    A. prevent short circuits from occurring
    B. keep all circuits at ground potential
    C. minimize shock hazards
    D. reduce the effects of electrolytic corrosion

27. A foreman explains a technical procedure to a new employee. If the employee does not understand the instructions he has received, it would be BEST if he were to   27._____

    A. follow the procedure as best he could
    B. ask the foreman to explain it to him again
    C. avoid following the procedure
    D. ask the foreman to give him other work

28. Of the following, the BEST connectors to use when mounting an electrical panel box directly onto a concrete wall are   28._____

    A. threaded studs   B. machine screws
    C. lag screws   D. expansion bolts

29. Of the following, the BEST instrument to use to measure the small gap between relay contacts is   29._____

    A. a micrometer   B. a feeler gage
    C. inside calipers   D. a plug gage

30. A POSSIBLE result of mounting a 40 ampere fuse in a fuse box for a circuit requiring a 20 ampere fuse is that the 40 ampere fuse may   30._____

    A. provide twice as much protection to the circuit from overloads
    B. blow more easily than the smaller fuse due to an overload
    C. cause serious damage to the circuit from an overload
    D. reduce power consumption in the circuit

KEY (CORRECT ANSWERS)

1.	D	16.	D
2.	D	17.	C
3.	D	18.	B
4.	D	19.	B
5.	B	20.	B
6.	A	21.	A
7.	B	22.	D
8.	B	23.	B
9.	D	24.	A
10.	A	25.	A
11.	D	26.	C
12.	D	27.	B
13.	C	28.	D
14.	C	29.	B
15.	C	30.	C

MECHANICAL APTITUDE
Tools and Their Use

EXAMINATION SECTION
TEST 1

DIRECTIONS: Each question or incomplete statement is followed by several suggested answers or completions. Select the one that BEST answers the question or completes the statement. *PRINT THE LETTER OF THE CORRECT ANSWER IN THE SPACE AT THE RIGHT.*

Questions 1-10.

DIRECTIONS: Questions 1 through 10 refer to the tools shown below. The numbers in the answers refer to the numbers beneath the tools.
NOTE: These tools are NOT shown to scale.

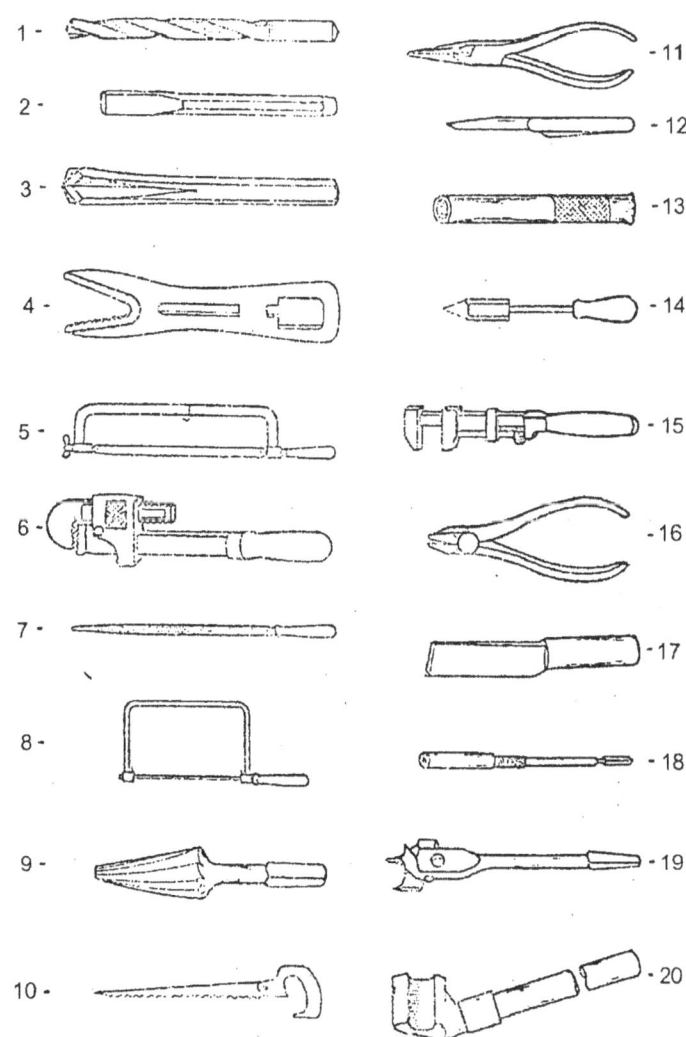

1. The tool that should be used for cutting a 1 7/8" diameter hole in a wood joist is number   1._____
   A. 3   B. 9   C. 14   D. 19

2. The tool that should be used for cutting thin-wall steel conduit is number qq   2._____
   A. 5   B. 8   C. 10   D. 16

3. The tool that should be used for soldering splices in electrical wire is number   3._____
   A. 3   B. 7   C. 13   D. 14

4. After cutting off a piece of a 3/4" diameter electrical conduit, the tool that should be used for removing a burr from the inside of the conduit is number   4._____
   A. 9   B. 11   C. 12   D. 14

5. The tool that should be used for turning a coupling onto a threaded conduit is number   5._____
   A. 6   B. 11   C. 15   D. 16

6. The tool that should be used for cutting wood lathing in plaster walls is number   6._____
   A. 5   B. 7   C. 10   D. 12

7. The tool that should be used for drilling a 3/8" diameter hole in a steel beam is number   7._____
   A. 1   B. 2   C. 3   D. 9

8. Of the following, the BEST tool to use for stripping insulation from electrical hook-up wire is number   8._____
   A. 11   B. 12   C. 15   D. 20

9. The tool that should be used for bending an electrical wire around a terminal post is number   9._____
   A. 4   B. 11   C. 15   D. 16

10. The tool that should be used for cutting electrical hook-up wire is number   10._____
    A. 5   B. 12   C. 16   D. 17

KEY (CORRECT ANSWERS)

1. D   6. C
2. A   7. A
3. D   8. B
4. A   9. B
5. A   10. C

TEST 2

DIRECTIONS: Each question or incomplete statement is followed by several suggested answers or completions. Select the one that BEST answers the question or completes the statement. *PRINT THE LETTER OF THE CORRECT ANSWER IN THE SPACE AT THE RIGHT.*

1. Round-nose pliers are *especially* useful for

    A. forming wire loops
    B. tightening small nuts
    C. crimping wires
    D. gripping small screws

    1._____

2. A slight coating of rust on small tools is BEST removed by

    A. rubbing the tool with a dry cloth
    B. scraping the tool with a sharp knife
    C. scraping the tool with a small file having vaseline on it
    D. rubbing the tool with fine steel wool moistened with kerosene

    2._____

3. The stake that should be used for hand-forming a small sheet metal cone is a _____ stake.

    A. hatchet   B. bottom   C. solid mandrel   D. blowhorn

    3._____

4. Of the following types of pliers, the BEST one to use to clamp down sheet metal to the top of a work bench is the

    A. channel-lock   B. vise grip   C. slip-joint   D. duck bill

    4._____

5. Angle brackets for supporting ductwork are *commonly* anchored to concrete walls by means of _____ bolts.

    A. carriage   B. J-   C. expansion   D. foot

    5._____

6. Of the following bolts, the *one* that should be used when attaching a hanger to a wooden joist is a _____ bolt.

    A. dead   B. lag   C. dardalet   D. toggle

    6._____

7. When bending sheet metal by hand, the BEST tool to use is a

    A. hand groover
    B. hand seamer
    C. hand ball tooler
    D. hand plier

    7._____

8. Of the following types of steel rivets of the same size, the STRONGEST is the _____ rivet.

    A. tinners'   B. flathead   C. roundhead
    D. countersunk

    8._____

9. Of the following snips, the one that can cut relatively thick sheet metal with the LEAST effort is _____ snips.

    A. straight   B. aviation   C. duck bill   D. hawk bill

    9._____

10. Of the following, the BEST tool to use to make a hole in a concrete floor for a machine hold-down bolt is a

    A. counterboring tool B. cold chisel
    C. drift punch D. star drill

11. Of the following, the BEST type of saw to use to cut a 4" diameter hole through a 5/8" wooden partition is a _____ saw.

    A. back B. saber C. circular D. cross-cut

12. While using a hacksaw to cut through a 1" diameter steel bar, a helper should not press down too heavily on the hacksaw because this may

    A. break the blade B. overheat the bar
    C. permanently distort the frame
    D. cause the hacksaw to slip

13. A miter box is used

    A. for locating dowel holes in two pieces of wood to be joined together
    B. to hold a saw at a fixed angle while sawing
    C. to hold a saw while sharpening its teeth
    D. to clamp two pieces of wood together at 90 degrees

14. Wing nuts are *especially* useful on equipment where

    A. the nuts must be removed frequently and easily
    B. the nuts are locked in place with a cotter pin
    C. critical adjustments are to be made frequently
    D. a standard hex head wrench cannot be used

15. The BEST device to employ to make certain that two points, separated by an unobstructed vertical distance of 12 feet, are in the best possible vertical alignment is a

    A. carpenter's square B. level
    C. folding ruler D. plumb bob

16. In a shop, snips should be used to

    A. hold small parts steady while machining them
    B. cut threaded pipe
    C. cut thin gauge sheet metal
    D. remove nuts that are seized on a bolt

17. A clutch is a device that is used

    A. to hold a work piece in a fixture
    B. for retrieving small parts from hard-to-reach areas
    C. to disengage one rotating shaft from another
    D. to level machinery on a floor

18. Of the following, the BEST device to use to determine whether the surface of a work bench is horizontal is a

    A. surface gage B. spirit level
    C. dial vernier D. profilometer

19. Of the following, the machine screw having the SMALLEST diameter is the 19.____

   A. 10-24 x 3/4" B. 6-32 x 1 1/4"
   C. 12-24 x 1"   D. 8-32 x 1 1/2"

20. To close off one opening in a pipe tee when the line connecting into it is to be temporarily 20.____
    removed, it is necessary to use a

   A. pipe cap   B. pipe plug   C. nipple   D. bushing

21. The tool that should be used to cut a 1" x 4" plank down to a 3" width is a _____ saw. 21.____

   A. hack   B. crosscut   C. rip   D. back

22. Sharpening a hand saw consists of four major steps, *namely,* 22.____

   A. jointing, shaping, setting and filing
   B. adzing, clinching, forging and machining
   C. brazing, chiseling, grinding and mitering
   D. bushing, dressing, lapping, and machining

23. If it is necessary to shorten the length of a bolt by cutting through the threaded portion, 23.____
    the SIMPLEST procedure to avoid difficulty with the thread is to

   A. cut parallel to the threads in the groove of the thread
   B. run on a die after cutting
   C. turn on a nut past the cutting point prior to cutting
   D. clear the injured thread with a 3-cornered file

24. The wrench that would prove LEAST useful in uncoupling several pieces of pipe is a 24.____
    _____ wrench.

   A. socket   B. chain   C. strap   D. stillson

25. Gaskets are *commonly* used between the flanges of large pipe joints to 25.____

   A. provide space for assembly
   B. take up expansion and contraction
   C. prevent the flanges from rusting together
   D. make a tight connection

KEY (CORRECT ANSWERS)

1.	A	11.	B
2.	D	12.	A
3.	D	13.	B
4.	B	14.	A
5.	C	15.	D
6.	B	16.	C
7.	B	17.	C
8.	C	18.	B
9.	B	19.	B
10.	D	20.	B

21. C
22. A
23. C
24. A
25. D

———

SAFETY
EXAMINATION SECTION
TEST 1

DIRECTIONS: Each question or incomplete statement is followed by several suggested answers or completions. Select the one that BEST answers the question or completes the statement. *PRINT THE LETTER OF THE CORRECT ANSWER IN THE SPACE AT THE RIGHT.*

1. Which one of the following is an INCORRECT safety guideline? 1.____

   A. All working conditions and equipment should be considered carefully before beginning an operation.
   B. Aisles should be lighted properly.
   C. Personnel should be provided with protective clothing essential to safe performance of a task.
   D. In manual lifting, the worker must keep his knees straight and lift with the arm muscles.

2. Of the following, the supply item with the GREATEST susceptibility to spontaneous heating is 2.____

   A. alcohol, ethyl B. kerosene
   C. candles D. turpentine

Questions 3-7.

DIRECTIONS: Questions 3 through 7 are descriptions of accidents that occurred in a warehouse. For each accident, choose the letter in front of the safety measure that is MOST likely to prevent a repetition of the accident indicated.

SAFETY MEASURE

   A. Posting warning signs
   B. Redesign of layout or facilities
   C. Repairing, improving or replacing supplies, tools or equipment
   D. Training the staff in safe practices

3. After a new all-glass door was installed at the entrance to the warehouse, one of the employees banged his head into the door causing a large lump on his forehead when he failed to realize that the door was closed. 3.____

4. While tieing up a package with manila rope, an employee got several small rope splinters in his right hand and he had to have medical treatment to remove the splinters. 4.____

5. An employee discovered a small fire in a wastepaper basket but was unable to prevent it from spreading because all the nearby fire extinguishers were inaccessible due to skids of material being stacked in front of the extinguishers. 5.____

6. When a laborer attempted to drop the tailgate of a delivery truck while the truck was being backed into the loading dock, he had his fingers crushed when the truck continued to move while he was working on lowering the tailgate. 6.____

75

7. An employee carrying a carton with both hands tripped over a broom which had been left lying in an aisle by another employee after the latter had swept the aisle.

8. Safety experts agree that accidents can probably BEST be prevented by

    A. developing safety consciousness among employees
    B. developing a program which publicizes major accidents
    C. penalizing employees the first time they do not follow safety procedures
    D. giving recognition to employees with accident-free records

9. The accident records of many agencies indicate that most on-the-job injuries are caused by the unsafe acts of their employees.
    Which one of the following statements pinpoints the MOST probable cause of this safety problem?

    A. Responsibility for preventing on-the-job accidents has not been delegated.
    B. Lack of proper supervision has permitted these unsafe actions to continue.
    C. No consideration has been given to eliminating environmental job hazards.
    D. Penalties for causing on-the-job accidents are not sufficiently severe.

10. Which of the following methods is LEAST essential to the success of an accident prevention program?

    A. Determining corrective measures by analyzing the causes of accidents and making recommendations to eliminate them
    B. Educating employees as to the importance of safe working conditions and methods
    C. Determining accident causes by seeking out the conditions from which each accident has developed
    D. Holding each supervisor responsible for accidents occurring during the on-the-job performance of his immediate subordinates

11. The effectiveness of a public relations program in a public agency is BEST indicated by the

    A. amount of mass media publicity favorable to the policies of the agency
    B. morale of those employees who directly serve the patrons of the agency
    C. public's understanding and support of the agency's program and policies
    D. number of complaints received by the agency from patrons using its facilities

12. Buttered bread and coffee dropped on an office floor in a terminal are

    A. minor hazards which should cause no serious injury
    B. unattractive, but not dangerous
    C. the most dangerous types of office hazards
    D. hazards which should be corrected immediately

13. A laborer was sent upstairs to get a 20-pound sack of rock salt. While going downstairs and reading the printing on the sack, he fell, and the sack of rock salt fell and broke his toe.
    Which of the following is MOST likely to have been the MOST important cause of the accident?
    The

A. stairs were beginning to become worn
B. laborer was carrying too heavy a sack of rock salt
C. rock salt was in a place that was too inaccessible
D. laborer was not careful about the way he went down the stairs

14. A COMMONLY recommended safe distance between the foot of an extension ladder and the wall against which it is placed is

    A. 3 feet for ladders less than 18 feet in height
    B. between 3 feet and 6 feet for ladders less than 18 feet in length
    C. 1/8 the length of the extended ladder
    D. 1/4 the length of the extended ladder

15. The BEST type of fire extinguisher for electrical fires is the _____ extinguisher.

    A. dry chemical   B. foam
    C. carbon monoxide   D. baking soda-acid

16. A Class A extinguisher should be used for fires in

    A. potassium, magnesium, zinc, sodium
    B. electrical wiring
    C. oil, gasoline
    D. wood, paper, and textiles

17. The one of the following which is NOT a safe practice when lifting heavy objects is:

    A. Keep the back as nearly upright as possible
    B. If the object feels too heavy, keep lifting until you get help
    C. Spread the feet apart
    D. Use the arm and leg muscles

18. In a shop, it would be MOST necessary to provide a fitted cover on the metal container for

    A. old paint brushes   B. oily rags and waste
    C. sand   D. broken glass

19. Safety shoes usually have the unique feature of

    A. extra hard heels and soles to prevent nails from piercing the shoes
    B. special leather to prevent the piercing of the shoes by falling objects
    C. a metal guard over the toes which is built into the shoes
    D. a non-slip tread on the heels and soles

20. Of the following, the MOST important factor contributing to a helper's safety on the job is for him to

    A. work slowly   B. wear gloves
    C. be alert   D. know his job well

21. If it is necessary for you to lift one end of a piece of heavy equipment with a crowbar in order to allow a maintainer to work underneath it, the BEST of the following procedures to follow is to

    A. support the handle of the bar on a box
    B. insert temporary blocks to support the piece
    C. call the supervisor to help you
    D. wear heavy gloves

22. Of the following, the MOST important reason for not letting oily rags accumulate in an open storage bin is that they

    A. may start a fire by spontaneous combustion
    B. will drip oil onto other items in the bin
    C. may cause a foul odor
    D. will make the area messy

23. Of the following, the BEST method to employ in putting out a gasoline fire is to

    A. use a bucket of water
    B. smother it with rags
    C. use a carbon dioxide extinguisher
    D. use a carbon tetrachloride extinguisher

24. When opening an emergency exit door set in the sidewalk, the door should be raised slowly to avoid

    A. a sudden rush of air from the street
    B. making unnecessary noise
    C. damage to the sidewalk
    D. injuring pedestrians

25. The BEST reason to turn off lights when cleaning lampshades on electrical fixtures is to

    A. conserve energy
    B. avoid electrical shock
    C. prevent breakage of lightbulbs
    D. prevent unnecessary eye strain

KEY (CORRECT ANSWERS)

1. D
2. D
3. A
4. D
5. B

6. D
7. D
8. A
9. B
10. D

11. C
12. D
13. D
14. D
15. A

16. D
17. B
18. B
19. C
20. C

21. B
22. A
23. C
24. D
25. B

TEST 2

DIRECTIONS: Each question or incomplete statement is followed by several suggested answers or completions. Select the one that BEST answers the question or completes the statement. *PRINT THE LETTER OF THE CORRECT ANSWER IN THE SPACE AT THE RIGHT.*

1. The MOST important reason for roping off a work area in a terminal is to 1.____

    A. protect the public
    B. protect the repair crew
    C. prevent distraction of the crew by the public
    D. prevent delays to the public

2. Shoes which have a sponge rubber sole should NOT be worn around a work area because such a sole 2.____

    A. will wear quickly
    B. is not waterproof
    C. does not keep the feet warm
    D. is easily punctured by steel objects

3. When repair work is being done on an elevated structure, canvas spreads are suspended under the working area MAINLY to 3.____

    A. reduce noise
    B. discourage crowds
    C. protect the structure
    D. protect pedestrians

4. It is poor practice to hold a piece of wood in the hands or lap when tightening a screw in the wood.
   This is for the reason that 4.____

    A. sufficient leverage cannot be obtained
    B. the screwdriver may bend
    C. the wood will probably split
    D. personal injury is likely to result

5. Steel helmets give workers the MOST protection from 5.____

    A. falling objects
    B. eye injuries
    C. fire
    D. electric shock

6. It is POOR practice to wear goggles 6.____

    A. when chipping stone
    B. when using a grinder
    C. while climbing or descending ladders
    D. when handling molten metal

7. When using a brace and bit to bore a hole completely through a partition, it is MOST important to 7.____

A. lean heavily on the brace and bit
B. maintain a steady turning speed all through the job
C. have the body in a position that will not be easily thrown off balance
D. reverse the direction of the bit at frequent intervals

8. Gloves should be used when handling 8._____

   A. lanterns   B. wooden rules
   C. heavy ropes   D. all small tools

Questions 9-16.

DIRECTIONS: Questions 9 through 16, inclusive, are based on the ladder safety rules given below. Read these rules fully before answering these items.

LADDER SAFETY RULES

When a ladder is placed on a slightly uneven supporting surface, use a flat piece of board or small wedge to even up the ladder feet. To secure the proper angle for resting a ladder, it should be placed so that the distance from the base of the ladder to the supporting wall is 1/4 the length of the ladder. To avoid overloading a ladder, only one person should work on a ladder at a time. Do not place a ladder in front of a door. When the top rung of a ladder rests against a pole, the ladder should be lashed securely. Clear loose stones or debris from the ground around the base of a ladder before climbing. While on a ladder, do not attempt to lean so that any part of the body, except arms or hands, extends more than 12 inches beyond the side rail. Always face the ladder when ascending or descending. When carrying ladders through buildings, watch for ceiling globes and lighting fixtures. Avoid the use of rolling ladders as scaffold supports.

9. A small wedge is used to 9._____

   A. even up the feet of a ladder resting on an uneven surface
   B. lock the wheels of a roller ladder
   C. secure the proper resting angle for a ladder
   D. secure a ladder against a pole

10. An 8 foot ladder resting against a wall should be so inclined that the distance between 10._____
    the base of the ladder and the wall is _____ feet.

    A. 2   B. 5   C. 7   D. 9

11. A ladder should be lashed securely when 11._____

    A. it is placed in front of a door
    B. loose stones are on the ground near the base of the ladder
    C. the top rung rests against a pole
    D. two people are working from the same ladder

12. Rolling ladders 12._____

    A. should be used for scaffold supports
    B. should not be used for scaffold supports
    C. are useful on uneven ground
    D. should be used against a pole

13. When carrying a ladder through a building, it is necessary to

    A. have two men to carry it
    B. carry the ladder vertically
    C. watch for ceiling globes
    D. face the ladder while carrying it

14. It is POOR practice to

    A. lash a ladder securely at any time
    B. clear debris from the base of a ladder before climbing
    C. even up the feet of a ladder resting on slightly uneven ground
    D. place a ladder in front of a door

15. A person on a ladder should NOT extend his head beyond the side rail by more than _____ inches.

    A. 12   B. 9   C. 7   D. 5

16. The MOST important reason for permitting only one person to work on a ladder at a time is that

    A. both could not face the ladder at one time
    B. the ladder will be overloaded
    C. time would be lost going up and down the ladder
    D. they would obstruct each other

17. Many portable electric power tools, such as electric drills, have a third conductor in the power lead which is used to connect the case of the tool to a grounded part of the electric outlet.
    The reason for this extra conductor is to

    A. have a spare wire in case one power wire should break
    B. strengthen the power lead so it cannot easily be damaged
    C. prevent the user of the tool from being shocked
    D. enable the tool to be used for long periods of time without overheating

18. Protective goggles should NOT be worn when

    A. standing on a ladder drilling a steel beam
    B. descending a ladder after completing a job
    C. chipping concrete near a third rail
    D. sharpening a cold chisel on a grinding stone

19. When the foot of an extension ladder, placed against a high wall, rests on a sidewalk or another such similar surface, it is advisable to tie a rope between the bottom rung of the ladder and a point on the wall opposite this rung.
    This is done to prevent

    A. people from walking under the ladder
    B. another worker from removing the ladder
    C. the ladder from vibrating when ascending or descending
    D. the foot of the ladder from slipping

20. In construction work, practically all accidents can be blamed on the   20._____
    A. failure of an individual to give close attention to the job assigned to him
    B. use of improper tools
    C. lack of cooperation among the men in a gang
    D. fact that an incompetent man was placed in a key position

21. If it is necessary for you to do some work with your hands under a piece of heavy equip-   21._____
    ment while a fellow worker lifts up and holds one end of it by means of a pinch bar, one
    important precaution you should take is to
    A. wear gloves
    B. watch the bar to be ready if it slips
    C. insert a temporary block to support the piece
    D. work as fast as possible

22. Employees of the transit system whose work requires them to enter upon the tracks in   22._____
    the subway are cautioned not to wear loose fitting clothing.
    The MOST important reason for this caution is that loose fitting clothing may
    A. interfere when men are using heavy tools
    B. catch on some projection of a passing train
    C. tear more easily than snug fitting clothing
    D. give insufficient protection against subway dust

23. The MOST important reason for insisting on neatness in maintenance quarters is that it   23._____
    A. keeps the men busy in slack periods
    B. prevents tools from becoming rusty
    C. makes a good impression on visitors and officials
    D. decreases the chances of accidents to employees

24. Maintenance workers whose duties require them to do certain types of work generally   24._____
    work in pairs.
    The LEAST likely of the following possible reasons for this practice is that
    A. some of the work requires two men
    B. the men can help each other in case of accident
    C. there is too much equipment for one man to carry
    D. it protects against vandalism

25. A foreman reprimands a helper for actions in violation of the rules and regulations.   25._____
    The BEST reaction of the helper in this situation is to
    A. tell the foreman that he was careful and that he did not take any chances
    B. explain that he took this action to save time
    C. keep quiet and accept the criticism
    D. demand that the foreman show him the rule he violated

KEY (CORRECT ANSWERS)

1. A
2. D
3. D
4. D
5. A

6. C
7. C
8. C
9. A
10. A

11. C
12. B
13. C
14. D
15. A

16. B
17. C
18. B
19. D
20. A

21. C
22. B
23. D
24. D
25. C

ARITHMETICAL REASONING

EXAMINATION SECTION
TEST 1

DIRECTIONS: Each question or incomplete statement is followed by several suggested answers or completions. Select the one that BEST answers the question or completes the statement. *PRINT THE LETTER OF THE CORRECT ANSWER IN THE SPACE AT THE RIGHT.*

1. A canvas tarpaulin measures 6 feet by 9 feet.
   The LARGEST circular area that can be covered completely by this tarpaulin is a circle with a diameter of _____ feet.

   A. 9   B. 8   C. 7   D. 6

2. The population of Maple Grove was 1,000 in 2006. In 2007, the population increased 40 percent, but in 2008, 2009, and 2010, the population decreased 20 percent, 10 percent, and 25 percent, respectively. (For each year, the percentage change in population is based upon a comparison with the preceding year.)
   At the end of this period, the population was MOST NEARLY

   A. 900   B. 850   C. 800   D. 750

3. The ratio of boys to girls in one school is 6 to 4. A second school contains half as many boys and twice as many girls as the first.
   The one of the following statements that is MOST accurate is that

   A. both schools have the same number of pupils
   B. the first school has 10 percent more pupils than the second
   C. the second school has 10 percent more pupils than the first
   D. there is not sufficient information to reach any conclusion about which school has more pupils

4. In a certain city, X number of cases of malaria have occurred over a 10-year period, resulting in Y number of deaths.
   The AVERAGE annual death rate from malaria in this city is

   A. Y/10   B. 10/X   C. 10-X/Y   D. $\frac{Y(10X)}{X+Y}$

5. A firemen's softball team wins 6 games out of the first 9 played. They go on to win all their remaining games and finish the season with a final average of games won of .750.
   The TOTAL number of games they played that season was

   A. 10   B. 12   C. 15   D. 18

6. While inspecting a cylindrical gravity tank for an automatic sprinkler system, a chief observes that the water in the tank is 10 feet deep and that the tank has a diameter of 9 feet. He asks the building manager how many gallons are in the tank and receives the reply, *About 10,000.* (Cubic foot of water contains 7 1/2 gallons.) Based on his own observation and calculations, the chief should

A. agree that the manager's answer is probably correct
B. disagree with the manager's answer; the answer is more nearly 20,000 gallons
C. disagree with the manager's answer; the answer is more nearly 15,000 gallons
D. disagree with the manager's answer; the answer is more nearly 5,000 gallons

7. The diagram at the right represents the storage space of a fire engine. The amount of space available for the storage of hose in the fire engine is MOST NEARLY _____ cubic feet.
   A. 40
   B. 75
   C. 540
   D. 600

8. If a piece of rope 100 feet long is cut so that one piece is 2/3 as long as the other piece, the length of the longer piece must be _____ feet.
   A. 60   B. 66 2/3   C. 70   D. 75

9. A water tank has a discharge valve which is capable of emptying the tank when full in two hours. It also has an inlet valve which can fill the tank, when empty, in four hours and a second inlet valve which can fill the tank, when empty, in six hours.
   If the tank is full and all three valves are opened fully, with water flowing through each valve to capacity, the tank will be emptied in _____ hours.

   A. 2
   B. 6
   C. 12
   D. a period of time which cannot be determined from the information given

10. Final grades in a history course are determined as follows:
      Class recitations - weight 50
      Weekly quizzes - weight 25
      Final examination - weight 25
    A student has an average of 60 on a class recitation and 80 on weekly quizzes.
    In order to receive a final grade of 75, he must obtain on his final examination a grade of

    A. 75   B. 80   C. 90   D. 100

11. Suppose that 8 inches of snow contribute as much water to the reservoir system as one inch of rain.
    If, during a snowstorm, an average of 12 inches of snow fell during a six-hour period, with drifts as high as three feet, the addition to the water supply as a result of this snowfall ultimately will be the equivalent of _____ inches of rain.

    A. 1 1/2
    B. 3
    C. 4 1/2
    D. an amount of rain which cannot be determined from the information given

12. A fire engine carries 900 feet of 2 1/2" hose, 500 feet of 2" hose, and 350 feet of 1 1/2" hose.
    Of the total hose carried, the percentage of 1 1/2" hose is MOST NEARLY

    A. 35   B. 30   C. 25   D. 20

13. An engine company made 96 runs in the month of April, which was a decrease of 20% from the number of runs made in March.
    The number of runs made in March was MOST NEARLY

    A. 136   B. 128   C. 120   D. 110

14. A water tank has a capacity of 6,000 gallons. Connected to the tank is a pump capable of supplying water at the rate of 25 gallons per minute, which goes into operation automatically when the water in the tank falls to the one-half mark.
    If we start with a full tank and drain the water from the tank at the rate of 50 gallons a minute, the tank can continue supplying water at the required rate for_____ hours.

    A. 2 1/2   B. 3   C. 3 1/2   D. 4

15. Three firemen are assigned the task of cleaning fire apparatus which usually takes three men five hours to complete. After they have been working three hours, three additional firemen are assigned to help them. Assuming that they all work at the normal rate, the assignment of the additional men will reduce the time required to complete the task by _____ minutes.

    A. 20   B. 30   C. 50   D. 60

16. Assume that at the beginning of the calendar year, an employee was earning $48,000 per year. On July 1st, he received an increase of $2,400 per year. On November 1st, he was promoted to a position paying $60,000 per year. The total earnings for the year were MOST NEARLY

    A. $51,000   B. $49,000   C. $50,000   D. $53,000

17. Engine A leaves its firehouse at 1:48 P.M. and travels 3 miles to a fire at an average speed of 30 miles per hour. Engine B leaves its firehouse at 1:51 P.M. and travels 6 miles to the same fire at an average speed of 40 miles per hour.
    From the above facts, we may conclude that Engine A arrives _____ minutes _____ Engine B.

    A. 3; before   B. 6; before
    C. 3; after   D. 6; after

18. A widely used formula for calculating the quantity of water discharged from a hose is $GPM = 29.7 d^2 \sqrt{P}$, where GPM = gallons per minute, d = diameter of the nozzle in inches, and P = pressure at the nozzle in pounds per square inch.
    If it takes 1 minute to extinguish a fire using a 1 1/2" nozzle at 100 pounds pressure per square inch, the number of gallons discharged is, according to the above formula, MOST NEARLY

    A. 730   B. 650   C. 690   D. 670

19. The spring of a spring balance will stretch in proportion to the amount of weight placed on the balance.
    If a 2-pound weight placed on a certain balance stretches the spring 1/4", then a stretch in the spring of 1 3/4" will be caused by a weight of _____ lbs. 19._____

    A. 10 B. 12 C. 14 D. 16

20. In a yard 100 feet by 60 feet, a dog is tied by a leash to a stake driven into the ground in the center of the yard. 20._____
    If the dog is to be kept from going off the property, the MAXIMUM acceptable length of the leash is _____ feet.

    A. 60 B. 50 C. 30 D. 28

21. From a length of pipe 10 feet long, a 3 1/3 foot piece is to be cut. 21._____
    If the diameter of the 10-foot length is 5 inches, the diameter of the piece to be cut will be

    A. 5" B. 2 1/3" C. 2" D. 1 2/3"

22. A certain crew consists of one foreman who is paid $15.00 per hour, 2 carpenters who are paid $12.60 per hour, 4 helpers who are paid $10.50 per hour, and 10 laborers who are paid $7.50 per hour. 22._____
    The average hourly earnings of the members of the crew is MOST NEARLY

    A. $11.40 B. $10.50 C. $10.05 D. $9.30

23. The fraction which is equivalent to the sum of .125, .25, .375, and .0625 is 23._____

    A. 5/8 B. 13/16 C. 7/8 D. 15/16

24. If the pay period of an employee is changed from every two weeks to twice a month, his gross pay (before deductions) from each pay period will 24._____

    A. increase by one-tenth
    B. increase by one-twelfth
    C. decrease by one-thirteenth
    D. decrease by one-fifteenth

25. In a certain state, the automobile license tags consist of two letters followed by three digits, e.g., AA-122. The MAXIMUM number of different combinations of numbers and letters which can be obtained under this system is MOST NEARLY 25._____

    A. 13,500 B. 75,000 C. 325,000 D. 675,000

KEY (CORRECT ANSWERS)

1. D
2. D
3. C
4. A
5. B

6. D
7. C
8. A
9. C
10. D

11. A
12. D
13. C
14. B
15. D

16. A
17. B
18. D
19. C
20. C

21. A
22. D
23. B
24. B
25. D

SOLUTIONS TO PROBLEMS

1. The largest circular area completely covered by the tarpaulin would have a diameter of the lesser of 6 ft. and 9 ft.

2. At the end of 2010, the population was $(1000)(1.40)(.80)(.90)(.75) = 756 \approx 750$.

3. Let 6x and 4x represent the number of boys and girls, respectively, at the first school. Then, 3x and 8x will represent the number of boys and girls, respectively, at the second school. The enrollment of the second school, 11x, is 10% higher than the enrollment at the first school, 10x.

4. Since Y deaths have occurred over a 10-year period due to malaria, the annual death rate caused by malaria is Y/10. X, the number of cases of malaria, has no effect on the annual death rate.

5. Let x = number of games played, after the first 9 games. Then, $(6+x)/(9+x) = .750$. Solving, x = 3. The total number of games played = 9 + 3 = 12.

6. Volume = $(\pi)(4.5)^2(10) \approx 636$ cu.ft. Then, $(636)(7\ 1/2) = 4770 \approx 5000$

7. 15x8x3 = 360; 15x6x2 = 180; 360 + 180 = 540 cu.ft.

8. Let 2x and 3x represent the two pieces. Then, 2x + 3x = 100. Solving, x = 20. The longer piece = (3)(20) = 60 ft.

9. Let x = number of hours required. Then, $\frac{x}{2} \cdot \frac{x}{4} \cdot \frac{x}{6} = 1$ Simplifying, x/12 = 1. Thus, x = 12

10. Let x = final exam grade. Then, $(60)(.50) + (80)(.25) + (x)(.25) = 75$. Simplifying, 50 + ,25x = 75. Solving, x = 100

11. If 8 in. of snow contribute 1 in. of rain, then 12 in. of snow contribute (1)(12/8) = 1 1/2 in. of rain.

12. $350 \div (900+500+350) = .20 = 20\%$

13. The number of runs in March was $96 \div .80 = 120$

14. The time required to extract 3000 gallons at 50 gallons per minute = $3000 \div 50 = 60$ min. = 1 hour. At this point, the tank is half full. Also, a pump begins replenishing the tank at 25 gallons per minute. Thus, the effect on draining has been slowed to 50 - 25 = 25 gallons per minute. To drain the remaining 3000 gallons will require $3000 \div 25 = 120$ minutes = 2 hours. Total draining time = 3 hours.

15. (3)(5) = 15 man-hours. After 3 hours, 9 man-hours have been used. At this point, 6 men are working, and since only 6 man-hours remaining, the time needed is 1 hour = 60 minutes.

16. ($48,000)(1/2) + ($50,400)(1/3) + ($60,000)(1/6) = $50,800 ≈ $51,000

17. Engine A requires (3)(60/30) = 6 minutes to get to the fire.
So, Engine A arrives at 1:54 PM. Engine B requires (6)(60/40) = 9 minutes to get to the fire. So, Engine B arrives at 2:00 PM. Thus, Engine A arrives 6 minutes before Engine B.

18. GPM = $(29.7)(1.5)^2(\sqrt{100})$ = 668.25 ≈ 670

19. Let x = required number of pounds. Then, 2/x = 1/4/1 3/4.
So, 1/4x = 3 1/2. Solving, x = 14

20. The shorter of the two dimensions is 60 ft. If the dog is in the center of the yard, the maximum length allowed for the leash is 60/2 = 30 ft.

21. The diameter of the cut piece = diameter of entire pipe = 5"

22. [($15.00)(1)+($12.60)(2)+($10.50)(4)+($7.50)(10)]/17 = $157.20/17 9.25 (closest answer in answer key is $9.30).

23. .125 + .25 + .375 + .0625 = .8125 = 13/16

24. Let x = annual pay. Then, x/26 = pay every two weeks, whereas pay every half month. His increase is $\frac{x}{24} - \frac{x}{26} = \frac{x}{312}$, which represents a fractional increase of $\frac{x}{312} / \frac{x}{26} = \frac{1}{12}$

25. The number of different license tags = (26)(26)(10)(10)(10) = 676,000 (closest answer in answer key is 675,000).

TEST 2

DIRECTIONS: Each question or incomplete statement is followed by several suggested answers or completions. Select the one that BEST answers the question or completes the statement. *PRINT THE LETTER OF THE CORRECT ANSWER IN THE SPACE AT THE RIGHT.*

1. If cast iron weighs 450 pounds per cubic foot, the weight of a solid cast iron manhole cover 2 feet in diameter and 1 inch thick is MOST NEARLY _____ pounds.

    A. 94   B. 118   C. 136   D. 164

    1._____

2. The sum of 2 5/8, 3 3/16, 1 1/2, and 4 1/4 is

    A. 9 13/16   B. 10 7/16   C. 11 9/16   D. 13 3/16

    2._____

3. A pump is able to fill a tank holding 15,000 gallons in 2 hours and 30 minutes. Pumping at the same rate, an empty 60,000 gallon tank can be filled in

    A. 10 hours   B. 10 hours, 30 minutes
    C. 11 hours   D. 11 hours, 30 minutes

    3._____

4. Assume you want to add 10,000 gallons of water to a tank. If you pump water into the tank at the rate of 100 gallons per minute for one hour and 50 gallons per minute after the first hour, the total time required to add the 10,000 gallons is MOST NEARLY

    A. 1 hour, 20 minutes   B. 2 hours
    C. 2 hours, 20 minutes   D. 3 hours

    4._____

5. A tank 25 feet long, 15 feet wide, and 10 feet deep is enlarged by extending the length another 25 feet.
   The enlarged tank will be able to hold _____ more than the original tank.

    A. 50%   B. 100%   C. 150%   D. 200%

    5._____

6. If cast iron weighs 450 pounds per cubic foot, the weight of a solid cast iron manhole cover 4 feet in diameter and 1 inch thick is MOST NEARLY _____ pounds.

    A. 188   B. 236   C. 328   D. 471

    6._____

7. If four men work seven hours during the day, the number of man-hours of work done is

    A. 4   B. 7   C. 11   D. 28

    7._____

8. If it takes four men fourteen days to do a certain job, seven men working at the same rate should be able to do the same job in _____ days.

    A. 8   B. 7   C. 6   D. 5

    8._____

9. A truck leaves the garage at 9:26 A.M. and returns the same day at 3:43 P.M. The period of time that the truck was away from the garage is MOST NEARLY _____ hours, _____ minutes.

    A. 5; 17   B. 5; 43   C. 6; 17   D. 6; 26

    9._____

10. Assume that it takes 6 men 8 days to do a certain job. Working at the same speed, the number of days that it will take 4 men to do this job is

    A. 9 B. 10 C. 12 D. 14

11. The sum of 3 5/8 + 4 1/4 + 6 1/2 + 7 1/8 is

    A. 20 7/8 B. 21 1/4 C. 21 1/2 D. 22 1/8

12. The fraction which is equal to .0625 is

    A. 1/64 B. 3/64 C. 1/16 D. 5/8

13. The volume, in cubic feet, of a rectangular coal bin 8 feet long by 5 feet wide by 7 feet high is MOST NEARLY

    A. 40 B. 56 C. 186 D. 280

14. Assume that a car travels at a constant speed of 36 miles per hour.
    The speed of this car, in feet per second, is MOST NEARLY (one mile equals 5,280 ft.)

    A. 3 B. 24.6 C. 52.8 D. 879.8

15. If one-third of a 19-foot length of lumber is cut off, the length of the remaining piece will measure APPROXIMATELY

    A. 8'8" B. 9'8" C. 12'8" D. 13'8"

16. The circumference of a circle having a diameter of 10" is MOST NEARLY _____ inches.

    A. 3.14 B. 18.72 C. 24.96 D. 31.4

17. Assume that in the purchase of paint, the seller quotes a discount of 10%.
    If the price per gallon is $19.05, the actual payment, in dollars per gallon, is MOST NEARLY

    A. $17.15 B. $17.85 C. $18.75 D. $19.50

18. Assume that a cubic foot of water contains 7 1/2 gallons. The number of gallons of water which could be contained in a rectangular tank 3 feet long, 2 feet wide, and 2 feet deep is MOST NEARLY

    A. 12 B. 45 C. 90 D. 120

19. The volume, in cubic feet, of a slab of concrete that is 5'0" wide, 6'0" long, and 0'6" in depth is MOST NEARLY

    A. 15.0 B. 13.5 C. 12.0 D. 10.5

20. The sum of the following pipe lengths, 22 1/8", 7 3/4", 19 7/16", and 43 5/8", is

    A. 91 7/8" B. 92 1/16" C. 92 1/2" D. 92 15/16"

21. The area, in square feet, of a plant floor that is 42 feet wide and 75 feet long is

    A. 3,150 B. 3,100 C. 3.075 D. 2,760

22. The sum of the following dimensions, 1 5/8, 2 1/4, 4 1/16, and 3 3/16, is

    A. 10 15/16 B. 11 C. 11 1/8 D. 11 1/4

23. Assume that six men, working together at the same rate of speed, can complete a certain job in 3 hours.
If, however, there were only four men available to do this job, and they all worked at the same rate of speed, to complete this job would take MOST NEARLY _____ hours.

   A. 4 1/4   B. 4 1/2   C. 4 3/4   D. 5

24. Due to unforeseen difficulties, a job which would normally take 17 hours to complete was actually completed in 21 hours.
This represents a percent increase over the normal time of MOST NEARLY

   A. 19%   B. 2.4%   C. 24%   D. 124%

25. Truck A costs $30,000 and gets 12 mpg and truck B costs $35,000 and gets 15 mpg. After 1 year driving 12,000 miles, how much would be saved by purchasing truck A if gasoline costs $1.50 per gallon?

   A. $1,000   B. $3,000   C. $4,700   D. $6,000

KEY (CORRECT ANSWERS)

1. B
2. C
3. A
4. C
5. B

6. D
7. D
8. A
9. C
10. C

11. C
12. C
13. D
14. C
15. C

16. D
17. A
18. C
19. A
20. D

21. A
22. C
23. B
24. C
25. C

SOLUTIONS TO PROBLEMS

1. $(450)(\pi)(1)^2(1/12) \approx 118$ pounds. (Note: $V = \pi R^2 H$)

2. 2 5/8 + 3 3/16 + 1 1/2 + 4 1/4 = 10 25/16 = 11 9/16

3. To fill a 60,000 gallon tank would require (4)(2 1/2 hrs.) = 10 hrs.

4. After 1 hour, (100)(60) = 6000 gallons have been added. To add the remaining 4000 gallons will require 4000 ÷ 50 = 80 minutes = 1 hour 20 minutes. Thus, total time needed is 2 hrs. 20 min.

5. The original volume = (25)(15)(10) = 3750 cu.ft., and the new volume = (50)(15)(10) = 7500 cu.ft. The increased volume of 3750 represents an increase of (3750/3750)(100) = 100%.

6. $(450)(\pi)(2)^2(1/12) \approx 471$ pounds

7. (4)(7) = 28 man-hours

8. (4)(14) = 56 man-days. Then, 56 ÷ 7 = 8 days

9. From 9:26 A.M. to 3:43 P.M. = 6 hrs. 17 min.

10. (6)(8) = 48 man-days. Then, 48 ÷ 4 = 12 days

11. 3 5/8 + 4 1/4 + 6 1/2 + 7 1/8 = 20 12/8 = 21 1/2

12. .0625 = 625/10,000 = 1/16

13. (8)(5)(7) = 280 cu.ft.

14. (36)(5280) = 190,080 ft. per hour. Since there are 3600 seconds in 1 hour, the speed = 190,080 ÷ 3600 = 52.8 ft. per second.

15. 19' - 1/3(19') = 12 2/3, = 12'8"

16. Circumference = $(\pi)(10")$ 31.4"

17. ($19.05)(.90) ≈ $17.15

18. (7 1/2)(3)(2)(2) = 90 gallons

19. (5)(6)(1/2) = 15 cu.ft.

20. 22 1/8" + 7 3/4" + 19 7/16" + 43 5/8" = 9l 31/16" = 92 15/16"

21. Area = (42)(75) = 3150 sq.ft.

22. 1 5/8 + 2 1/4 + 4 1/16 + 3 3/16 = 10 18/16 = 11 1/8

23. (6) (3) = 18 man-hours. Then, 18 / 4 = 4 1/2 hours

24. 21 - 17 = 4. Then, 4/17 ≈ 24%

25. For Truck A, the expenses are $30,000 + (1000)($1.50) = $31,500 For Truck B, the expenses are $35,000 + (800)($1.50) = $36,200. $36,200 - $31,500 = $4,700

TEST 3

DIRECTIONS: Each question or incomplete statement is followed by several suggested answers or completions. Select the one that BEST answers the question or completes the statement. *PRINT THE LETTER OF THE CORRECT ANSWER IN THE SPACE AT THE RIGHT.*

1. Assume that a light maintainer and his helper replaced 25 lamps on one round of their assigned territory.
   If it took two hours to complete this round, and the maintainer's pay rate was $9.60 per hour and the helper's rate was $8.40 per hour, the labor cost of replacing each burned out lamp averaged _____ cents.

    A. 18   B. 36   C. 72   D. 144

2. A certain power distribution job will require two main-tainers at $16.00 per hour and two helpers at $13.20 per hour. The job will take three 8-hour days to complete and will require 6 hours of planning and supervision by a foreman at $19.60 per hour.
   The TOTAL labor cost for this job is

    A. $264.80   B. $501.60   C. $818.40   D. $1,519.20

3. Two identical containers are partly filled with bolts and weigh 40 lbs. and 75 lbs., respectively. To save storage space, all the bolts are put in one of the containers. The two containers now weigh 5 lbs. and 110 lbs., respectively.
   If three bolts weigh 1/2 lb., the TOTAL number of bolts is

    A. 210   B. 450   C. 630   D. 660

4. The sum of the following dimensions, 2'7 1/2", 1'8 1/2", 2'1/16", and 3/4", is

    A. 5'15 9/16"   B. 5'15 11/16"
    C. 5'7/16"   D. 6'4 9/16"

5. If a 3-foot length of contact rail weighs 150 pounds, then 39 feet of contact rail weighs _____ pounds.

    A. 1,850   B. 1,900   C. 1,950   D. 2,000

6. The sum of the following dimensions, 3'2 1/2", 8 7/8", 2'6 3/8", 2'9 3/4", and 1'0", is

    A. 9'3 1/4"   B. 10'3 1/4"   C. 10'7 1/4"   D. 16'7 1/4"

7. If a drawing for a contact rail installation is made to a scale of 1 1/2" to the foot, the drawing is said to be one _____ size.

    A. sixteenth   B. eight   C. quarter   D. half

8. If a drawing has a scale of 1/4" = 1', a dimension of 1 3/4" on the drawing would be equal to

    A. 4'   B. 5'   C. 6'   D. 7'

9. A reel weighs 600 lbs. when fully loaded with cable and 200 lbs. when empty.
   If the cable weighs 2.5 lbs. per foot, the number of reels a foreman should order for a job requiring 700 feet of this cable is _____ reels.

    A. 2   B. 3   C. 4   D. 5

10. If the scale on a working drawing is shown as 1/4" = 1', a scaled measurement of 4 1/2 inches represents an actual length of _____ feet.

    A. 8   B. 9   C. 16   D. 18

11. A gap on the third rail starts at a subway column marked 217+79. The gap extends 68 feet to another column marked 217+11.
    A column midway between these columns would be marked 217+_____

    A. 34   B. 39   C. 45   D. 68

12. Assume a foreman decided that 100 contact rail ties need replacing. Each tie measures 9' x 6" x 8".
    In providing room for storing these ties at the job site, the MINIMUM storage volume required is APPROXIMATELY _____ cubic feet.

    A. 300   B. 360   C. 432   D. 576

13. Assume a certain job was done a year ago and took 8 men a total of 5 days to complete. The records show that each day involved 5 hours of overtime for half the men. Your assistant supervisor now assigns you the identical job to be done using 6 men and no overtime.
    The MINIMUM number of regular work days that should be scheduled for this job is _____ days.

    A. 13   B. 11   C. 9   D. 6

14. The sum of the following dimensions, 12'11 3/16", 9'8 5/8", 7'3 3/4", 5'2 1/2", and 3'1 1/4", is

    A. 39'5 9/16"   B. 38'3 5/16"
    C. 36'2 3/8"   D. 35'1 7/8"

15. If the scale on a drawing is 1/4" to the foot, then a 5/8" measurement would represent an actual length of

    A. 5'4"   B. 4'8"   C. 2'6"   D. 1'3"

16. The sum of 1 9/16", 3 1/2", 7 3/8", 10 3/4", and 12 5/8" is

    A. 33 11/16"   B. 34 13/16"   C. 35 11/16"   D. 35 13/16"

17. A reel containing an unknown length of cable weighs 340 pounds.
    If the empty reel weighs 119 lbs. and the cable weighs 0.85 lb. per foot, the number of feet of cable on the reel is

    A. 140   B. 260   C. 400   D. 540

18. If the scale on a shop drawing is 1/4" to the foot, then a part which measures 3 3/8 inches long on the drawing has an actual length of _____ feet _____ inches.

    A. 12; 6   B. 13; 6   C. 13; 9   D. 14; 9

19. Taking into account time and one-half payment for time over 40 hours of work, the gross pay of an employee who works 43 hours in a week at a rate of pay of $5.34 per hour is

    A. $213.60   B. $229.62   C. $237.63   D. $245.64

20. The sum of 0.365 + 3.941 + 10.676 + 0.784 is   20._____

    A. 13.766   B. 15.666   C. 15.756   D. 15.766

21. An air conditioning unit is rated at 1000 watts. The unit is run for 10 hours per day, five   21._____
    days per week. If the cost for electrical energy is 50 cents per kilowatt-hour, the weekly
    cost for electricity should be

    A. $2.50   B. $5.00   C. $25.00   D. $250.00

22. Assume that the cost of a certain wiring installation is broken down as follows: Materials   22._____
    $1,200, Labor $800, and Rental of equipment $400.
    The percentage of the total cost of the job that can be charged to Labor is MOST
    NEARLY

    A. 12.3   B. 33.3   C. 40.0   D. 66.6

23. Assume that it takes 4 electrician's helpers 6 days to do a certain job.   23._____
    Working at the same rate of speed, the number of days it will take 3 electrician's help-
    ers to do the same job is

    A. 6   B. 7   C. 8   D. 9

24. Assume that a 120-volt, 25-cycle magnetic coil is to be rewound to operate properly on   24._____
    60-cycles at the same voltage.
    If the coil at 25-cycles has 1,000 turns, at 60-cycles the number of turns should be
    MOST NEARLY

    A. 2,400   B. 1,200   C. 416   D. 208

25. A light maintainer whose rate is $14.40 per hour is assigned to replace burned-out sta-   25._____
    tion and tunnel lamps. During 4 hours, he replaces 28 lamps.
    The average labor cost for replacing each of these burned-out lamps was NEAREST
    to

    A. 56¢   B. $1.04   C. $2.00   D. $3.60

KEY (CORRECT ANSWERS)

1. D
2. D
3. C
4. D
5. C

6. B
7. B
8. D
9. D
10. D

11. C
12. A
13. C
14. B
15. C

16. D
17. B
18. B
19. C
20. D

21. C
22. B
23. C
24. C
25. C

5 (#3)

SOLUTIONS TO PROBLEMS

1. (2)($9.60+$8.40) = $36.00. Then, $36.00 ÷ 25 = $1.44 or 144 cents.

2. (2)($16.00)(24) + (2)($13.20)(24) + (6)($19.60) = $1519.20

3. An empty container weighs 5 lbs., so the container which contains bolts and weighs 110 lbs. actually has 105 lbs. of bolts. Since 3 bolts weigh 1/2 lb., 105 lbs. would contain (105/1/2)(3) = 630 bolts.

4. 2'7 1/4" + 1'8 1/2" + 2'1/16" + 3/4" = 5'15 25/16" = 6 '4 9/16"

5. 39 feet of rail weighs (13)(150) = 1950 pounds

6. 3'2 1/4" + 8 7/8" + 2'6 3/8" + 2'9 3/4" + 1'0" = 8'25 18/8" = 10'3 1/4"

7. 1 1/2"/1" = 3/2.1/12=1/8

8. l 3/4" ÷ 1/4" = 7 Then, (7)(1') = 7'

9. 600 - 200 = 400. Then, 400 ÷ 2.5 = 160 ft. of cable per reel. Since 700 ft. of cable is needed, 700/160 = 4.375, which means 5 reels will be required (must round up).

10. 4 1/2" ÷ 1/4" = 9/2 4/1 = 18 Then, (18)(1') = 18'

11. Half of 68 = 34; 11 + 34 = 45; 79 - 34 = 45

12. (100)(9')(1/2')(2/3') = 300 cu.ft.

13. Number of man-days = (4)(5) + (4)(5)(1 5/8) =52.5
    For 6 men working only 8-hour days, 52.5 ÷ 6 = 8.75 = 9 days needed.

14. 12'11 3/16" + 9'8 5/8" + 7'3 3/4" + 5'2 1/2" + 3'1 1/4" = 36'25 37/16" = 38'3 5/16"

15. 5/8" ÷ 1/4" = 5/8 . 4/1 = 2 1/2. Then, (2 1/2)(1') = 2'6"

16. 1 9/16" + 3 1/2" + 7 3/8" + 10 3/4" + 12 5/8" = 33 45/16" = 35 13/36"

17. 340 - 119 = 221 lbs. Then, 221 ÷ .85 = 260 ft.

18. 3 3/8" ÷ 1/4" = 27/8 . 4/1 = 13/ 1/2. Then, (13 1/2) (1') = 13 ft. 6 in.

19. (40)($5.34) + (3)($5.34)(1.5) = $237.63

20. 0.365 +3.941 + 10.676 + 0.784 = 15.766

21. (1000)(10)(5) = 50,000 watt-hours = 50 kilowatt-hours. Then, (50)($.50) = $25.00

22. $800 / ($1200+$800+$400) = 1/3 ≈ 33.3%

23. (4)(6) = 24. Then, 24/ 3 = 8 days

24. Let x = number of required turns. Since the number of cycles varies inversely as the number of turns, 25/60 = x/1000.
    Solving, x 416 (actually 416 2/3)

25. ($14.40)(4) = $57.60. Then, $57.60 ÷ 28 ≈ $2.06

BASIC FUNDAMENTALS OF ELECTRICITY

CONTENTS

UNIT 1 – ELECTRICITY	1
UNIT 2 – MAGNETISM	6
UNIT 3 – BATTERIES	13
UNIT 4 – USING ELECTRICITY	17

BASIC FUNDAMENTALS OF ELECTRICITY

Electricity
Unit 1

When you use a small hand drill, the energy that turns the drill comes from your body. When you snap the switch on an electric drill, another form of energy spins the bit of the drill. We call this form of energy *electricity*. Electrical energy plays a vital part in our environment. It lights our houses, cooks our food, runs our factories, and carries messages for us.

Like other forms of energy, electricity is something that we cannot create. We get it by converting another form of energy into electrical energy. The energy in running water is often used to produce, or *generate*, electricity. Waterpower can be used to turn a generator, which converts the energy in running water into electrical energy. Plants which use this process are called *hydroelectric* plants.

In the United States most of our electricity is produced by changing heat energy into electrical energy. A plant which uses this process is called a thermoelectric plant. In a *thermoelectric* plant, heat energy is first changed into mechanical energy. A steam turbine is often used for this purpose. Then the mechanical energy, produced by the turbine, is changed into electrical energy by a large *generator*. Today we produce some electricity also by changing atomic energy into electric energy.

Electrical Charges

Electricity is a form of energy produced when an electrical charge moves along a wire. Let us try to explain what an electrical charge is. If you lift a brick into the air, the brick acquires potential energy. You have separated the brick from the ground by using energy in your body. If you drop the brick, it will move to the ground, expending the energy it picked up when it was lifted. If the brick strikes a pane of glass on the way down, the energy in the brick will break the glass. The moving brick has kinetic energy; it will do work.

Electricity depends on this same principle. Inside the atom the tiny particles called *protons and electrons* are attracted to one another just as the brick is attracted to the ground. The proton and electron are called *charged particles*. The proton carries a *positive* charge. The electron carries a *negative* charge. They attract one another. If we force them apart, we must use energy, just as we use energy to raise a brick. When we release them, the electrons and protons move back together. While they are moving they can do work. For convenience sake, we say that the electrons move toward the protons.

Whenever electrons are moving, electricity is present. As they move, electrons can do work. They have energy. The reason they have energy is the same as the reason the brick has energy. Work must be done to separate electrons and protons. When they come back together, the energy they picked up is released.

Eletrical Energy

Let's take a simple example. Suppose we have a small heap of protons and electrons. We take all the electrons in one hand, and all the protons in the other hand. Then we pull them apart. Since they attract each other, we must use energy when we pull them apart. The electrons and protons then have potential energy. If they can, they will move back together again.

If we connect the two piles with a wire, the electrons will move along the wire and return to the protons. Like the falling brick, the electrons have energy as they move back to the protons. If we put a glass pane under the brick, we can make the brick use some of its energy to break the glass.

If we put a hurdle in front of the electrons, we can make them work as they move back toward the protons. That is the basis of all electricity-powered equipment. Electrons are made to use some of their energy as they try to return to the protons.

Suppose we connect electrons and protons by a wire, but we put in a high hurdle that the electrons must cross. As the electrons move over the hurdle, they release some of their energy. The electron must use energy to jump the hurdle just as we do. This energy is not destroyed. It is converted into heat. A "hot spot" will appear in the wire at the hurdle we placed in the road. If we put the resistance inside a glass bulb, and take out most of the air, the spot will glow white. We will have made an electric light bulb. By making the electrons work as they returned to the protons, we have created a light that we can use.

Electron flow

This illustration is a little too simple. But all electricity works on this general principle. Actually, one electron usually does not move the whole length of a wire. It moves only a short distance. The effect is like one billiard ball striking a long row of billiard balls. The shock is passed from one ball to the next, but each ball does not move very far. Another example is the way a shock runs through a long train when the engine stops. In any electric wire there are millions and millions of electrons that pass the movement along. This is called electron flow. The flow of electrons is the form of energy we call electricity.

The flow of electrons along a wire depends upon the way electrons are placed in an atom. You remember that electrons are arranged in shells around the nucleus of the atom. The nucleus has a positive charge. The electrons have a negative charge. In some atoms the electrons in the outer shell can be knocked loose very easily. Loose electrons are called *free electrons*, and they are the carriers of electrical energy. When the wire connects a supply of protons and a supply of electrons, these free electrons move along the wire-or drift-toward the protons. This movement produces an *electric current*.

Conductors and Insulators

If there are no free electrons, no electric current can be produced. Some materials produce hirge numbers of free electrons. They can carry an electric current very easily. These materials are called *conductors* because they conduct electricity. Other materials contain few free electrons. Little or, no electricity can flow through them. They are called *insulators*. They do not conduct electricity. Materials like silver, copper, aluminum, and gold possess many free electrons. They are good electrical conductors. Because copper is inexpensive, it is used most often for electrical wire. Materials like glass, rubber, wood, air, and paper are *insulators*. They do not carry electricity because they have few free electrons.

Measuring Electricity

When electrons flow along a conductor, we have electrical energy. Energy passes along the wire at the same speed as light, 186,000 miles each second. But how much electrical energy is passing through the wire? How much work can the electricity do? To answer these questions, we must measure electricity. To measure, we must have standards.

To find out how much electricity we have, we need only count the number of electrons available. If there are 6¼ billion billion electrons separated from protons, we have one *coulomb* of electrical charge. This sounds like a large number of electrons. But it is only a small amount of electricity.

A second question we must answer is, "How hard are the electrons trying to get back to the protons? How much pressure do they exert?" If we have electrons in one hand and protons in the other, how hard do they pull? The standard unit used by science to measure electrical pressure is based on the coulomb. If one coulomb of electrons is available, the amount of pressure they produce is defined as one *volt*. This is our standard for electrical pressure. If we have five coulombs of electrons in one hand, they will exert five volts of pressure trying to return to the protons. The volt is often called an *electromotive* force, and abbreviated as *emf*, or just a capital *E*. In our formulas, we will always abbreviate volts as *E*.

The coulomb and the volt measure potential energy. They tell us how many electrons we are holding. This is like weighing a rock we have lifted off the ground. But we would also like to know about electricity when it is in action. How fast are the electrons moving in our wire? To find this, we simply measure the number of electrons that pass one point in one second. If one coulomb of electrons flows past in one second, we say that one *ampere* of electric current is flowing in the wire. In other words, if one coulomb of electrons moves past a point in one second, one ampere of electricity is flowing.

Notice that all of these definitions are tied together. One coulomb is equal to 6¼ billion billion electrons. This number of electrons produces one volt of pressure. If one coulomb of electrons flows each second, the current is called one ampere. Of course, electricity will flow only when two points are connected. It will flow only if there is some separation of electrons and protons. If the number of electrons and the number of protons are equal at the same ends of a wire, no electricity will flow.

Resistance

When you apply energy to a machine like the wheel and axle, you lose some of the energy inside the machine because of friction. If you apply electrical energy to a wire, you also lose some energy in the wire. This loss is due to the *resistance* of the wire. The wire must have free electrons to carry electrical energy through the wire. But the electrons are tied to the nucleus of the atom by a small force. This force must be overcome before the electrons are free. The energy to free the electrons must be supplied from the energy in the electrons moving into the wire.

In a machine we must know how much energy we lose to friction to know the efficiency of the machine. We also measure the amount of loss in an electrical conductor. To do this, we measure the resistance of the conductor. Now, we know that the energy lost was used to pull electrons loose from their shells. And we know that this energy is converted into heat. So if we measure the amount of heat generated in a conductor, we know how much energy we have lost.

The standard unit used to measure resistance is called the ohm. This is the amount of resistance that generates 0.24 calories of heat when one ampere of electrical current flows through a wire. In other words, we run one ampere of current through a wire and measure the heat that is produced. If the heat equals 0.24 calories, then the resistance of the wire is one ohm. This definition of the unit of resistance ties it to all the other measuring standards in electricity. Look at the following table.

NAME OF UNIT	MEANING	UNINT	ABBREVIATION
Voltage	Pressure, or potential difference	Volt	*E*
Current	Flow of Electrons	Ampere	*I*
Resistance	Opposition to the flow of electrons	Ohm	*R*

Ohm's Law

If we separate electrons and protons and keep them separated, we have a potential difference between them. If we connect these two points with a conductor, we have an *electrical circuit*. When the two points are connected, electrons will flow through the conductor. We can find the voltage, the current, and the resistance in any electrical circuit by using a simple formula called *Ohm's Law*. This is one of the basic laws in all electricity, and you should learn it thoroughly. Ohm said that in any electrical circuit:
1. The current flowing is equal to the voltage divided by the resistance.
2. The resistance is equal to the voltage divided by the current.

3. The voltage is equal to the resistance multiplied by the current.

These three rules apply simply because they are defined that way. We know that one volt of electricity will push one ampere of current across a resistance of one ohm. Ohm produced his three rules by combining the definitions into one general rule. The formula is:

$$\text{Current}(I) \frac{(E) \text{voltage}}{(R) \text{resistance}}$$

We can write this in three ways:

1. $I = \frac{E}{R}$ 2. $E = I \times R$ 3. $R \frac{E}{R}$

Learn all three forms of Ohm's Law thoroughly.

Using Ohm's Law

In the United States most of our houses are wired for 110 volts of electricity. Suppose you had a heater that had a resistance of eleven ohms. But you did not know how many amperes of current the heater used. Ohm's Law could tell you the answer easily. You know the voltage and resistance. You want to know the current. Using formula 1 above:

$$I = \frac{E}{R} \qquad I = \frac{110}{11} \qquad I = 10 \text{ amperes}$$

Your heater would need a ten ampere fuse. You can solve any other problems of this type using the same formula.

Power

If we know the voltage, current, and resistance in an electrical current, we still do not know how much energy the circuit is using. This can be a serious problem when we want to figure out our own electricity bills.

The unit of electrical power is the watt. This is the amount of work done in one second when one volt of electricity moves one ampere of current through a circuit. In other words, if we have one volt of pressure and it moves one ampere of current through the circuit, we are using one watt of electrical energy. When larger units are needed, we use the unit called the kilowatt which is equal to one thousand watts.

To find the power (in watts) used in a circuit, simply multiply the voltage of the circuit by the current flowing through a circuit. The power formula is written:

$$\text{Power } (W) = (E) \text{ Voltage} \times (I) \text{ Current}$$

Almost every electrical problem can be solved by using the power formula, or combining the power formula with Ohm's Law.

Examples

1. An air conditioner has a tag which states that the unit uses 2,200 watts of power. The unit plugs into 110 volt electricity. How large must the fuse be in the line?

a. $W = E \times I$ or $2,200 = 110 \times I$

b. $I = \frac{2,200}{110}$ or $I = 20$ ampers

The air conditioner will use a twenty ampere fuse. This is a very heavy load for house wiring, and the wiring should be checked before adding this much current to a line.

2. You have just bought a new electric heater. It operates on 110 volt electricity, and it has a resistance of ten ohms. You pay five cents for each kilowatt of electricity. How much will it cost to run the heater for thirty days?

a. First, you must use Ohm's Law to find the current that flows through the heater:

$$I = \frac{E}{R} \qquad I = \frac{110}{10} \qquad I = 11 \text{ amperes}$$

b. Then you find the number of watts the heater uses, using the power formula:

$$W = E \times I \qquad W = 110 \times 11 \qquad W = 1{,}210 \text{ watts}$$

c. Now you know that the heater uses 1.21 kilowatts every hour. This electricity costs five cents for each kilowatt hour. You can figure that the heater will cost about six cents per hour to run. If it ran day and night for thirty days, the total cost would be approximately forty-three dollars ($43.56, to be exact). This is the way you can use the two formulas to work out electrical problems in the home.

Words Used in Unit 1

abbreviated (ə brē´vĭ āt əd), shortened
convenience (kən vēn´ yəns), saving of trouble
electron (ĭ lĕk´trŏn), a tiny particle carrying one unit of negative electricity
expending (ĕks pĕnd´ĭng), i using up
hurdle (hər´ dəl), an obstacle in one's way
illustration (ĭl əs trā´shən), story, example
proton (prō´tŏn), tiny particle carrying one unit of positive electricity
thermoelectric (thər mō ĭ lĕk´trĭk), having to do with electricity produced by heat

Magnetism
Unit 2

If you take a small piece of the mineral magnetite and hold it near some iron filings, the iron filings will cling to the magnetite. This material is called a *natural magnet.* Since this magnet actually pulls the iron filings toward it, we know that it can do work. So we know that a magnet contains energy of some sort.

We can make a magnet with electricity, too. If we wrap some wire around an iron spike and run an electric current through the wire, the spike will also attract iron filings. But the spike will attract iron only while the electric current is flowing. When the current is shut off, the spike loses its magnetism. Such a magnet is called an electromagnet.

What is this mysterious force that draws the iron to the magnet? We know that it is related to electricity because we can produce magnetism by electricity.

What's a Magnet?

Like most basic questions about our universe, this is a hard question to answer. We know that the molecules inside a magnet are organized. They are so arranged that there is potential difference between the two ends of the magnet. That is, one end has a positive charge and the other end has a negative charge. We know that energy must have been used to make this arrangement. Each end of the magnet is called a pole. We say that one pole is positive and the other is negative. The two poles act like electrons and protons. That is, likes repel each other; opposites attract. Two positive poles repel each other, and two negative poles repel each other. But a positive· pole and a negative pole will attract one another.

The charges at the poles of a magnet are probably due to the movement of electrons inside the magnet. We are not exactly certain what bring this about. But we do know a great deal about the way magnets work. And we know many of the relations between magnetism and electricity. These are the things we will study in this unit.

Magnetic fields

A magnet attracts an iron filing *before* it touches the filing. The area around a magnet is charged, and the charge around the magnet pulls the iron toward the magnet. This charged area is called a magnetic field. Without these magnetic fields there could be no electricity as we know it.

The magnetic field increases in strength as we move closer to the surface of the magnet. If we place a magnet beneath a sheet of paper, and sprinkle tiny iron particles on the paper, the iron particles will arrange themselves along field lines of the magnet. Notice the pattern the lines form. Near the poles the lines are close together. The field is very strong here. At the center point between the poles, the lines are spread apart. The field is weakest here.

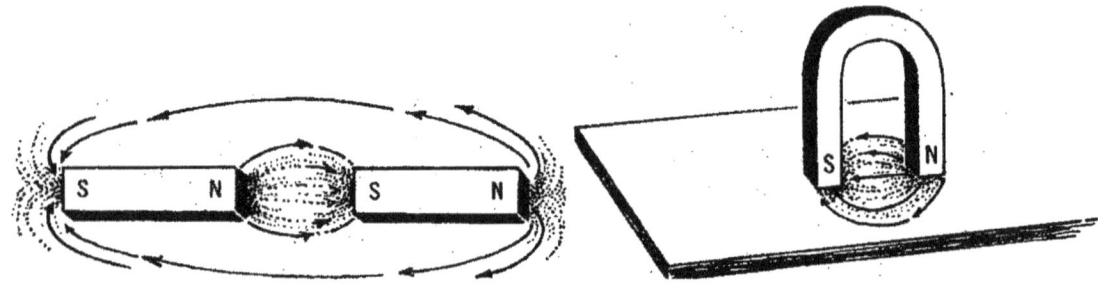

Fig. 1 a

Fig. 1 b

Figures 1a, 1 b Magnetic Lines of Force-Bar Magnet and Horseshoe Magnet.

The strength of the magnet determines the strength of the field. If we place a pieee of iron in the field, it concentrates the lines of force and increases the strength of the field. A magnetic field can attract certain objects through solid wood and some other materials. It can exert force through a perfect vacuum. Every magnet or electromagnet produces a magnetic field.

Induction

We have the whole science of electronics because a magnet produces a magnetic field. Yet we cannot really explain magnetism very well. We can only say how magnetism works, not why it works. One property of a magnetic field is of outstanding importance. If a small piece of wire is moved across the lines of force of a magnetic field, a small electric current flows in the wire. The kinetic energy of the moving wire is changed into electrical energy. The wire does not have to touch the magnet. All it must do is cut *across* the lines of force. The faster the wire moves the more electrical current runs in the wire. The more lines of force the wire cuts, the more electric current runs in the wire. This principle is called *induction*. An electric current is *induced* in the moving wire. Actually, the magnetic field is able to change mechanical energy into elctrical energy. Every electric motor, every electric generator, and every transformer depends upon this principle of induction.

REMEMBER

- A moving wire cutting the lines of force in a magnetic field produces an electric current in the wire.

- The more lines of force the wire cuts, the more current generated.

- The faster the wires move, the more electric current generated.

Electromagnetism

If a wire is passed through a magnetic field, an electric current is produced. To reverse the process, if an electric current is run through a wire, a magnetic field is produced. This is called an electromagnet. You can test this principle by connecting the two terminals on a small battery with a bare wire. The wire will pick up iron filings while it is connected. If the wire is shaped into a loop, the shape of the magnetic field changes. Figure100 (A) shows the effect of the loop. Th lines of force are increased inside the loop. If more loops are added, the magnetic field grows stronger. A coiled wire carrying electricity that has more than one loop is usually called a *solenoid, or coil*. The coil will act like any other magnet. One end of the coil is positive; the other end is negative. Because the coil has two poles, we say that it shows *polarity*.

A solenoid acts just like a bar magnet. The strength of the magnet depends upon the size of the wire, the number of turns of wire, and the amount of electrical current running through the wire. An increase in any of these factors makes the magnet stronger. If an iron bar is placed inside the coiled wire, it concentrates the lines of force and makes the magnet much stronger. Most electromagnets have an Iron core.

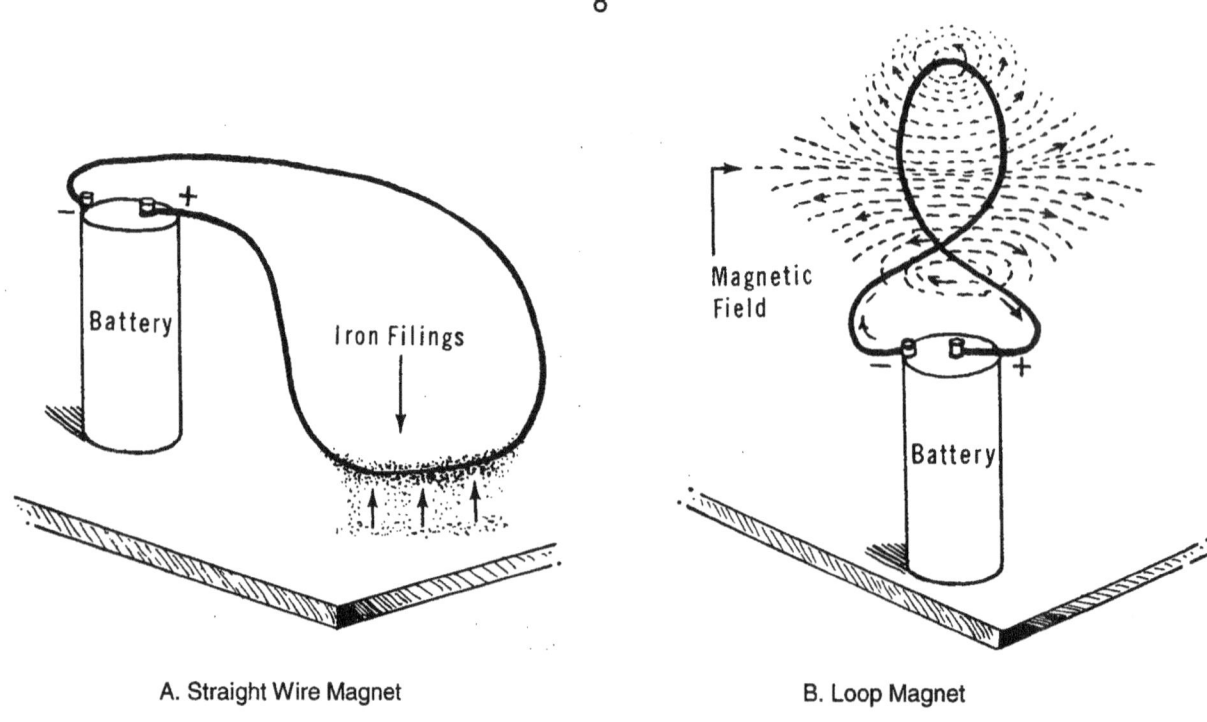

A. Straight Wire Magnet   B. Loop Magnet

FIGURE 2

Making Electricity

When electrons flow through wire, an electric current is present. That is what we mean by electricity. Before electrons will flow, there must be an excess of electrons in one place, separated from an excess of protons. This makes a potential difference between the two points. To make electricity we must create a potential difference between two points. We can do this with a magnet and a length of Wire.

Let us place a large U-shaped magnet in a vice. Then we take a piece of copper wire and attach the wire to a sensitive meter that measures electric current. Now we move the wire down between the poles of the magnet. We have cut the lines of force, and we have created a potential difference inside the wire. For electrons will move from one end of the wire to the other. An electric current flows in the wire. If we move the wire back up between the poles of the magnet, the electrons flow back in the other direction. The magnetic field holds the electrons in position. When the wire moves, the electrons are strained apart. This produces the potential difference that causes electrical current to flow. And this is the way we change the mechanical energy of the moving wire into electrical energy.

The Alternating Current Generator

Now let us put this principle to work. In figure 101, a simple electric generator is shown. There is a large magnet, with a loop of wire that rotates between the poles of the magnet. We must have some source of energy to spin the wire loop. The energy that spins the loop is converted into electrical energy by the generator. The generator is called an *alternating current generator*. The electrons flow first in one direction along the wire and then in the reverse direction.

Each complete turn of the wire loop is called one *cycle*. As the loop turns, the amount of electric current flowing in the wire varies in a regular pattern. If we follow the wire loop through one complete turn, or cycle, we can see how this change takes place.

In position A the wire loop is horizontal. It is not cutting any lines of force in the magnetic field. Therefore no electric current is flowing in the wire. As the loop turns from A to B, it begins to cut lines of force. More and more electric current flows in the wiare. When the loop reaches position

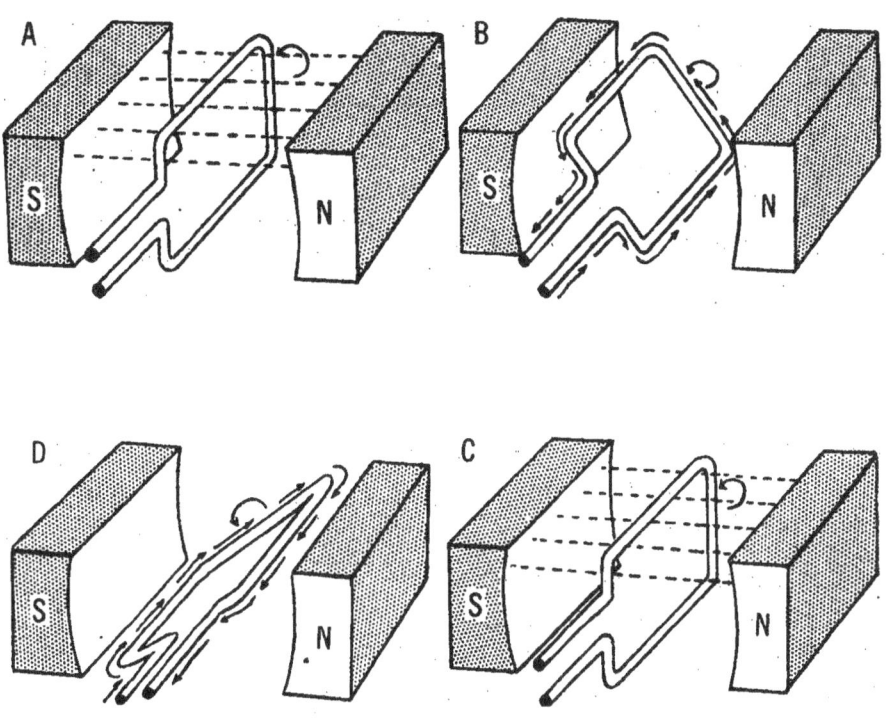

FIGURE 3. Loop Generator-Four Positions.

B, it is cutting all of the lines of force, and the current in the wire reaches a peak. Moving from B to C, the amount of current in the wire drops away to zero. The number of lines of force cut by the wire drops away to zero. When the wire is in position C, no current is flowing in the wire

The wire loop continues to turn from position C to position D. But this time the wires are reversed, and the current is flowing in the opposite direction. The amount of current increases once again to a peak at position D, but the current is flowing in the opposite direction in the wire. From position D back to position A, the current drops off once again. Back at position A, the current in the wire is zero, and one full cycle is complete.

Tile Current Cycle

We can draw a graph to show the amount of current flowing in the wire loop at different parts of the cycle. This graph is shown in figure 102. The graph begins at position A in figure 101. Each quarter turn of the loop is marked. Notice that the current reaches a peak after one quarter turn, and then returns to zero. In the next quarter turn, it reaches a second peak--*in the opposite direction*. Then it returns again to zero. Alternating current always has peaks in both directions because the current flows in both directions in the wire loop. The graph in figure 102 is called a sine wave. It shows one full cycle of electric current, produced by an alternating current generator.

The number of cycles of current produced each second is called the *frequency* of the electricity. In the United States most generators produce sixty full cycles of current each second. This is written sixty cps. For radio broadcasting, much higher frequencies are used. The radio

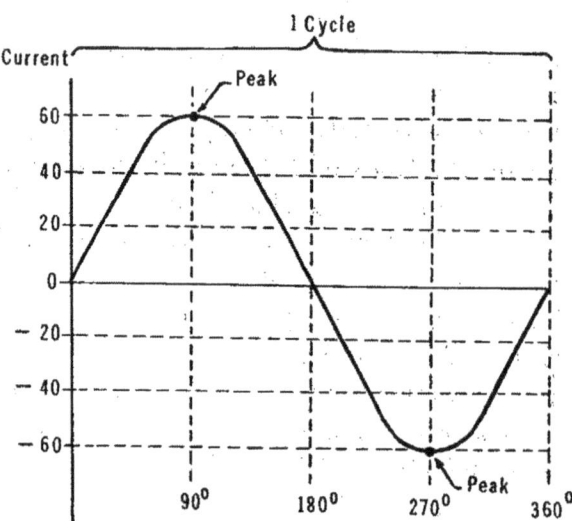

FIGURE 4. Graph: Sine Wave.

broadcasting band begins at 550 kilocycles, or 550,000 cycles per second. One kilocycle is equal to one thousand cycles. For special types of radio, a unit of one million cycles is used. This is called a *megacycle*. The human ear cannot hear these electrical frequencies. Our ears can be stimulated by mechanical energy only. Electrical energy has no effect on the ear.

The Electric Generator

An electric motor and electric generator are nearly the same. The electric generator converts mechanical energy into electrical energy. An electric motor converts electrical energy into mechanical energy. Actually, electricity is not very useful until it is changed into another form. But it is easy to transport and store, and cheap to produce. This makes it an ideal form of energy for many purposes.

The magnetic field in an electric generator is supplied by an electromagnet called the field coil. This coil lies just inside the housing of the generator. The moving part of the generator (the loop) is called the *armature*. The armature is wound with many loops of wire. Some wire is always cutting the lines of force of the magnetic field and producing electric current. The ends of the loop of wire wound on the armature are attached to two *slip rings*. The electric current generated in the generator is taken off the armature from these two rings. They are in contact with two *brushes* which carry the current away from the rings. When the generator is used to produce *direct current*, which flows in only one direction, a device is used to reverse the connections after each half turn of the armature. This device is called a *commutator*.

The generator cannot produce energy. It can only convert mechanical energy into electrical energy. Some outside power must turn the armature. In large electric plants a steam turbine is used to turn the armature in a very heavy generator. In an automobile, the small generator is attached to the drive shaft of the car.

The Electric Motor

The electric generator changes mechanical energy into electrical energy. The electric motor changes electrical energy into mechanical energy. The parts in a motor and a generator are nearly the same. But an electric motor depends on a different principle. A pole that has a positive charge is attracted to a pole with a negative charge. But it is repelled by another positive pole. This is the principle that runs an electric motor.

In an electric motor, electricity is fed into the field coil and into the winding of the armature. This creates two electromagnets, each with a positive pole and a negative pole. When the electricity is connected, the positive pole of the armature moves toward the negative pole of the field coil. This turns the armature. But the turning would stop as soon as the positive armature pole reached the negative field coil pole. So, when the positive pole has nearly reached its goal, the commutator on the motor reverses the current.

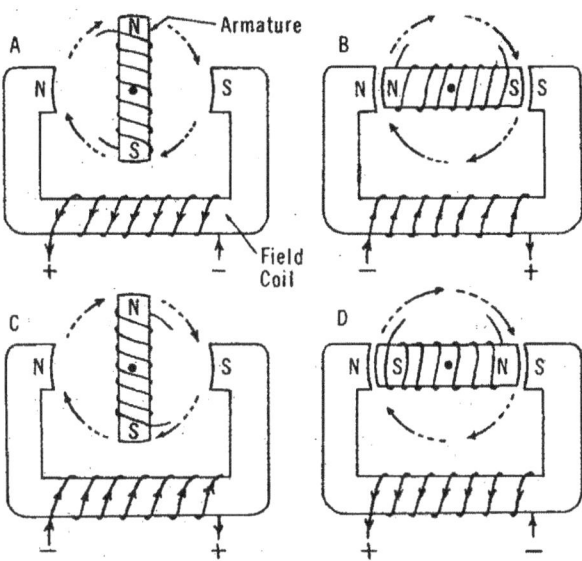

FIGURE 5. Electric Motor Showing Rotation

The positive pole on the armature is now facing a positive pole and is pushed away toward the negative pole. Again, just as it reaches its goal, the commutator reverses the connections. Again the armature pole is shoved away. So the armature keeps turning, trying to bring a positive and negative pole together. Because of the commutator it never succeeds. The pole on the armature is like a dog chasing a mechanical rabbit at a race track. Just as the dog reaches the rabbit, the rabbit's speed is increased and the dog falls bechind. The turning armature of the motor produces mechanical energy which can be used to do work.

Transformers

The electric line that passes your house carries about eighteen thousand volts. But inside the house it is a safe 110 volts. This voltage is produced by a transformer. A transformer also uses the principle of induction. But it uses it to move electricity from one wire to another even though the two wires are not touching. Inside a transformer there are two solenoids or coils. They are often wound around the same center.

One solenoid is connected to a source of alternating current. As the current moves through the coil, it produces an electric field around the coil. The electric field passes through the second coil nearby. As the current moving through the coil rises and falls with each cycle, the magnetic field

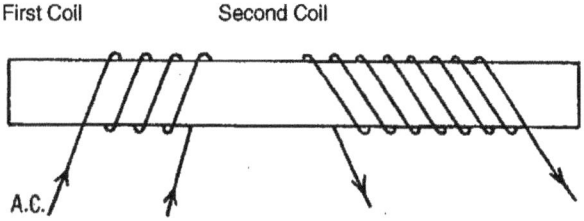

FIGURE 6. Principle of the Transformer.

around the coil also rises and falls. This produces an electric current in the second coil which is an exact duplicate of the electric current in the first coil. Although neither of the coils moves, the lines of force move as the field expands and collapses. As the lines of force cut across the wire in the second coil, they induce an electric current in the second coil.

The voltage in the second coil depends upon the number of turns of wire used in each coil. If there is the same number of turns in each coil, the voltage will not change as it moves from one to the other. If the second coil has ten times as many turns as the first coil, the voltage will be increased ten times. This is called a s*tep-up* transformer. If the number of turns in the second coil is 1/10 as large as the number in the first coil, only 1/10 as much voltage will be produced in the second coil. This is called a *step-down* transformer. Transformers can be used any time the voltage must be changed in an electric circuit. They are manufactured in a wide variety of sizes for different types of voltage changes.

Words Used in Unit 2

armature (ăr´məchər), the moving part of a generator
arranged (ərănjd´), put into proper order
collapses (kə lăps´əz), shrinks together
commutator (kŏm´ū tă tər), device which reverses the direction of flow of electricity
concentrates (kŏn´sən trăts) , brings together to one place
induced (in dūst´), produced, caused to appear
organized (ŏr´gən ĭzd), put into working order
repel (rĭ pĕl´), force back, move away from
terminals (tər´mə nəlz), the ends of a battery where an electrical connection is made

Batteries

Unit 3

Science is full of surprises. We learned in the last unit that a spinning loop of wire in a magnetic field can produce electricity. It does this by separating electrons and protons to produce an electrical potential in the spinning wire. No liquids are used. No chemical reaction takes place. Yet electricity is produced. This seems to be a long way from the chemist's laboratory. Yet the chemist only smiles to himself. He fills a glass with a few chemicals dissolved in water. He places a rod of carbon and a rod of zinc in the water and attaches a wire to each rod. When the two wires are connected, an electric current flows through the wires. The chemist too can produce electricity.

There is a useful lesson in this for anyone who studies science. The chemist and the physicist start from different points. But they both deal with electricity, even though they use different approaches. You see nature is not divided into only chemistry and physics. Our environment is all one. We have divided our world into physical and chemical things. But electricity is only the flow of electrons along a wire. It does not matter how you cause the electrons to flow. The physicist does it one way; the chemist does it another. Both men produce electricity.

The Voltaic Cell

When you start your car, you must use a battery to turn the engine over until the small electrical generator gets going. This battery produces electricity by a chemical reaction. We know that electricity is produced when there is a potential difference between two points. This occurs when electrons and protons, or positive and negative charges, are separated. The chemist separates his charges in a unit called the *voltaic cell*. All batteries are a variation of this basic unit.

The voltaic cell consists of three parts:

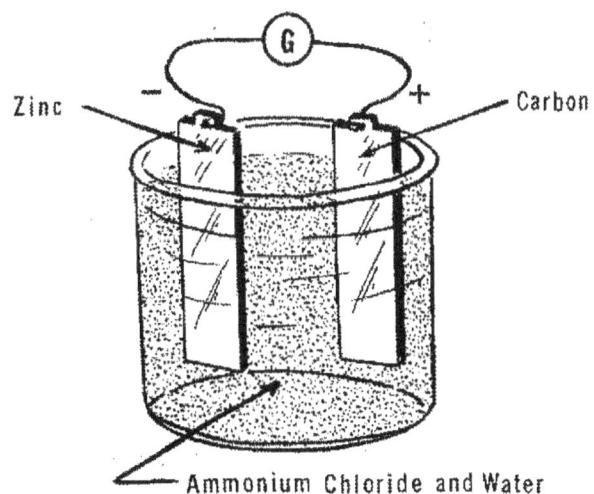

FIGURE 7. Voltaic cell

(1) a container made of insulating material-some material that will not conduct electricity; (2) a chemical solution called an electrolyte; and (3) two metal plates, called electrodes, which are placed in the solution. The electrodes must be conductors of electricity. When the electrodes are joined by a wire, electrons will flow along the wire. The voltaic cell will produce an electric current.

What happens inside the cell to produce electricity? One of the electrodes is made of the metal zinc. The other is made of pure carbon. The electrolyte is usually a mixture of water and sulfuric acid. Water is not a good electrical conductorthe sulfuric acid makes the solution a conducting material.

Chemical Action in Cell

When the electrodes are placed in the electrolyte, the zinc plate dissolves. It forms charged particles called irns. Ions can be either positively charged or negatively charged. If there is a surplus of eleetrons on the ion, it is negatively charged. If there is a shortage of electrons on the ion, it is positively charged. You can probably see the connection already. Electricity is produced by a flow of surplus electrons. Anyhow, the zinc forms ions with a surplus of electrons. These surplns electrons gather on the zinc electrode. This gives the zinc electrode a negative charge.

The electrons taken from zinc are added to the zinc strip. So the zinc electrode acquires a surplus of electrons. There is still one more step. The water in the electrolyte produces hydrogen ions, or negative charges. These hydrogen ions move to the carbon rod and collect electrons from it. So the carbon rod gets a surplus of protons, or positive charges.

By chemical action we thus produce a positive charge on the carbon rod and a negative charge on the zinc rod. The zinc rod has an excess of electrons. And so there is a potential difference between the carbon rod and the zinc rod. If we conned these two points, electrons will flow from the zinc rod to the carbon rod. An electric current will be produced in the wire. As the electrons move from the zinc plate, more zinc dissolves and the potential difference is maintained. Eleetric current will flow from zinc to carbon until the zinc has completely dissolved. Then the voltaic cell will be worn out. A new zinc rod must be added to make it work again.

This is the basic method which the chemist uses to produce electricity. He dissolves zinc and uses the energy to produce electricity. Many kinds of material can be used to make a voltaic cell. Usually electrodes are made of zinc and carbon because both minerals are cheap. The electrolyte is often a compound of ammonia and chlorine called *ammonium chloride.*

Primary Cells and Secondary Cells

When the zinc in the voltaic cell is used up, the battery is dead. A cell of this sort is called a *primary cell*. The chemical action inside the battery moves only in one direction. When the cell is unable to produce more electricity, nothing can be done to make the battery useful again.

There is another type of battery, however, which can solve this problem. The chemical action inside this battery cell can be reversed. When the cell is producing electricity, a chemical reaction takes place.

When the cell runs down, the chemical action can be reversed. We say that the battery is *discharging* when it is producing electricity. When the process is reversed, the cell is being charged. This type of battery is called a *secondary cell*. We know many examples of both batteries. A flashlight battery is a primary cell. When it is used up, we throw it away. An automobile battery is a secondary cell. It can be recharged again and again before it must be thrown away.

The Primary Cell --- A Dry Cell Battery

The most common primary cell is the small battery we use in a flashlight. Usually it is made in the shape of a small cylinder. The outer shell of the battery is a small can made of zinc. This is the negative electrode of the battery. The positive electrode is a solid carbon rod suspended in the can. The carbon rod is insulated from the zinc can-they do not touch. Inside the can there is a damp paste of ammonium chloride and water. The cell is not completely dry, but it can be turned upside down without spilling. The top of the can is sealed with some plastic insulating material. This separates the carbon rod from the zinc can and holds in the electrolyte.

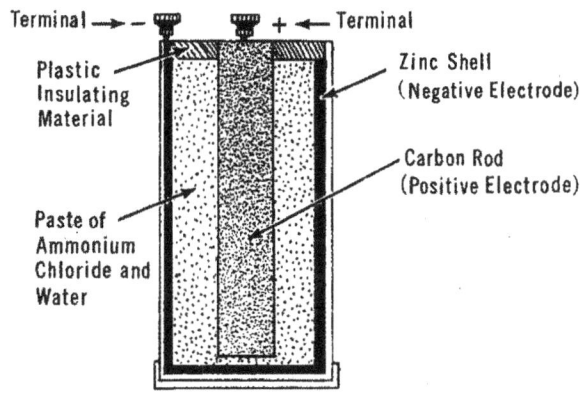

FIGURE 8. Dry Cell Battery

The dry cell works just like the voltaic cell. The zinc dissolves, and excess electrons form on the zinc can, and hydrogen ions take electrons from the carbon rod, creating a shortage of electrons on the rod. This produces a potential difference between the two points. When they are connected, electricity is produced in the connecting wire. When all of the zinc has dissolved, the cell is used up. These cells produce about one volt of electrical pressure and a small amount of electrical current.

Electrolysis

The secondary battery cell is based on another principle. When an electric current is passed through a solution of water, the process is called *electrolysis.* The results of *electrolysis* depend on the dissolved materials in the solution. If the solution is a mixture of water and sulfuric acid, electrolysis produces hydrogen at one electrode and oxygen at the other electrode. In other words, electrolysis separates water into hydrogen and oxygen molecules. If the solution contains copper sulfate, electrolysis will produce pure copper on the negative electrode. The electric current separates the dissolved materials so they have an electrical charge. They then move toward the terminal of the opposite polarity, or opposite charge.

Because electrolysis will separate dissolved materials, it is often used to place a thin metal coating on a metal base. Silver plating and chromium plating are done by electrolysis. This is called *electroplating.* Let us look at one example of the process. When electricity is passed through a solution of copper sulfate, copper ions and sulfate ions are formed. The copper ions have a positive charge; the sulfate ions have a negative charge. The positive copper ions move to the negative plate, and the negative sulfate ions move to the positive plate. This movement takes place when electric current is flowing.

Direct current must always be used for electrolysis to keep the current moving in just one direction. If the negative plate in the tank is a piece of metal, a layer of pure copper will be deposited on the plate. Because the ions of copper are pure, this is a good method for separating copper from any impurities it may contain. So electrolysis is widely used in the copper industry to produce pure metal.

The Storage Battery

The principle of electrolysis is used by the secondary cell to produce electricity. Electrolysis is made to produce a chemical change in a battery. When this chemical change is reversed, electricity is produced by the battery. Actually, the battery gives up the energy that caused the first chemical change. That is why it is often called a storage battery. It "stores" the electrical energy until its chemical process is reversed. Then it releases the energy.

How is this done? Let us take the automobile battery as an example. This is called a lead-acid battery because its main parts are lead and acid. This battery is an insulated case, containing an electrolyte and two plates. Both plates are made of the same material-lead. The electrolyte is a mixture of sulfuric acid and water.

Now, when the battery is made, both terminals are attached to lead plates. There is no potential difference between the two plates, and no electricity can be produced by the cell. Before the cell will produce electricity, it must go through electrolysis. A direct current is run through the battery. This causes a chemical change in one of the lead plates. It creates a potential difference between the two plates. This potential difference will produce electricity when the chemical reaction is reversed. Electrolysis is called *charging the battery*.

Grouping Battery Cells

A single battery cell provides a small voltage and a little current. A commercial battery usually contains several separate cells, tied together into one unit. There are various ways to tie the batteries together. Each method gives different voltage and current ratings for the battery. If all the positive terminals and all the negative terminals are tied together, the connection is called a *parallel* connection. If the positive terminal of one cell is tied to the negative terminal of the next cell, the connection is called a *series* connection. If a combination of the two eonncctions is used, it is called a *series-parallel* connection. Each method has advantages and disadvantages. In general, a parallel circuit supplies high current rating, but no increase in voltage. A series circuit supplies high voltage and low current ratings. A series-parallel circuit can combine the advantages of both types of connection.

Batteries

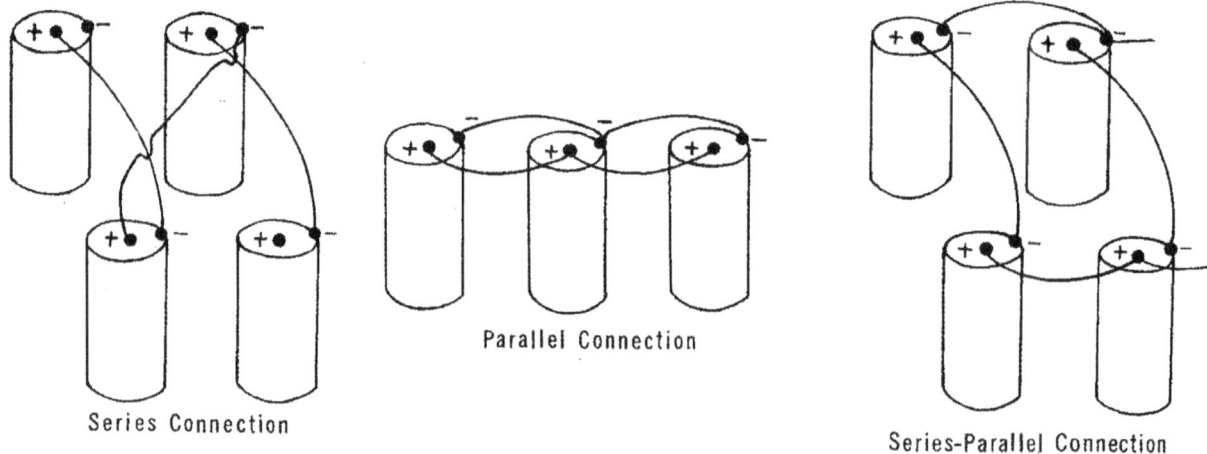

FIGURE 9. Series, Parallel, and Series-Parallel Connections.

Words Used in Unit 3

approaches (əprōch´əz), ways of getting to something
commercial (kə mėr´shăl), made to be sold
electrolysis (ĭ lĕktr´ŏlə sĭs), the passing of an electric current through a solution of water
ions (ī´ənz), electrically charged particles
laboratory (lăb´rə tŏ rĭ), place equipped for scientists to work
surplus (sėr´pləs), amount over and above what is needed
voltaic (vŏl tā´ĭk), basic type of battery

Using Electricity

Unit 4

Electricity is energy. It can be used to do work. Electricity is probably the most convenient form of energy we have. It can be produced easily and cheaply. It can be transported from place to place rapidly and. economically. It can be changed into mechanical energy by a simple and inexpensive electric motor. Electric heat is clean and quickly produced. In many ways electricity is an ideal form of energy.

Producing Electricity

Every year the United States uses about 600 billion kilowatt-hours of electricity. One kilowatt-hour is the amount of electricity needed to burn a thousand watt bulb for one full hour. Some of our electricity is produced by converting water power into electric power. Running or falling water is used to spin a large turbine. A generator converts this spinning energy into electrical energy.

Most of the electricity used in the United States is produced by burning coal. In the last few years, we have begun to use atomic power to produce electricity. Most atomic plants use the heat energy in a nuclear reactor to produce steam. The steam is used in a turbine, and the turbine spins a large generator. The generators used to make electricity commercially are very large and heavy. The armature may weigh thousands of pounds. The coils are made of thick heavy wire. A large generator can produce thousands of amperes of electric current under a pressure of ten thousand to fifteen thousand volts.

Transporting Electricity

When electricity is transmitted for long distances, the voltage is always increased. The electricity is run through a step-up transformer. Then high voltage electricity is sent along heavy wires. This reduces the loss of energy in the transmission lines.

Electricity can also be transmitted without wires. But air has a very high resistance to electricity, and the losses are high. Wireless transmission of electric power is not yet practical. Radio waves are really electrical energy moving through air. But they must be produced at high frequencies. And the amount of energy that reaches a radio reeeiver is very small.

Long-distance electric power lines usually carry electricity at about 300,000 volts pressure. This high pressure cuts down losses. But it is too dangerous to use in the home. Three hundred thousand volts of pressure can force electricity through several inches of air, and cause an arc. This can be very dangerous. So the voltage is dropped for home use to 110 volts or 220 volts. Heavy appliances like stoves use 220 volt electricity because this reduces the relative amount of current flowing in the wires of the house. If a stove needs twenty amperes of 110 volt electricity, it needs only ten amperes of 220 volt electricity to produce the same energy. You can prove this by looking at Ohm's Law again. When the voltage is doubled, the current needed to produce the same power is cut in half. This makes for safer electrical operation.

Heating with Electricity

Electricity is produced when electrons flow through a wire. The electrons are carrying energy, and they can do work as they flow. If we place a high resistance in the path of the electrons, they will work hard to get past it. This work generates heat. This is the basic principle behind all electrical heating systems. The higher the resistance, the more work the electrons must do to pass. This produces more heat. An English physicist named Joule studied the relation between resistance and heating power in electricity. He discovered three basic laws that seem to explain what happens when we heat by electricity. The three laws are:
- ❖ The amount of heat produced is directly proportional to resistance.
    - o If one ohm of resistance in a cir- cuit produces one joule of heat, ten ohms of resistance will produce ten joules of heat. One joule is equal to 0.24 calories.

- ❖ The amount of heat produced is directly proportional to the time the current flows.
  - o If one joule of heat is produced in one second, ten joules of heat will be produced in ten seconds.
- ❖ Heat produced in a circuit is directly proportional to the square of the current flowing in the circuit.
  - o If two amperes of current produce four joules of heat, three amperes of current will produce nine joules of heat.

These three laws tell us that we can increase the amount of heat that is produced by an electrical circuit if we:
1. increase the resistance in the circuit.
2. increase the current in the circuit.
3. increase the time that current flows in the circuit.

Notice that an increase in current causes the greatest change in the amount of heat produced. That is why 220 volt electricity is used for heavy appliances. It reduces the current in the house wiring and reduces the amount of heat produced in the wires. This cuts down the danger of fire in the house.

Lighting

The electric light bulb was invented by an American, Thomas A. Edison. A light bulb is simply a piece of wire with a very high resistance and a high melting point which is placed inside an evacuated glass bulb. When electrons pass through the wire, they heat it white hot. The material must have a high resistance to produce the white heat. So it must have a high melting point too, or it will melt in the high temperature. Most light bulb filaments are made of tungsten wire. The filament is placed in a glass bulb, and most of the air is pumped out of the bulb. If the air remained in the bulb, the oxygen would burn the hot filament. Usually some inert gas like argon or nitrogen is placed in the bulb. This saves the filament and allows the use of higher temperatures.
Inert Gas

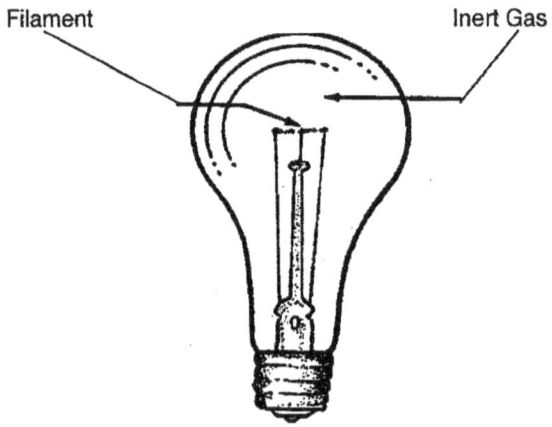

FIGURE 10. Light Bulb.

The Telegraph

Electricity travels at the speed of light --186,000 miles per second. This makes it an ideal carrier for messages. The first method of using electricity to carry messages was invented by Samuel F. B. Morse in 1837. Morse called his invention the *telegraph*. It uses the principle of an electromagnet. When an electric current flows through a coil of wire, the coil becomes a magnet, and it will attract metal. When the current is shut off, the magnet stops working. Morse used this simple principle to send his messages along electric wires.

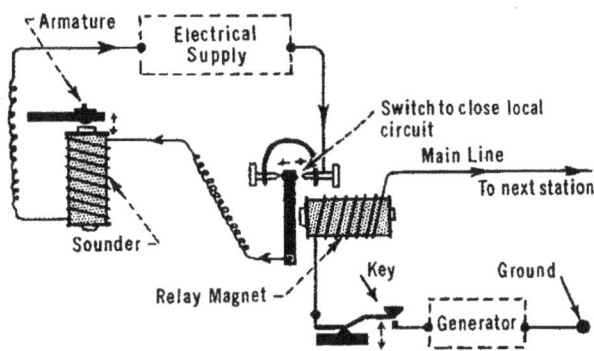

FIGURE 11. Simplified Telegraph with Key.

The main parts of a telegraph system are the key, the sounder, the wires, and a supply of electricity. These parts are shown in figure 109. When the key is pushed down, electricity flows through the wires and produces an electromagnet in the coil. This draws the sounder down with a sharp click. When the key is released, the magnet releases the sounder. By spacing the sounds made on the sounder, we can send messages. Morse also invented an alphabet made of long and short signals which is called the *Morse Code*. Using this code, we can send messages from one place to another. Of course, both the sender and the receiver must understand the Morse Oode-but it can be learned in a short time.

The old key and sounder system is not used much today. Instead, we use a machine that looks like a typewriter to send and receive messages. Each key of the machine sends a special signal along the wire. When that signal is received, the receiving machine types out the same message. These machines are called *teletype* machines. They are much faster and more accuurate than a key and sounder. They are used by the Armed Forces, police, news services, and many other organizations.

The Telephone

The telephone is more complex than the telegraph. The telegraph works by changing the *amount* of energy sent over a wire. The telephone must do more than this. First, it must change mechanical energy, produced by the voice, into electrical energy. Then the electrical energy is transmitted over a wire. Finally, the telephone must change the electrical energy back to mechanical energy that our ears can hear.

The principle that a telephone uses to change mechanical energy into electrical energy is a simple one. According to Ohm's Law, when the resistance in a circuit changes, the amount of current flowing through the circuit changes. A telephone transmitter uses the mechanical energy in sound to change the electrical resistance in a circuit. The method is quite simple.

A round disc, or diaphragm, is attached to a small box filled with carbon particles. Carbon is a resistor, and it is part of the electrical circuit of the telephone. When the sound waves strike the disc, it vibrates. This compresses the particles of carbon. As the carbon particles are pressed together, the resistance in the circuit drops. When the pressure is released, the resistance in the circuit rises. This causes changes in the current flowing in the circuit. They follow the same pattern as the vibrations of the disc

The telephone receiver must change the electrical energy carried by the electric current into mechanical energy. We cannot hear electrical waves. Our ears respond only to mechanical waves in the air. The telephone receiver uses the principle of the electromagnet. The variations in electric current produced by the transmitter cause variations in the strength of the electromagnet in the receiver.

In a telephone receiver there is a small electromagnet. This magnet holds the thin disc in place. As the strength of the magnet varies, the disc vibrates. Since the strength of the magnet is varied by the electric current produced by the vibrating disc in the transmitter, the disc in the receiver vibrates in exactly the same way. These vibrations produce mechanical sound waves exactly like those that activated the transmitter. Electrical energy is changed into mechanical energy, and our ears hear the sound coming from the receiver.

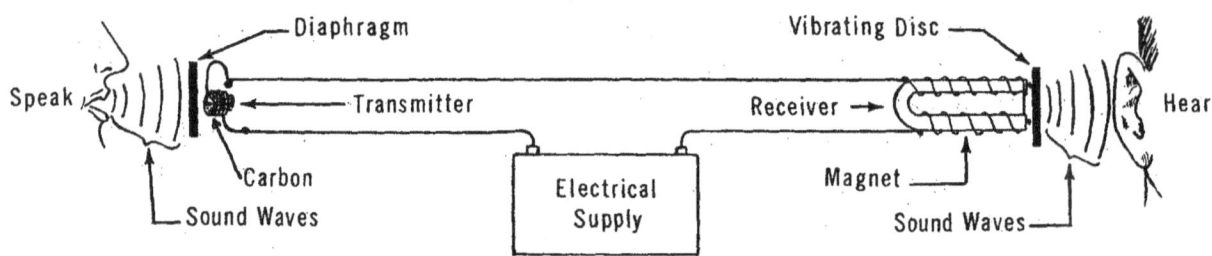

FIGURE 12 Simplified Telephone Circuit

Arc Welding

There are so many possible uses of electricity that we can cover only a very few of them. In this unit we are looking at a few nonelectronic uses of electricity. One of the most important of these uses is arc welding. In modern industry arc welding is a very important process. It is employed to build auto bodies, airplanes, and thousands of other things that we use every day.

Electric welding works on the same principle as the electric arc light. High voltage and very heavy electric currents are needed for welding. Usually this requires a special transformer and a special electric line into the building. One end of the electric line is attached to the material to be welded. The other end is run through a special tip or rod made of high resistance metal. This rod is held by the man who does the welding.

There are different kinds of welding rods for each type of welding, depending upon the material to be welded. The composition of the tip or rod determines the strength of the joint and the temperature at the arc. A skilled welder chooses the rod that will best do the particular job. When the metal rod is touched against the material to be welded, the electric circuit is closed and electric current runs through the rod. The high resistance produces a high temperature, and the material in the rod is vaporized. This produces a trail of metal vapor between the rod and the material being welded. The heavy electric current runs through this vapor arc, producing a white heat.

As in the carbon arc light, the metal tip keeps melting as electricity flows along the rod. The vaporized metal forms a solid deposit on the joint, called a "bead." The tip of the rod must be kept an even distance from the material to produce a smooth, even joint. This takes experience and a steady hand. When the metal hardens and cools, it produces a joint that is very strong. In fact, the welded part of a joint is often stronger than the metal that is joined together.

Other Uses of Electricity

Some of the special uses of electricity are often overlooked. It can be used to reduce smoke in cities, for example. If an electric device is placed inside a large chimney, it can be used to charge dirt particles as they move up the chimney. A collector higher up the chimney that has an opposite charge will collect the particles as they pass by. The amount of smoke and dirt that leaves the chimney is, thus, cut to a minimum. The collector must be emptied from time to time.

Electricity is very useful in the field of medicine. Special light bulbs are used to kill germs in hospitals. These lights produce energy of a particular frequency that is deadly to germs. Electric energy is used to provide heating for therapy machines, used to ease the pain when bones or muscles are seriously injured. There is even an electric knife that seals as it cut, thus eliminating the need for sewing. It is an excellent instrument for certain kinds of operations.

Radar and television, calculating machines, and weather satellites all come under the area of *electronics.* Yet all of these complex machines are built upon the same principles that are stated in Ohm's Law. The study of electronics is based on our study of electricity. The one great difference between electricity and electronics lies in making use of the effect that can be produced by a vacuum tube. But all electricity, whether it is passed through a vacuum tube or not, must obey the same general law.

Words Used in Unit 4

economically (ē kə nŏm´ĭk lĭ), inexpensively
evacuated (ĭ văk´ū ăt əd), emptied
filament (fĭl´ə mənt), the wire in a light bulb
inert (ĭn ərt´), not active
reduces (rĭ dūs´əs), makes less
transformer (trăns fôrm´ər), an apparatus for increasing or decreasing voltage
vaporized (vă´pər ĭzd), changed into vapor, or a gas
welded (wĕld´əd), joined together by pressing while soft and hot

GENERAL PRINCIPLES OF WIRING

Section I. DESIGN AND LAYOUT OF INTERIOR WIRING

47. General

The different wiring systems in common use for civilian and armed forces construction are often called open-wire, cable, and conduit systems.

Many installation methods and procedures used in the wiring processes are common to all systems, and these are described in this chapter. In most wiring installations the type of wiring to be installed will be specified on the blueprints. If not so specified the installation method must be determined. In general, the type of wiring used should be similar to that installed in adjacent or nearby buildings.

48. Load Per Outlet

The first step in planning the circuit for any wiring installation is the determination of the connected load per outlet. The load per outlet can be obtained in several different ways:

a. The most accurate method of determining load per outlet is made by obtaining the stated value from the blueprints or specifications.

   (1) Commonly, the lighting outlets shown on the blueprints are listed in the specifications along with their wattage rating.

     (*a*) If the lights used are of the incandescent type, this figure represents the total wattage of the lamp.

     (*b*) When fluorescent type lights are specified, the wattage drain (also called load per outlet) should be increased approximately 20 percent to provide for the ballast load. For example, when the fixture is rated as a 2-lamp, 100-watt unit, the actual wattage drain is 200 watts plus approximately 20 watts for each lamp ballast, or a total load of 240 watts.

   (2) If the specifications are not available, the blueprints in many cases designate the type of equipment to be connected to specific outlets. Though the equipment ultimately used in the outlet may come from a different manufacturer, equipment standards provide the electrician with assurance that the outlets will use approximately the same wattage. If the equipment is available, the nameplate will list the wattage used or ampere drain. If not, table VII should be used to obtain the average wattage consumption of electrical appliances. Table VIII lists the current requirements for small motors of various horsepower ratings.

b. To provide adequate wiring for systems where the blueprints or specifications do not list any special or appliance loads, the following general rules will apply:

   (1) For heavy duty outlets or mogul size lampholders, the load per outlet should be figured at 5 amperes each.

   (2) For all other outlets, both ceiling and wall, the wattage drain (load per outlet) should be computed at 1.5 amperes per outlet.

c. The total outlet load may also be determined on a watts-per-square-foot basis. In this load-determination method, the floor area of the building to be wired is computed from the outside dimensions of the building. This square footage area is then multiplied by the standard watts-per-square-foot requirement based on the type of building to be wired. Table IX lists these constants along with a feeder-demand factor which is explained in paragraph 53 for various types of building occupancies.

49. Type of Distribution

a. The electrical power load in any building cannot be properly circuited until the type and voltage of the central power-distribution system is known. The voltage and the number of wires from the

Table VII. Wattage Consumption of Electrical Appliances

Appliance	Average wattage
Blanket	150
Clock	3
Coffeemaker	550
Chafing dish	600
Dishwasher	100
Egg boiler	250
Fan, 8-inch	30
Fan, 10-inch	35
Fan, 12-inch	50
Frying pan	600
Griddle	450
Grill	600
Heater (radiant)	1000
Heating pad	50
Hotplate	660
Humidifier	500
Immersion heater	300
Iron	1000
Ironer	1320
Mixer	200
Phonograph	40
Range	8000
Refrigerator	250
Radio	100
Roaster	1320
Sewing machine	75
Soldering iron	200
Sunlamp	450
Television	300
Toaster	450
Vacuum cleaner	160
Washing machine	175
Water heater	2000
Waffle iron	660

Table VIII. Motor Currents

Horse-power	Full-load amperes			
	120 v. 1 phase	240 v. 1 phase	208 v. 3 phase	416 v. 3 phase
⅙	3.1	1.6	...	...
¼	4.4	2.2	...	...
½	7.1	3.6	2.1	1.1
¾	9.8	4.9	3.0	1.5
1	12.5	6.3	3.7	1.9
1½	17.7	8.9	5.3	2.7
2	23.1	11.6	7.0	3.5
3	32.6	16.3	9.6	4.8
5	54.0	27.0	16.0	8.0

powerlines to the buildings are normally shown or specified on the blueprints. However, the electrician should check the voltage and type of distribution at the power-service entrance to every building in which wiring is to be done. This is especially necessary when he is altering or adding circuits. The voltage checks are usually made with an indicating voltmeter at the service-entrance switches or at the distribution load centers. The type of distribution is determined by visual check of the number of wires entering the building.

b. If only two wires enter the building, the service is either direct current or single-phase alternating current. The voltage is determined by an indicating voltmeter.

c. When three wires enter a building the service can either be single-phase, direct-current, or three-phase.

Table IX. Standard Loads for Branch Circuits and Feeders and Demand Factor for Feeders

Occupancy	Standard load, watts per square foot	Feeder demand factor, percent
Armories and auditoriums	1	100%
Banks	2	100%
Barber shops	3	100%
Churches	1	100%
Clubs	2	100%
Dwellings	3	100% for first 3,000 watts, 35% for next 117,000, 25% for excess above 120,000.
Garages	0.5	100%
Hospitals	2	40% for first 50,000 watts, 20% for excess over 50,000.
Office buildings	2	100% for first 20,000 watts, 70% for excess over 20,000.
Restaurants	2	100%
Schools	2	100% for first 15,000 watts, 50% for excess over 15,000.
Stores	3	100%
Warehouses	0.25	100% for first 12,500 watts, 50% for excess over 12,500.
Assembly halls	1	100%

(1) If the power distribution is single-phase alternating current or direct current the test leads over 2 of the wires in the service entrance will give an indicating voltmeter reading that will be exactly twice as much as when the voltmeter leads are applied between any 1 of these 2-wires and the third.

(2) A three-phase distribution system will show no change in voltage between any pair of leads when tested with an indicating voltmeter.

d. Four-wire distribution denotes 3-phase and neutral service. When tested, voltages between the neutral wires and each of the 3 hot wires should be all the same. The voltage readings between any 2 of these 3 wires are similar and should equal the neutral to hot wire voltage multiplied by 1.732. Common operating voltages for this type service are 120 and 208 volts.

50. Grounding

a. Requirements.
(1) All electrical systems must have the neutral wire grounded if the voltage between the hot lead and the neutral is less than 150 volts.
(2) It is recommended that all systems have a grounded neutral where the voltage to ground does not exceed 300 volts.
(3) Circuits operating at less than 50 volts need not be grounded, provided the transformer supplying the circuit is connected to a grounded system.

b. Types of Grounding.
(1) A system ground is the ground applied to a neutral wire. It reduces the possibility of fire and shock by reducing the voltage of 1 of the wires of a system to 0 volts potential above ground.
(2) An equipment ground is an additional ground which is attached to appliances and machinery located in such places as laundries and basements where wet or humid conditions could create dangerous short circuits. An equipment ground is advantageous in these areas for the appliances can be maintained at zero voltage, and if a short circuit does occur in a hot load, the fuse protection opens the circuit and prevents serious injury to operating personnel.

c. Methods of Grounding.
(1) A system ground is provided by the instal-

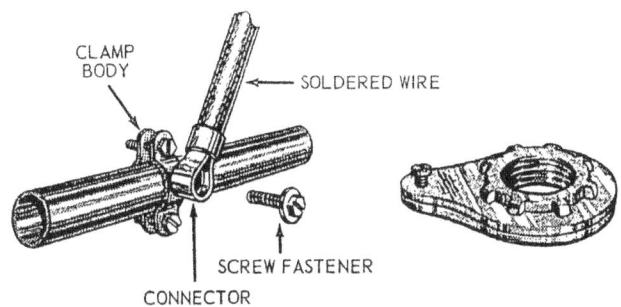

Figure 42. Typical grounding fixtures.

lation of a No. 6-gage bare wire connecting the neutral wire either with a water pipe or a ¾-inch conduit driven 8 feet into the ground. The wire is attached to the water pipe or conduit by a special clamp or bushing ground-connector clamp after the pipe or conduit has been filed or sandpapered clean to make a good electrical contact. A clamp type ground-connector has two semicircular sections which encircle the ground rod or conduit and are tightened by a machine screw. A bushing type ground connector clamp is screwed onto the ground rod in a manner similar to installing a bushing on a conduit. Figure 42 shows typical grounding fixtures.

(2) Equipment is grounded through the conduit in a permanent installation by utilizing the system ground, or through the use of a three-wire cord, plug, and matching receptacle. The third wire in the receptacle is attached to either the conduit or the system ground. Similarly, the third prong on the plug is connected to the metal structure of the equipment to be grounded.

d. Ground Detection. When testing or inspecting system installations, proper grounding can be determined visually and electrically as follows:
(1) The neutral wire, always grounded, should be a white-colored insulated wire. The equipment ground wire should always be green.
(2) If checked with an indicating voltmeter, the scale should indicate zero when the test prods are placed between the neutral wire and the building water pipes or ground rod.

51. Circuiting the Load

a. If all the power load in a building were con-

Table X. Requirements for Branch Circuits

Rating of circuit	15 amperes	20 amperes	25 amperes	35 amperes	50 amperes
Rubber-insulated conductors 2 or 3 per raceway or cable. Minimum gage number:					
(1) Type R	14	12	10	8	5
(2) Type RP	14	12	10	8	6
(3) Type RH	14	14	12	10	8
Receptacle rating (amperes)	15 (max.)	15 (min.)	20 (min.)	25 (min.)	50 (min.)
Type of lampholders (for exceptions, see National Electrical Code).	Any type.	Heavy duty.	Heavy duty.	Heavy duty.[1]	Heavy duty.[1]
Portable appliances. Maximum individual rating of one appliance, not motor-driven[2] (amperes).	12	15	20	Not permitted.	Not permitted.
Fixed appliances, total rating (amperes):					
(1) If lampholders or portable appliances are also supplied.	6	15	20	25	Combination not permitted.
(2) If fixed appliances only, with one or more being motor-driven, are supplied.	12	15	20	25	Not permitted.
(3) If fixed appliances only, none being motor-driven, are supplied.	15	20	25	35	50[3]

[1] No lampholder may be supplied by this circuit in dwellings.
[2] Can be motor-driven if time-lag fuses are used.
[3] Only appliances permitted on this circuit are fixed cooking appliances or a range and water heater.

nected to a single pair of wires and protected by a single fuse, the entire establishment would be without power in case of a breakdown, a short circuit, or a fuse blowout. In addition the wires would have to be large enough to handle the entire load, and, therefore, too large in some cases to make connections to individual devices. Consequently, the outlets in a building are divided into small groups known as branch circuits. These circuits normally are rated in amperes as shown in table X. This table contains a comparison of the various ampere requirements of the branch circuits with the standard circuit components.

b. The method of circuiting the building load varies with the size of the building and the power load.

   (1) In a small building with little load, the circuit breakers or fuses are installed at the power-service entrance and the individual circuits are run from this location.

   (2) For buildings of medium size with numerous wiring circuits, the fuse box should be located at the center of the building load so that all the branch runs are short, minimizing the voltage drop in the lines.

   (3) When buildings are large or have the loads concentrated at several remote locations, the ideal circuiting would locate fuse boxes at each individual load center. It is assumed that the branch circuits would be radially installed at each of these centers to minimize the voltage drops in the runs.

c. The number of circuits required for adequate wiring can be determined by adding the connected load in watts and dividing the total by the wattage permitted on the size of branch circuit selected. The total wattage is obtained from the sum of the loads of each individual outlet determined by one of the three methods outlined in paragraph 48. For example, if 15-ampere, 110-volt circuits are to be used, the maximum wattage permitted on each circuit equals 15 x 110 or 1650 watts. If the total connected load is assumed to be 18,000 watts, $\frac{18000}{1650}$ shows 11.5 circuits are required. Since we cannot have ½ of a circuit, twelve 15-ampere circuits are used to carry the connected load. The number of circuits determined by this method is the basic minimum. For long-range planning in permanent installations, the best practice requires the addition of several circuits to the minimum required, or the installation of the next larger modular-size fusing panel to allow for future wiring additions. If additional circuits over the minimum required are used, reducing the number of outlets per circuit, the electrical installation is more efficient. This is true because the voltage drop in the system is reduced allowing the apparatus to operate more efficiently.

d. Motors which are used on portable appliances are normally disconnected from the power source either by removal of the appliance plug from its receptacle or by the operation of an attached built-in switch. Some large-horsepower motors, however, require a permanent power installation with special controls. Motor switches, some of which are shown in figure 43, are rated in horsepower capacity. In a single motor installation a separate circuit must be run from the fuse or circuit breaker panel to the motor, and individual fuses or circuit breakers installed. For multiple motor installations the National Electrical Code requires that "Two or more motors may be connected to the same branch circuit, protected at not more than 20 amperes at 125 volts or less or 15 amperes at 600 volts or less, if each does not exceed 1 horsepower in rating and each does not have a full load rating in excess of 6 amperes. Two or more motors of any rating, each with individual overcurrent protection (provided integral with the motor start switches or an individual units), may be connected to one branch circuit provided each motor controller and motor-running overcurrent device be approved for group installation and the branch circuit fusing rating be equal to the rating required for the largest motor plus an amount equal to the sum of the full load ratings of the other motors".

52. Balancing the Power Load on a Circuit

The ideal wiring system is planned so that each wiring circuit will have the same ampere drain at all times. Since this can never be achieved, the circuiting is planned to divide the connected load as evenly as possible. Thus, each individual circuit uses approximately the average power consumption for the total system. This will make for minimum service interruption. Figure 44 demonstrates the advantage of a balanced circuit when a 3-wire single-phase, 110–220-volt distribution system is used. The current in the neutral conductor remains 0 as shown.

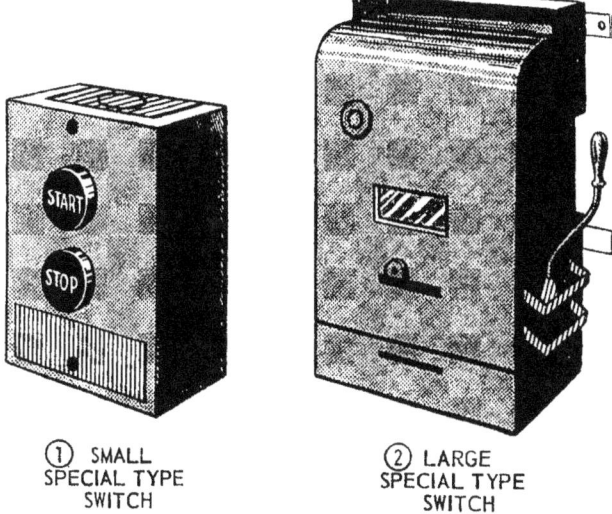

① SMALL SPECIAL TYPE SWITCH   ② LARGE SPECIAL TYPE SWITCH

Figure 43. Motor switches.

This 1 factor reduces the voltage drop in each circuit by 50 percent from what it would be if the load were on two 2-wire circuits.

53. Load Per Building

a. Maximum Demand. In some building installations the total possible power load may be connected to power at the same time. In this case, the generating capacity of the power supply, which must be kept available for these buildings, is equal to the connected load. In the majority of building installations where armed forces personnel will work, the maximum load which the system is required to service is much less than the connected load. This power load which is set at some arbitrary figure below the possible total connected load is called the "maximum demand" of the building.

b. Demand Factor. The ratio of "maximum demand" to total connected load in a building expressed as a percentage is termed demand factor. The determination of building loads can be obtained by the use of standard demand factors as shown in table IX. For example, if the connected load in a warehouse is 22,500 watts, using the demand factors listed in table IX for warehouses the actual building load can be obtained as follows: 100 percent of the first 12,500 watts equals 12,500, 50 percent of the remaining 10,000 watts equals 5,000; therefore, the total building load is 12,500 plus 5,000 watts or 17,500 watts.

54. Balancing the Power Load of a Building

The standard voltage distribution system from a generating station to individual building installations is the 3- or 4-wire, 3-phase type. Distribution transformers as shown in figure 45 on the powerline poles change the voltage to 110 or 220, and are designed to deliver 3-wire single-phase service. These transformers are then connected across the distribution phase leads in a balanced arrangement as shown. Consequently, for maximum transformer efficiency, the building loads assumed for power distribution as shown in figure 45 should also be balanced as previously illustrated in figure 44.

55. Additions to Existing Wiring

a. Circuit Capacity. In the installation of additions to existing wiring in a building the electrician determines first the available extra capacity of the present circuits. This can readily be obtained by ascertaining the fused capacity of the building and subtracting the present connected load. If all the outlets do not have connected loads, their average load should be used to obtain the connected load figure. When the existing circuits have available capacity for new outlets and are located near the additional outlet required, they should be extended and connected to the new outlets.

b. New Circuits. When the existing outlets cannot handle an additional load and a spare circuit has been provided in the local fuse or circuit breaker panel, a new circuit is installed. This is also done if the new outlet or outlets are so located that a new circuit can be installed more economically than an existing circuit extension. Moreover, the installation of a new circuit will generally decrease the voltage drop on all circuits, resulting in an increase in appliance operating efficiency. Figure 46 illustrates the addition of a new circuit from the spare circuit No. 4 in the circuit breaker panel.

c. New Load Center. In many wiring installations no provisions are made for spare circuits in the fuse panel. Moreover, the location of the new circuit required is often remote from the existing fusing or circuit breaker panel. In this case the most favorable method of providing service to the circuit is to install a new load center at a location close to the circuit outlets. This installation must not overload the incoming service and service-entrance switch. Should such an overload be indicated, the service equipment should also be changed to suit the new requirements. This sometimes can be accomplished in 2-wire systems by pulling in an additional wire from the powerline. This changes the service from 2-wire to 3-wire at 110 to 220 volts. In these cases the fuse or circuit breaker box should also be changed and enlarged to accommodate the increased circuit capacity. Figure 47 schematically illustrates the installation of an additional load center for a new circuit.

d. Concealed Installations. The addition of outlets in a building with finished interior walls having enclosed air spaces entails the use of a fish wire and drop chain. Figure 48 shows the addition of a wire run for an outlet accomplished by a drop from the attic space or as a riser from the basement. First

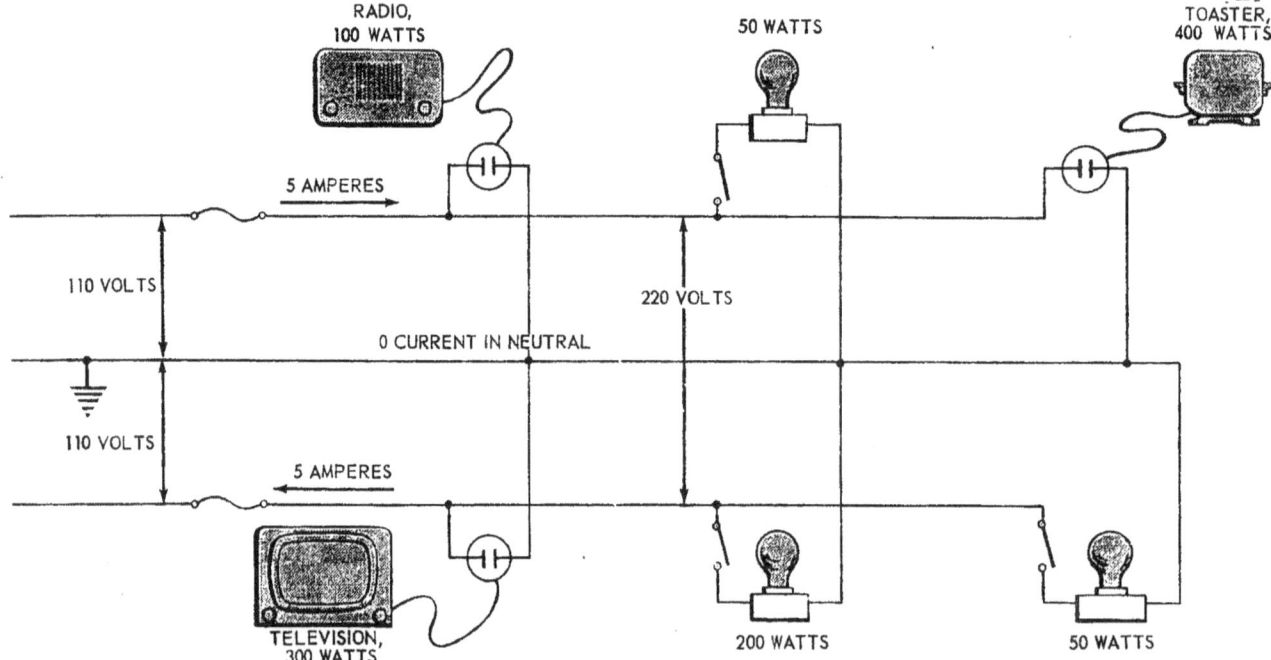

Figure 44. Diagram showing circuit balancing.

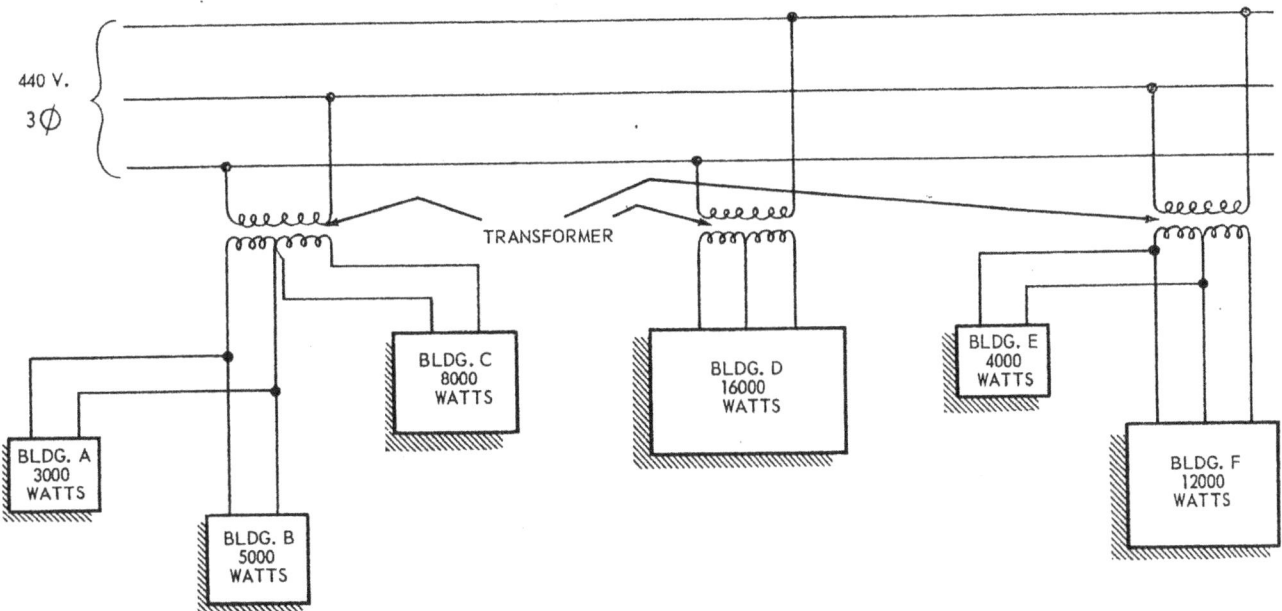

Figure 45. Diagram showing building load balancing.

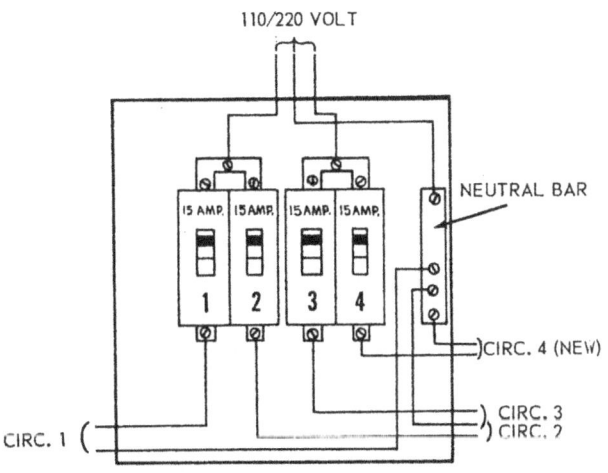

Figure 46. Addition of a new circuit.

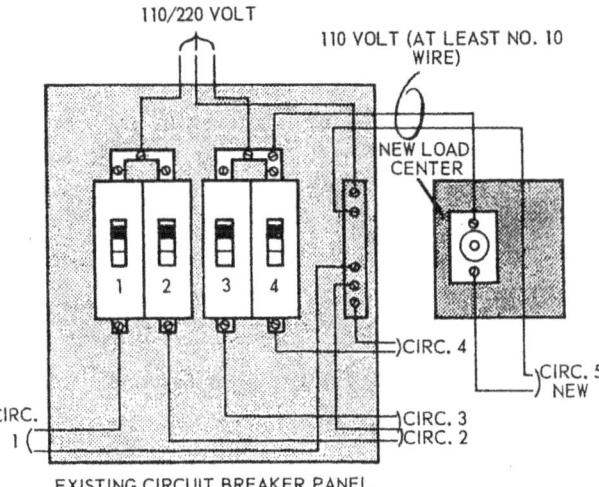

Figure 47. Addition of new load center.

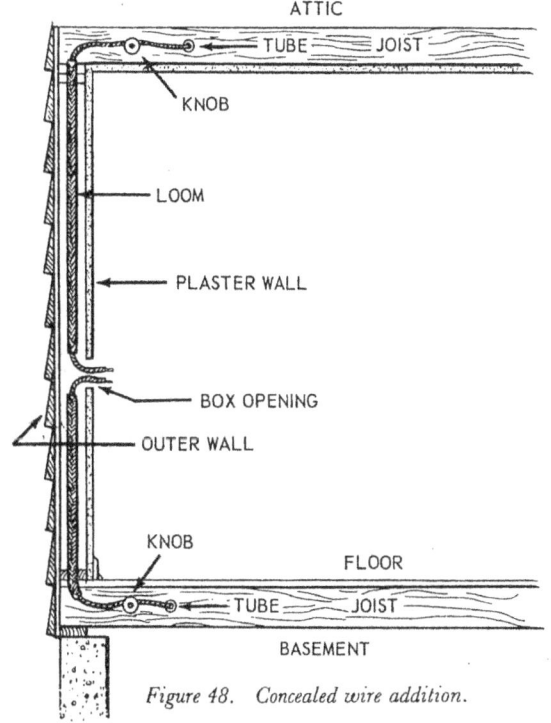

Figure 48. Concealed wire addition.

an opening is made in the interior finished wall at the desired outlet position. If the attic circuit is to be tapped, holes are drilled in the top plates of the wood studding, and a drop chain is lowered inside the wall and pulled through the box opening. The wire to be installed is then attached to the chain and pulled through, completing the rough-in operation for the outlet. Similarly when a wire is to be pulled in from the basement, a stiff wire, called a fish wire, is used. After drilling through the rough floor and bottom plate of the studding the fish wire is pushed up from the basement until it is grasped at the box opening. The wire to be pulled is then attached and pulled through the inner wall section.

56. Wire Size

a. Wire sizes No. 14 and larger are classified in accordance with their maximum allowable current-carrying capacity based on their physical behavior when subjected to the stress and temperatures of operating conditions. Fourteen-gage wire is the smallest wire size permitted for use in interior wiring systems.

b. The determination of the wire size to be used in circuits is dependent on the voltage drop coincident with each size. The size of the conductor used as a feeder to each circuit is also based on voltage drop, and should be selected so that the voltage drop from the branch circuit supply to the outlets will not be more than 3 percent for power loads and 1 percent for lighting loads. Table XI which is based on an allowable 3 percent voltage drop, lists the wire sizes required for various distances between supply and load, at the difference amperages.

c. Table XI also lists the service-wire requirements and capacities. The minimum gage for service-wire installation is No. 8 except for installations consisting of a single branch circuit in which case they shall not be smaller than the conductors of a branch circuit and in no case smaller than No. 12. Though this may seem to contradict the minimum wire size listed, the service-wire sizes are increased because they must not only meet the voltage-drop requirement but also be inherently strong enough to support their own weight, plus any additional loading caused by climatic conditions (ice, branches, and so on).

57. Special Switches

a. Three-Way Switching. A single-pole switch controls a light or a receptacle from only one location. When lights have to be controlled from more than one location, a 3-way switch is used. Three-way switches can be identified by a common terminal, normally color-coded darker than the other terminals and located alone at the end of the switch housing. A schematic wiring diagram of a 3-way switch with 3-wire cable is shown in figure 49. In the diagram terminals A and A' are the common terminals, and switch operation connects them either to B or C and B' and C' respectively. Either switch will operate to close or open the circuit, turning the lights on or off.

b. Four-Way Switching. Occasionally it is necessary to control an outlet or light from more than 2 locations. Two 3-way switches plus a 4-way switch for each location where control is desired and required in addition to that normally available in a 3-way circuit as illustrated in figure 50 (i. e., 3 control points, one 4-way switch, 4 control points, two 4-way switches). In figure 50 the switches must be installed with the 4-way units connected between the two 3-way units, and the 3-wire cable installed between the switches.

58. Wiring For Hazardous Locations

Hazardous locations requiring special wiring considerations are divided into four classes by the National Electric Code.

a. Class I. For locations in which highly flammable gasses and liquids are manufactured, used, or handled, such as hydrogen, gasoline, alcohol, etc., all wiring must be in rigid metal conduit with explosion-proof fittings. All equipment such as circuit breakers, fuses, motors, generators, controllers, etc., must be totally inclosed in explosion-proof housings.

b. Class II. In locations where combustible dust is likely to be thrown into suspension in the air in sufficient quantities to produce explosive mixtures, such as flour mills, grain elevators, coal pulverizing plants, etc., the wiring must be in rigid conduit with threaded fittings. All equipment must be in dust-proof cabinets with motors and generators totally inclosed or in totally inclosed fan-cooled housings.

c. Class III. Locations in which easily ignitible fibers or materials producing combustible flyings are handled or used, such as textile mills, cotton gins, or woodworking plants, require wiring of the same type as in Class II. If the atmosphere is such that lint and flyings will collect on motors or generators they must be inclosed as in Class II.

d. Class IV. In locations where easily combustible fibers are stored, such as warehouses for cotton waste, hemp, Spanish moss, excelsior, etc., all of the type of wiring described in this manual may be used. Open wiring is permitted when the conductors are protected where they are not run in roof spaces or well out of reach of mechanical damage. Rotating machines must be inclosed as in Class II.

59. Installation in Hazardous Locations

The Code further specifies standards for particular types of installations. For example, some of these special requirements for hospital operating room installation are listed in *a* through *f* below:

Table XI. Voltage Drop Tables

Wire size for 120-volt single-phase circuit

Load (amps.)	Minimum wire size (AWG)	Service wire size (AWG)	Wire size (AWG) Distance one way from supply to load (ft.)											
			50	75	100	125	150	175	200	250	300	350	400	450	500
15	14	10	14	12	10	8	8	6	6	6	4	4	4	2	2
20	14	10	12	10	8	8	6	6	6	4	4	2	2	2	2
25	12	8	10	8	8	6	6	4	4	4	2	2	2	1	1
30	12	8	10	8	6	6	4	4	4	2	2	1	1	0	0
35	12	6	8	6	6	4	4	4	2	2	1	1	0	0	2/0
40	10	6	8	6	6	4	4	2	2	2	1	0	0	2/0	2/0
45	10	6	8	6	4	4	2	2	2	1	0	0	2/0	2/0	3/0
50	10	6	8	6	4	4	2	2	2	1	0	2/0	2/0	3/0	3/0
55	8	4	6	4	4	2	2	2	1	0	2/0	2/0	3/0	3/0	4/0
60	8	4	6	4	4	2	2	1	1	0	2/0	3/0	3/0	4/0	4/0
65	8	4	6	4	4	2	2	1	0	2/0	2/0	3/0	4/0	4/0	
70	8	4	6	4	2	2	1	1	0	2/0	2/0	3/0	4/0	4/0	
75	6	4	6	4	2	2	1	0	0	2/0	3/0	4/0	4/0		
80	6	4	6	4	2	2	1	0	0	2/0	3/0	4/0	4/0		
85	6	4	4	4	2	1	1	0	2/0	3/0	3/0	4/0			
90	6	2	4	2	2	1	0	0	2/0	3/0	4/0	4/0			
95	6	2	4	2	2	1	0	2/0	2/0	3/0	4/0				
100	4	2	4	2	2	1	0	2/0	2/0	3/0	4/0				

Wire size for 220-volt three-phase circuits

Load (amps.)	Minimum wire size (AWG)	Service wire size (AWG)	Wire size (AWG) Distance one way from supply to load (ft.)											
			100	150	200	250	300	350	400	500	600	700	800	900	1,000
15	14	12	14	12	10	8	8	8	6	6	6	4	4	4	2
20	14	10	12	10	8	8	6	6	6	4	4	4	2	2	2
25	12	8	10	8	8	6	6	6	4	4	2	2	2	2	1
30	12	8	10	8	6	6	6	4	4	2	2	2	1	1	0
35	12	8	10	8	6	6	4	4	4	2	2	1	1	0	0
40	10	6	8	6	6	4	4	4	2	1	1	1	0	0	2/0
45	10	6	8	6	6	4	4	2	2	2	1	0	0	2/0	2/0
50	10	6	8	6	4	4	2	2	2	1	0	0	2/0	2/0	3/0
55	8	6	8	6	4	4	2	2	2	1	0	2/0	2/0	3/0	3/0
60	8	6	6	6	4	2	2	2	1	0	0	2/0	3/0	3/0	4/0
65	8	4	6	4	4	2	2	2	1	0	2/0	2/0	3/0	3/0	4/0
70	8	4	6	4	4	2	2	1	1	0	2/0	3/0	3/0	4/0	4/0
75	6	4	6	4	2	2	2	1	0	2/0	2/0	3/0	4/0	4/0	
80	6	4	6	4	2	2	1	1	0	2/0	3/0	3/0	4/0	4/0	
85	6	4	6	4	2	2	1	0	0	2/0	3/0	4/0	4/0		
90	6	4	6	4	2	2	1	0	0	2/0	3/0	4/0	4/0		
95	6	4	6	4	2	1	1	0	2/0	3/0	3/0	4/0			
100	4	2	4	2	2	1	0	0	2/0	3/0	4/0	4/0			
125	4	2	4	2	1	0	2/0	2/0	3/0	4/0					
150	2	2	2	2	0	2/0	2/0	3/0	4/0						
175	2	1	2	1	0	2/0	3/0	4/0	4/0						
200	1	0	1	0	2/0	3/0	4/0	4/0							
225	0	0	0	0	2/0	3/0	4/0								
250	2/0	2/0	2/0	2/0	3/0	4/0									
275	3/0	3/0	3/0	3/0	3/0	4/0									
300	3/0	3/0	3/0	3/0	4/0										
325	4/0	4/0	4/0	4/0											

Table is based upon approximately 3% voltage drop.

Table XI. Voltage Drop Tables—Continued

Wire size for 240-volt three-phase circuits.

Load (amps.)	Minimum wire size (AWG)	Service wire size (AWG)	Wire size (AWG) Distance one way from supply to load (ft.)												
			100	150	200	250	300	350	400	500	600	700	800	900	1,000
15	14	10	14	12	10	9	8	6	6	6	4	4	4	2	2
20	14	10	12	10	8	8	6	6	6	4	4	2	2	2	2
25	12	8	10	8	8	6	6	4	4	4	2	2	2	1	1
30	12	8	10	8	6	6	4	4	4	2	2	1	1	0	0
35	12	6	8	6	6	4	4	4	2	2	1	1	0	0	2/0
40	10	6	8	6	6	4	4	2	2	2	1	0	0	2/0	2/0
45	10	6	8	6	4	4	2	2	2	1	0	0	2/0	2/0	3/0
50	10	6	8	6	4	4	2	2	2	1	0	2/0	2/0	3/0	3/0
55	8	4	6	4	4	2	2	2	1	0	2/0	2/0	3/0	3/0	4/0
60	8	4	6	4	4	2	2	1	1	0	2/0	3/0	3/0	4/0	4/0
65	8	4	6	4	4	2	2	1	0	2/0	2/0	3/0	4/0	4/0	
70	8	4	6	4	2	2	1	1	0	0	2/0	3/0	4/0	4/0	
75	6	4	6	4	2	2	1	0	0	2/0	3/0	4/0	4/0		
80	6	4	6	4	2	2	1	0	0	2/0	3/0	4/0	4/0		
85	6	4	4	4	2	1	1	0	2/0	3/0	3/0	4/0			
90	6	2	4	2	2	1	0	0	2/0	3/0	4/0	4/0			
95	6	2	4	2	2	1	0	2/0	2/0	3/0	4/0				
100	4	2	4	2	2	1	0	2/0	2/0	3/0	4/0				
125	4	2	4	2	1	0	2/0	3/0	3/0	4/0					
150	2	1	2	1	0	2/0	3/0	4/0	4/0						
175	2	0	2	0	2/0	3/0	4/0	4/0							
200	1	0	1	0	2/0	3/0	4/0								
225	1/0	2/0	1/0	2/0	3/0	4/0									
250	2/0	2/0	2/0	2/0	3/0	4/0									
275	3/0	3/0	3/0	3/0	4/0										
300	3/0	3/0	3/0	3/0	4/0										
325	4/0	4/0	4/0	4/0											

Table is based on approximately 3% voltage drop.

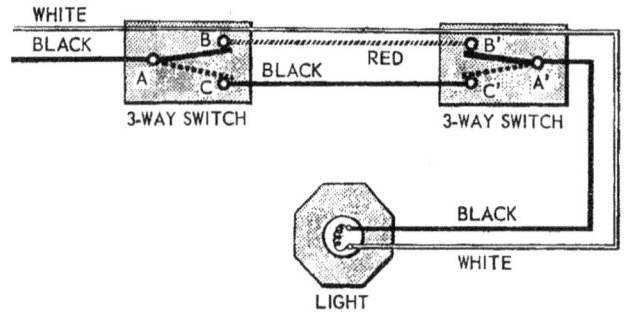

Figure 49. Three-way switch wiring.

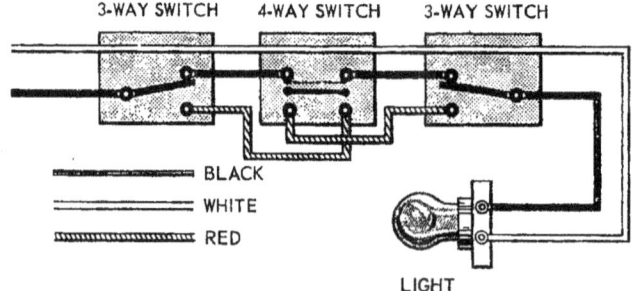

Figure 50. Four-way switch wiring.

a. All equipment installed in the operating room must be explosion proof and provided with a suitable equipment ground.

b. In anaesthetizing locations, an ungrounded electrical distribution system is required to reduce the hazards of electric shocks and arcs in the event of insulation failure. Alternating-current circuits shall be insulated from the conventionally grounded alternating supply by means of one or more transformers which isolate the circuits electrically from the main feeder line. Direct-current circuits shall be insulated from their grounded feeders by means of a motor generator set or suitable battery system.

c. All service equipment including switch and panel boards must be installed in nonhazardous locations.

d. Ceiling suspended lighting fixtures shall be suitably protected against mechanical injury.

e. Explosion-proof switches, receptacles, motors or similar conduit installations must be isolated from the rest of the conduit runs by sealing fittings. This type fitting has a removable plug which permits the insertion of a sealing compound, sealing off the points of possible explosion from the remaining conduit areas.

f. Nonmetallic tools such as rubber head hammers and spark free drills must always be used when making electrical repairs or installations in the area.

Section II. BASIC PROCEDURES COMMON TO ALL WIRING

60. Splices

A spliced wire must be as good a conductor as a continuous conductor. Figure 51 shows many of the variations of splicing used to obtain an electrically-secure joint. Though splices are permitted wherever accessible in wiring systems they should be avoided whenever possible. The best wiring practice (including open wiring systems) is to run continuous wires from the service box to the outlets. Under no conditions should splices be made in conductors encased in conduit.

61. Solderless Connectors

Figure 52 illustrates several types of connectors used in place of splices because of their ease of installation. Since heavy wires are difficult to tape and solder properly, split-bolt connectors (fig. 52 ①) are commonly used for wire joining. Figure 52 ②

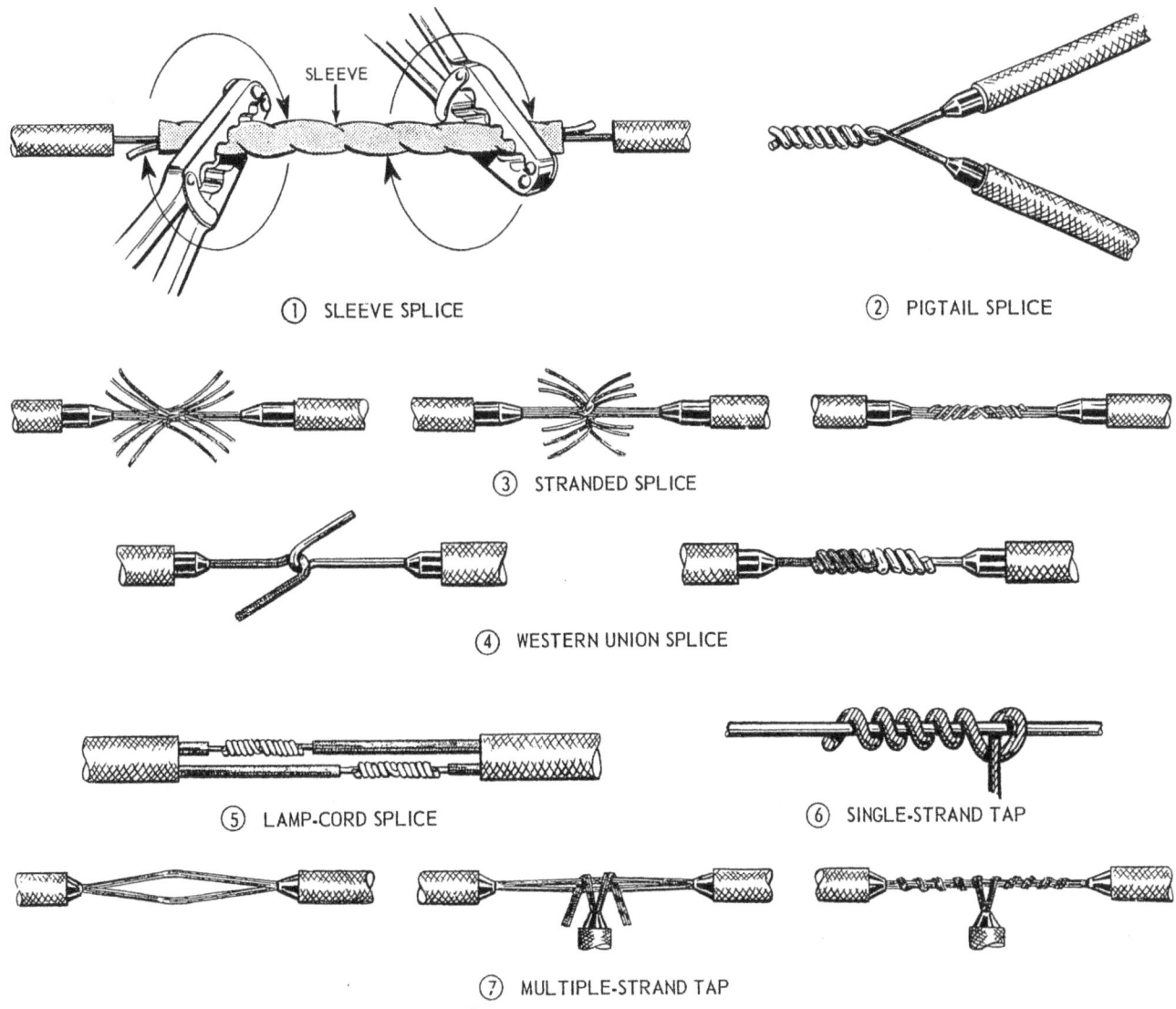

Figure 51. Typical wire splices and taps.

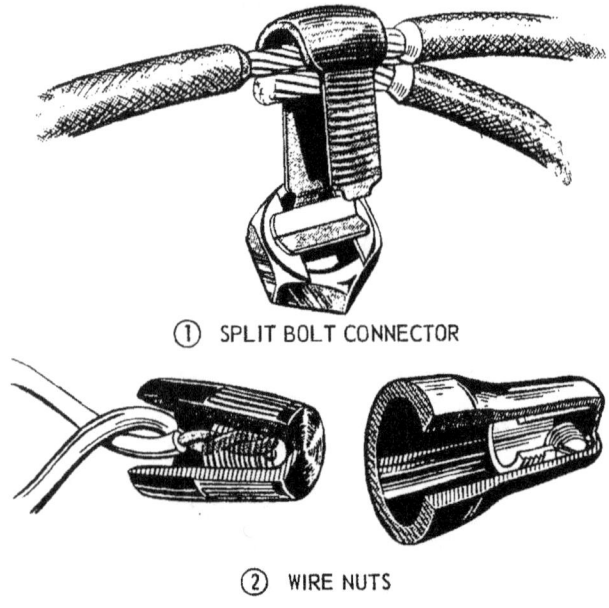

① SPLIT BOLT CONNECTOR

② WIRE NUTS

Figure 52. Solderless connectors.

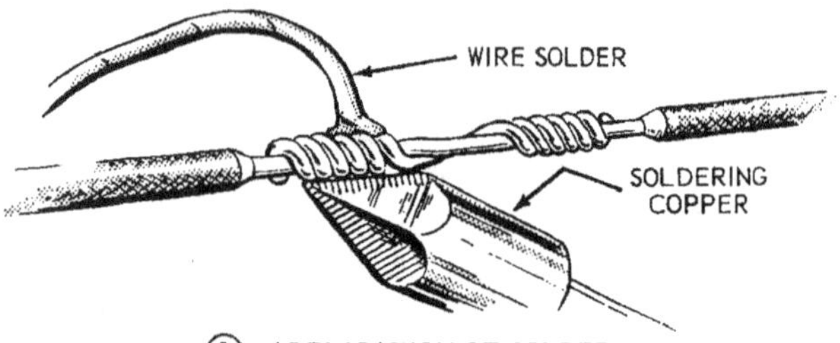

① APPLICATION OF SOLDER

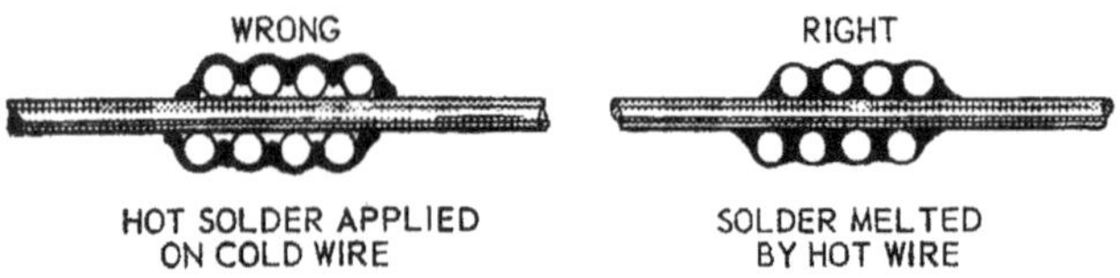

② RIGHT AND WRONG SOLDER JOINT

Figure 53. Soldering and solder joints.

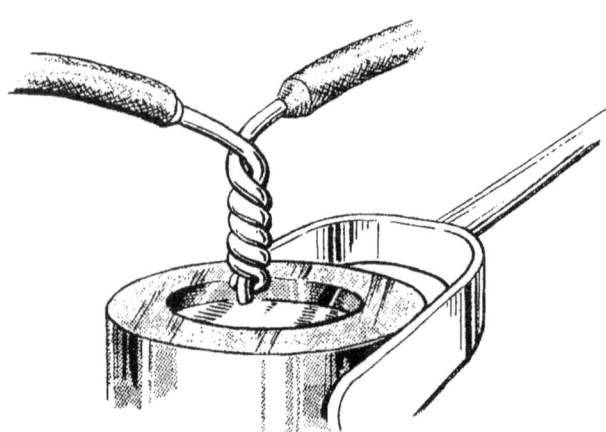

Figure 54. Dip soldering.

illustrates several types of solderless connectors popularly called wire nuts, which are used for connecting small-gage and fixture wire. One design shown consists of a funnel-shaped metal-spring insert molded into a plastic shell, into which the wires to be joined are screwed. The other type shown has a removable insert which contains a setscrew to clamp the wires. The plastic shell is screwed onto the insert to cover the joint.

62. Soldering

a. All splices must be soldered before they are considered to be as good as the original conductor. The primary requirements for obtaining a good solder joint are a clean soldering iron, a clean joint, and a nonacid flux. These requirements can be satisfied by using pure rosin on the joint, or by using a rosin-core solder.

b. To insure a good solder joint, the electric heated or copper soldering iron should be applied to the joint until the joint melts the solder by its own heat. Figure 53 ② shows the difference between a good and bad solder joint. The bad joint has a weak crystalline structure.

c. Figure 54 illustrates dip soldering. This method of soldering is frequently used by experienced electricians because of its convenience and relative speed for soldering pigtail splices. These splices are the most common type used in interior wiring.

63. Taping Joints

a. Every soldered joint must be covered with a coating of rubber, or varnished cambric, and friction tape to replace the wire insulation of the conductor. In taping a spliced solder joint (fig. 55) the rubber or cambric tape is started on the tapered end of the wire insulation and advanced toward the other end, with each succeeding wrap, by overlap-

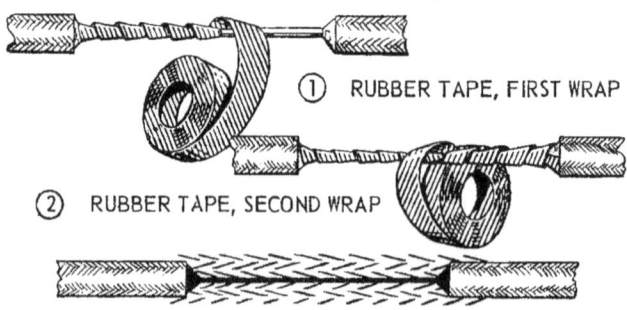

① RUBBER TAPE, FIRST WRAP

② RUBBER TAPE, SECOND WRAP

③ RUBBER AND FRICTION TAPED JOINT

Figure 55. Rubber- and friction-tape insulating.

ping the windings. This procedure is repeated from one end of the splice to the other until the original insulation thickness has been restored. The joint is then covered with several layers of friction tape.

b. Though the method in *a* above for taping joints is still considered to be standard, the scotch electrical tape, which serves as an insulation and a protective covering, should be used whenever available. This tape materially reduces the time required to tape a joint, and reduces the space needed by the joint because a satisfactory protective and insulation covering can be achieved with single-layer taping.

64. Insulation and Making Wire Connections

a. When attaching a wire to a switch or an electrical device or when splicing it to another wire, the wire insulation must be removed to bare the copper conductor. Figure 56 ① shows the right and wrong way to remove insulation. When the wire-stripping tool is applied at right angles to the wire, there is danger that the wire may be nicked and thus weakened. This may result in a short circuit. Consequently the cut is made at an angle to the conductor. After the protective insulation is removed, the conductor is scraped or sanded thoroughly to remove all traces of insulation and oxide on the wire.

b. Figures 56 ② and ③ show the correct method of attaching the trimmed wire to terminals. The wire loop is always inserted under the terminal screw, as shown, so that the tightening process tends to close the loop. The loop is made so that the wire insulation terminates close to the terminal.

65. Job Sequence

a. General. The installation of interior wiring is generally divided into two major divisions called roughing-in and finishing. Roughing-in is the installation of the outlet boxes, cable, wire, and conduit. Finishing is the installation of the switches, receptacles, covers, fixtures, and the completion of the service. The interval between these two work periods is used by other trades for plastering, inclosing walls, finishing floors, and trimming.

b. Roughing-In.

(1) The first step in the roughing-in phase of a wiring job is the mounting of outlet boxes. The mounting can be expedited if the locations of all boxes are first marked on the studs and joists of the building.

(2) All of the boxes are mounted on the building members on their own or by special brackets. For concealed installation, all boxes must be installed with the forward edge or plaster ring of the boxes flush with the finished walls. Figure 25 illustrates typical box mountings.

(3) The circuiting and installation of wire for open wiring, cable, or conduit should be the next step. This involves the drilling and cutting-out of the building members to allow for the passage of the conductor or its protective covering. The production-line method of drilling the holes for all runs, as the installations between boxes are called, at one time, and then installing all of the wire, cable, or conduit, will expedite the job.

(4) The final roughing-in step in the installation of conduit systems is the pulling-in of wires between boxes. This can also be included as the first step in the finishing phase, and requires care in the handling of the wires to prevent the marring of finished wall or floor surfaces.

c. Finishing.

(1) The splicing, soldering, and taping of joints in the outlet boxes is the intial step in the completion phase of a wiring job.

(2) Upon completion of the first finishing step, the proper leads to the terminals of

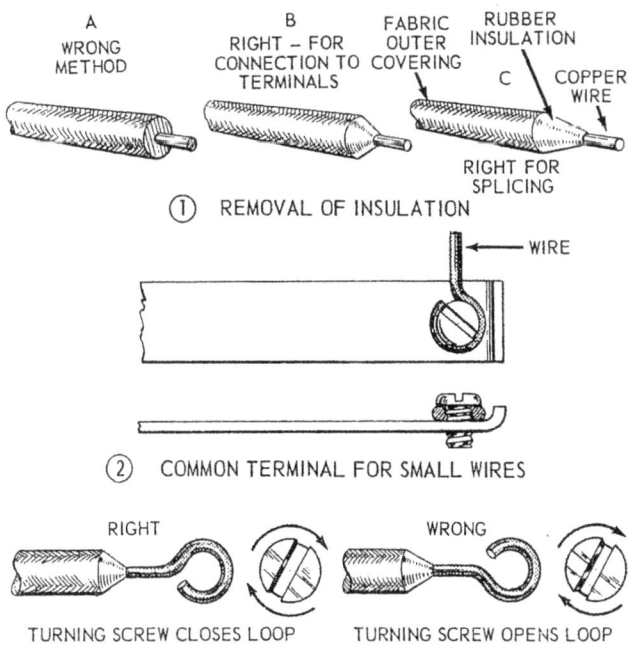

Figure 56. Removing insulation and attaching wire to terminals.

switches, ceiling and wall outlets, and fixtures are then installed.

(3) The devices and their cover plates are then attached to the boxes. The fixtures are generally supported by the use of special mounting brackets called fixture studs or hickeys.

(4) The service-entrance cable and fusing or circuit breaker panels are then connected and the circuits fused.

(5) The final step in the wiring of any building requires the testing of all outlets by the insertion of a test prod or test lamp, the operation of all switches in the building, and the loading of all circuits to insure proper circuiting has been installed.

OPEN WIRING, KNOBS, AND TUBES

Section I. INSTALLATION

66. Advantages and Uses

Open wiring is permitted by the National Electrical Code for interior use. A cost comparison of the four basic types of wiring indicates open wiring to be the most economical. This is true only because the costs of the materials used in installation are comparatively low when compared to the other systems. If the labor costs were computed, this system may be equal or higher in cost than the other methods of installation, especially when a great amount of damage-protection installation is needed. Installations of open wiring, however, are very common during wartime periods of material shortages.

67. Materials

a. Conductors. Conductors for open wiring in dry places may be any one of the rubber-covered (R, RP, RH, or RHT), slow-burning, weatherproof (SBW), varnish-cambric (V), or thermoplastic (T or TW) types. In damp locations, conductors should always be of the rubber-covered type.

b. Insulators. Insulators should be free of projections or sharp edges that might cut into and injure the insulation. They are commonly made of porcelain. Loom, which is a flexible nonmetallic tubing, is also used to protect the electrical conductors.

c. Boxes and Devices. Boxes and devices used with open wiring are described in paragraph 31.

68. Wire Spacing

In an exposed installation of knob-and-tube wiring, the wires must be separated from each other by at least 2½ inches. They must be spaced at least ½ inch from the building surface in a dry location, and at least 1 inch when in a wet or damp location. In a concealed installation the wires must be separated a distance of at least 3 inches and must be supported at least 1 inch from the mounting surface. The minimum spacing of wires in straight runs and at right angle turns is illustrated in figures 57 and 58.

69. Support Spacing

a. Run Spacing. When wiring is run over exposed flat surfaces, the knobs and cleats should be spaced no further than 4½ feet apart as shown in figure 59.

b. Tap Spacing. A support should be installed within 6 inches of a wire tap or takeoff. The wire of the tap circuit should always be secured to this support to insure a strain-free tap.

c. Support Spacing from Boxes. Supports should be installed within 12 inches of an outlet box. The wires to the box should be installed loosely so that there is no strain on the terminal connections.

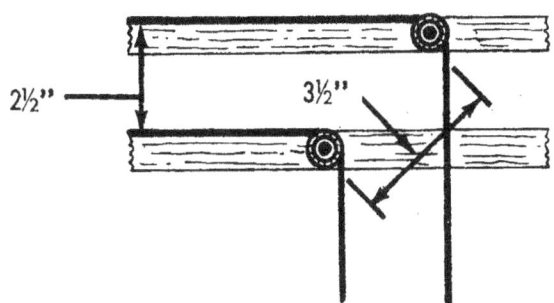

Figure 57. Wire spacing for exposed work.

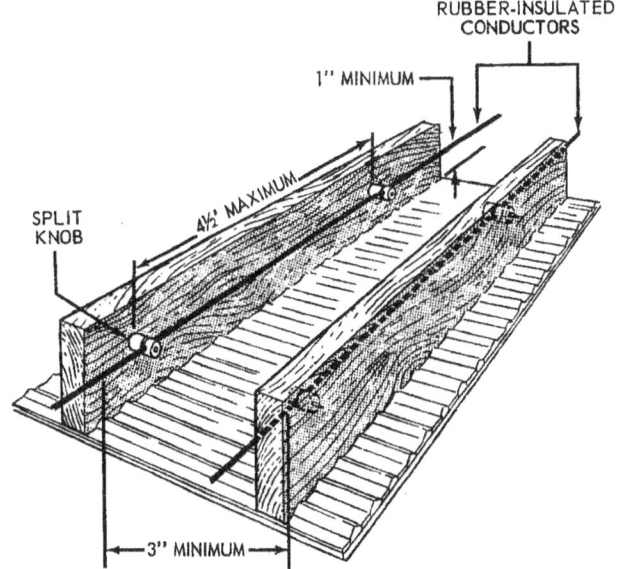

Figure 58. Minimum wire spacing for concealed installation.

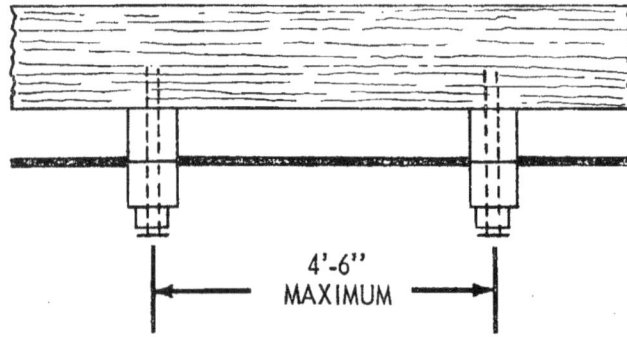

Figure 59. Knob and cleat spacing.

70. Installation

a. Typical Installation. Figure 60 shows a typical exposed knob-and-tube installation for a hospital unit, and demonstrates the circuiting and the methods of installing the conductors to each of the outlets.

b. Knobs and Cleats.

(1) Split knobs are used to support wire sizes 10 through 14 and can support 1 or 2 wires. They are used as 2-wire supports at splices and taps. Figure 61 ① illustrates the use of split knobs.

(2) Solid knobs are employed to support wire size No. 8 or larger. The wires must be supported on the solid knobs by tying. The conductors used for tying must have the same insulation as the supported conductors. A porcelain solid knob is shown in figure 61 ②.

(3) Two- or three-wire cleats are also used in supporting wire sizes No. 10 to 14. Single cleats must be used for wire size No. 8 or larger. Cleats are available which support the wires at distances of ½ to 1 inch from the surface on which the cleats are mounted.

(4) The installation steps used in mounting the split knobs or cleats for supporting wires are shown in figure 61. In the first operation, leather washers, to cushion the porcelain, are threaded on the nails of a 2-wire cleat. In the second step 2 wires are placed in the grooves of the cleat base section and the cleat head and nails are positioned above the wires. The third step shows the cleat in supporting position after the wires have been pulled tight and the nails driven firmly into the wood.

c. Wire Protectors.

(1) *Tubes.* When conductors pass through

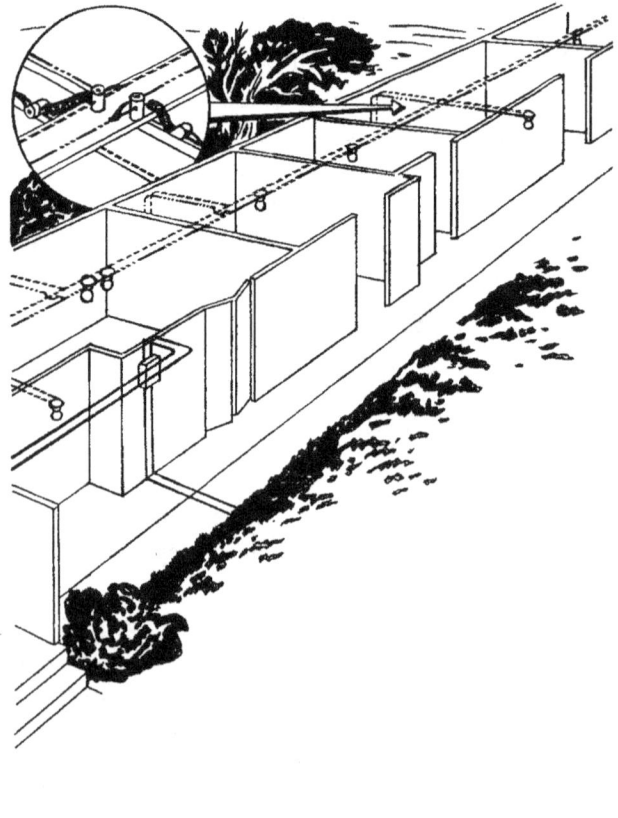

Figure 60. Typical knob-and-tube installation

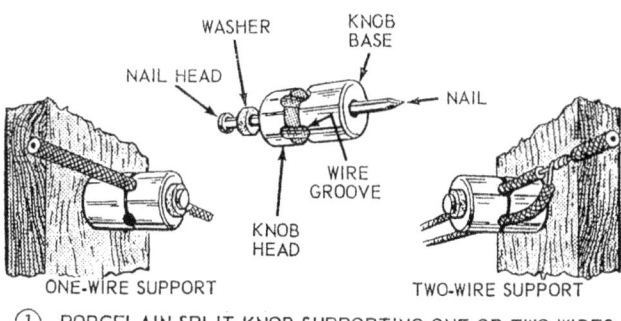

① PORCELAIN SPLIT KNOB SUPPORTING ONE OR TWO WIRES

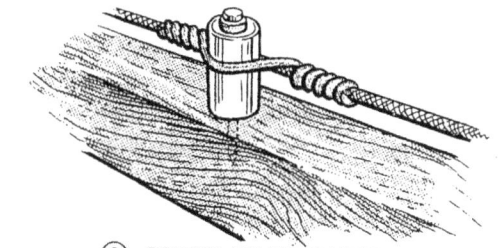

② PORCELAIN SOLID KNOB

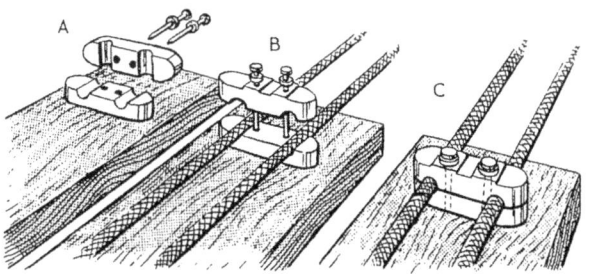

③ PORCELAIN CLEATS SUPPORTING TWO PARALLEL WIRES

Figure 61. Knob and cleat installation.

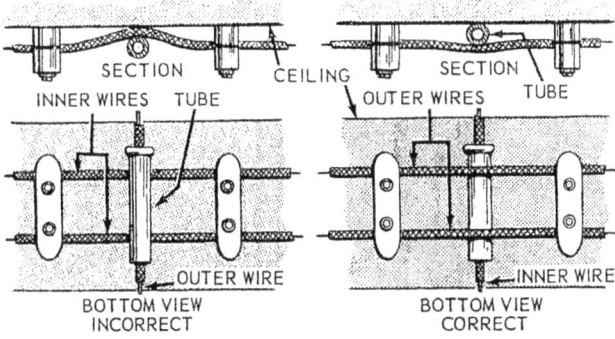

① CORRECT AND INCORRECT METHOD OF INSTALLING PROTECTIVE TUBE FOR WIRE CROSSOVER

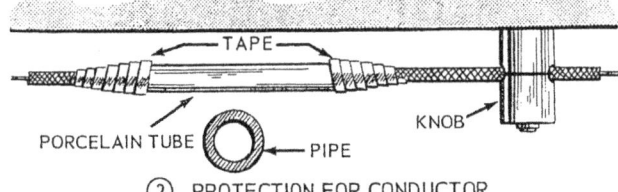

② PROTECTION FOR CONDUCTOR PASSING OVER PIPE

Figure 62. Protective tubes for conductors.

studs, joists, floors, walls, or partitions they must be protected by porcelain tubes installed in the hole through the supporting members. These tubes are available in standard sizes ranging from 1 to 24 inches long and ⁵⁄₁₆ to 1½ inch inner diameter. The tubes must be long enough to extend through the entire wall. If the wall is too thick to use porcelain bushings, standard iron pipe or conduit may be used, provided insulated bushings are installed at each end of the pipe. The holes in which the tubes are to be installed should be drilled at an angle so that the tube head can be placed on the high side of the hole to prevent it from being dislodged by gravity. The tubes may also be used to protect wires at points of crossover. As the tube is installed on the wire closest to the supporting surface, it is always installed on the inner wire, thus preventing the outer wires from making contact with the mounting surface.

Figure 62 illustrates the proper and improper use of tubes at points of wire crossover and also the use of a tube installation for protecting an electrical conductor passing over a pipe. Conductors passing through timber cross braces in plastered partitions must be protected by an additional tube extending at least 3 inches above the timber. The extra tubes (fig. 63) protect the conductors from plaster accumulation, which collects on the horizontal cross members when plastering.

(2) *Loom.* In some installations where it is difficult to support wires on knobs and cleats, the wires may be encased in a continuous flexible tubing, commonly called loom. This tubing which is fabricated of woven varnished cambric, should be supported on the building by means of knobs, spaced approximately 18 inches apart. Any such run should not exceed a distance of 15 feet. Loom is also used to insulate wires at crossovers when they are installed closer than ½ inch to supporting timbers, when 2 or more wires are spaced less than 2½ inches apart, or upon entry to an outlet box. Outlet boxes used in open wiring are designed for the secure clamping of the loom wire to the box. Figure 64 illustrates typical uses of loom.

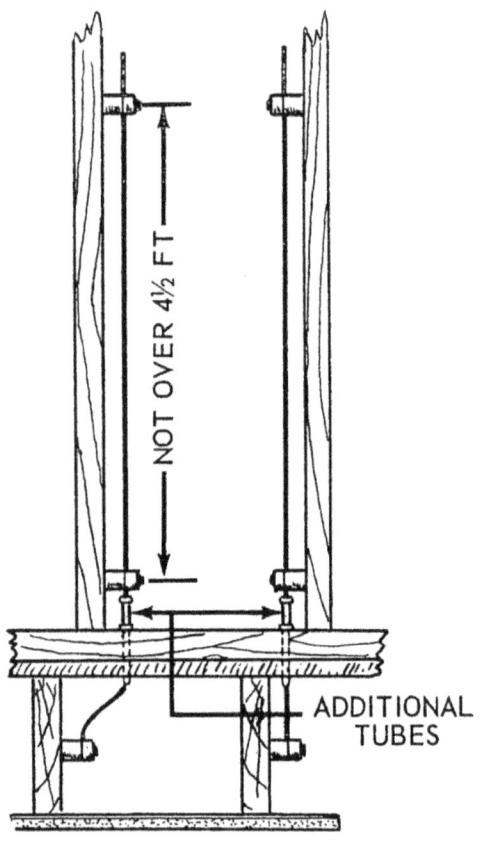

Figure 63. Additional tubes to protect against plaster accumulation.

d. *Damage Protection.*
  (1) *Running boards.* When conductors are installed where they may be subject to mechanical damage, protective shields called running boards must be used. Exposed open wiring located within 7 feet of the floor is considered to be subject to mechanical injury. The required installations of a running board on the rafters and below joists for preventing such injury is pictured in figure 65 ①. Running boards must be at least ½ inch thick and must extend at least 1 inch but not more than 2 inches outside of the conductors. This method of installation is used when the wires are threaded through the joists and rafters. In some installations the wires have to be installed on the running boards with protective sides called railings.
  (2) *Railings.* Railings should be at least ⅞ inch thick and when used alone are at least as high as the insulating supports. When used with running boards they are at least 2 inches high. Figure 65 ② illustrates the installation of railings with and without a running board.
  (3) *Boxing.* The preferred method of protecting open wiring on walls within 7 feet of the floor is called boxing. This method requires the installation of railings with a cover spaced at least 1 inch from the conductor. In this installation, the boxing should be closed at the top and bushings installed to protect the entering and leaving wire leads.
  (4) *Protection limitations.* As previously outlined and illustrated the labor and expense of installing damage protection in open wiring is extensive. Consequently, open wiring installations should be limited to wiring layouts whose outlet locations do not require damage protection. Nonconforming installations may be made in emergencies where the possibility of mechanical damage is not present.

e. *Three-Wire Installations.* The installation of wires in groups of 3 on joists and running boards requires that those surfaces be at least 7 inches wide to insure wire spacing of 2½ inches and a space of 1 inch for wood clearance beyond each outside wire. When joists are not large enough, 1 wire may be run on

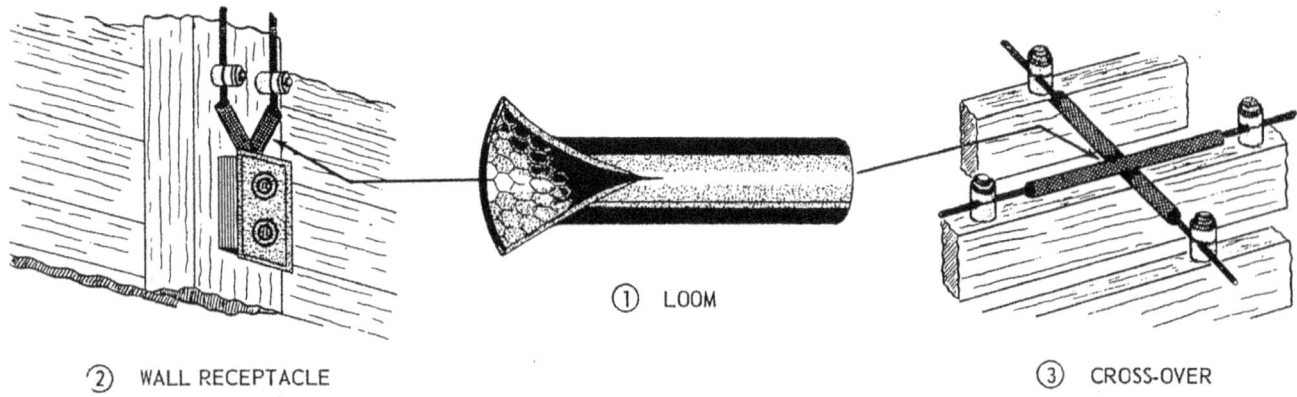

Figure 64. Typical insulation of wires with loom.

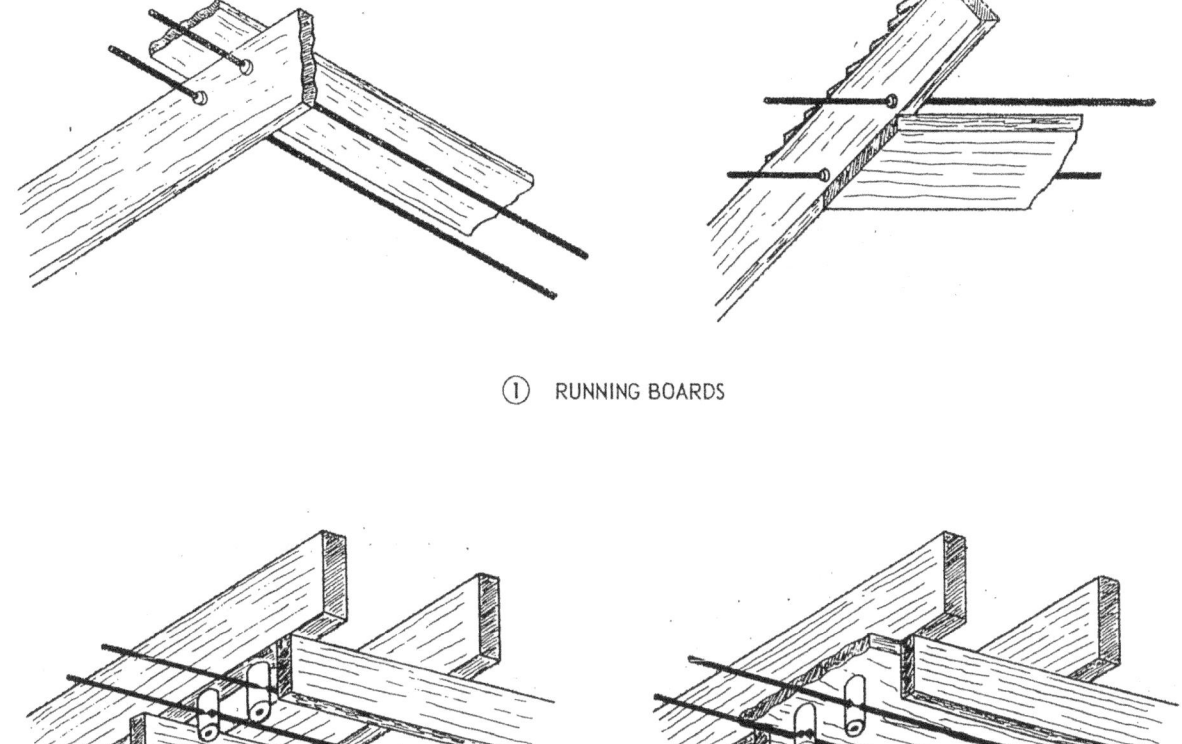

① RUNNING BOARDS

② RAILINGS

Figure 65. Protection for wiring subject to damage.

the top of the joist and the other 2 wires on the sides. Typical installations of 3 wires on joists and running boards are shown in figure 66.

f. Concealed Installation. Concealed knob-and-tube wiring consists of conductors supported in the hollow spaces of walls and ceilings. The wiring is installed in buildings under construction after the floors and studdings are in place, but before lathing or any other construction is completed. The wires are attached to devices in boxes which must have their front edges mounted flush with the finished surface. To facilitate this type of installation, the boxes are generally mounted on brackets or wooden cleats as shown in figure 67.

71. Connection to Devices

a. Figure 68 shows the procedure used in connecting electrical lighting devices to an open wiring circuit. The base of the porcelain lamp socket is first fastened by wood screws to the mounting member. The wires are then stripped of insulation and looped around the screw terminals. Finally, the porcelain head is attached to the base.

b. A typical duplex receptacle installation for an open wiring installation (fig. 69) illustrates the required knob mounting 12 inches from the box, and the placement of loom over the wire at the box entry. The standard mounting height of a receptacle is either 1 foot or 4 feet above the floor depending upon the location of the outlet.

c. The installation and connection of lampholders commonly used in exposed open wiring is shown in figure 70. The pigtail socket has permanently attached leads of No. 14 wire size or larger. These are paired, but are not twisted together unless they are longer than 3 feet. The pendant lampholder is a device to which the lamp cord is attached and supported by means of an underwriters knot. Both the pendant and pigtail lampholder sockets are keyless (no switch) and are operated by wall switches to prevent additional strain on the lead wires supporting the sockets.

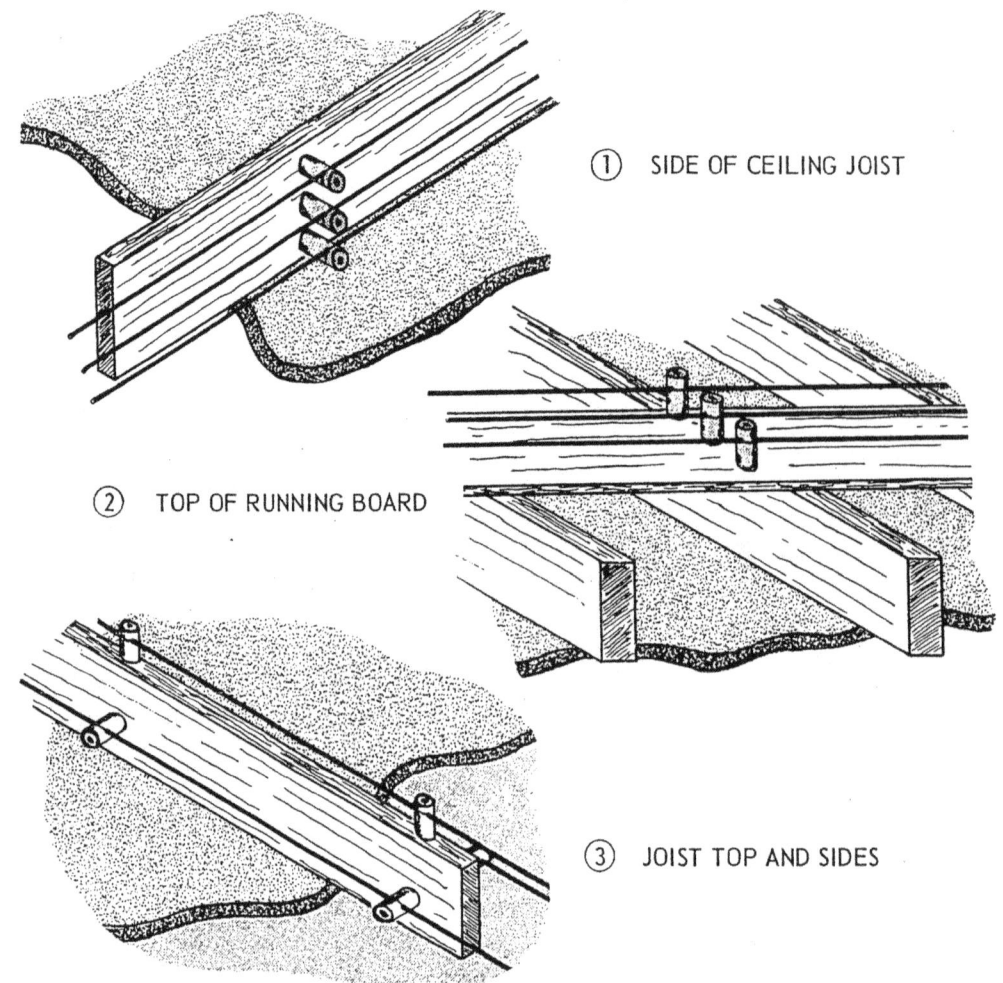

Figure 66. Knob mounting for three-wire circuits.

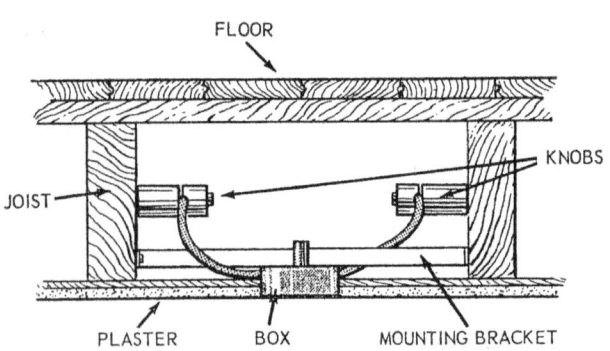

Figure 67. Installation of box in plaster.

d. Figure 71 illustrates a typical service-entrance installation and figure 72 shows the procedures in circuit breaker wiring. If a service-entrance switch were used instead of a main circuit breaker, a separate fuse cabinet would be required to provide individual circuit protection. The wires from the powerline should be secured to the building at least 10 feet from the ground for normal installations. When the service entrance is located above a roadway this height should be increased to 18 feet. If the building is not high enough to meet these requirements, the entrance height may be less, provided all conductors within 8 feet of the ground are rubber-insulated. The line wires at the service entrance to a building should be spaced at least 6 inches apart and should be supported at least 2 inches from the building by service-entrance insulators or brackets. Upon entering the building, the line wires should be threaded upward through slanting noncombustible tubes so that moisture will not follow the conductor into the service-entrance switch.

e. Motors are often located with permanent power leads of exposed open wiring, requiring extensive damage protection. To minimize both time and expense the tap from the open-wiring ceiling circuits should be made with armored cable or conduit. Figure 73 shows a diagrammatic installation of the power connections and operating switch for a three-phase motor connected to exposed knob-and-tube wiring.

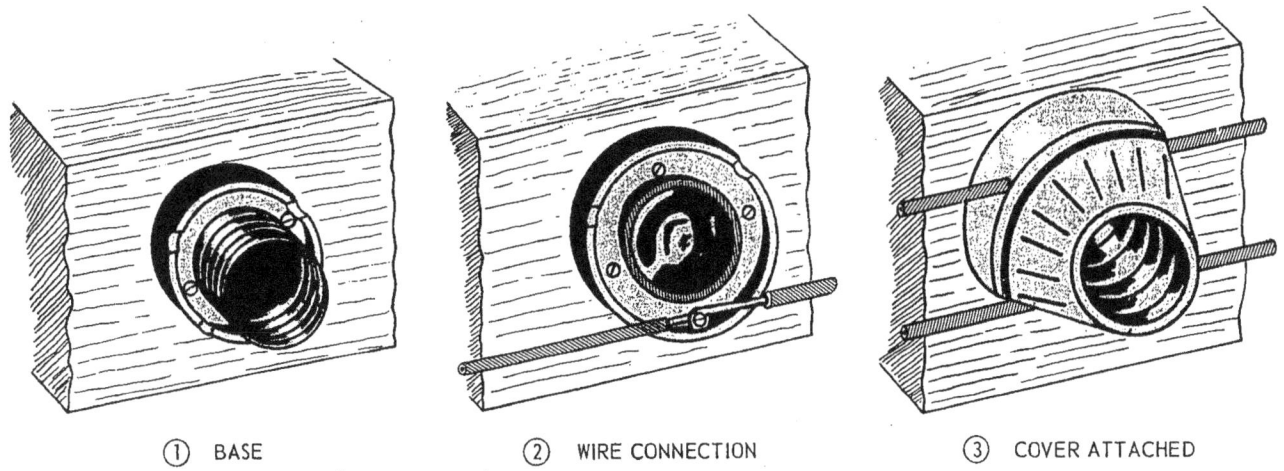

Figure 68. Porcelain fittings used with knob and tube wiring.

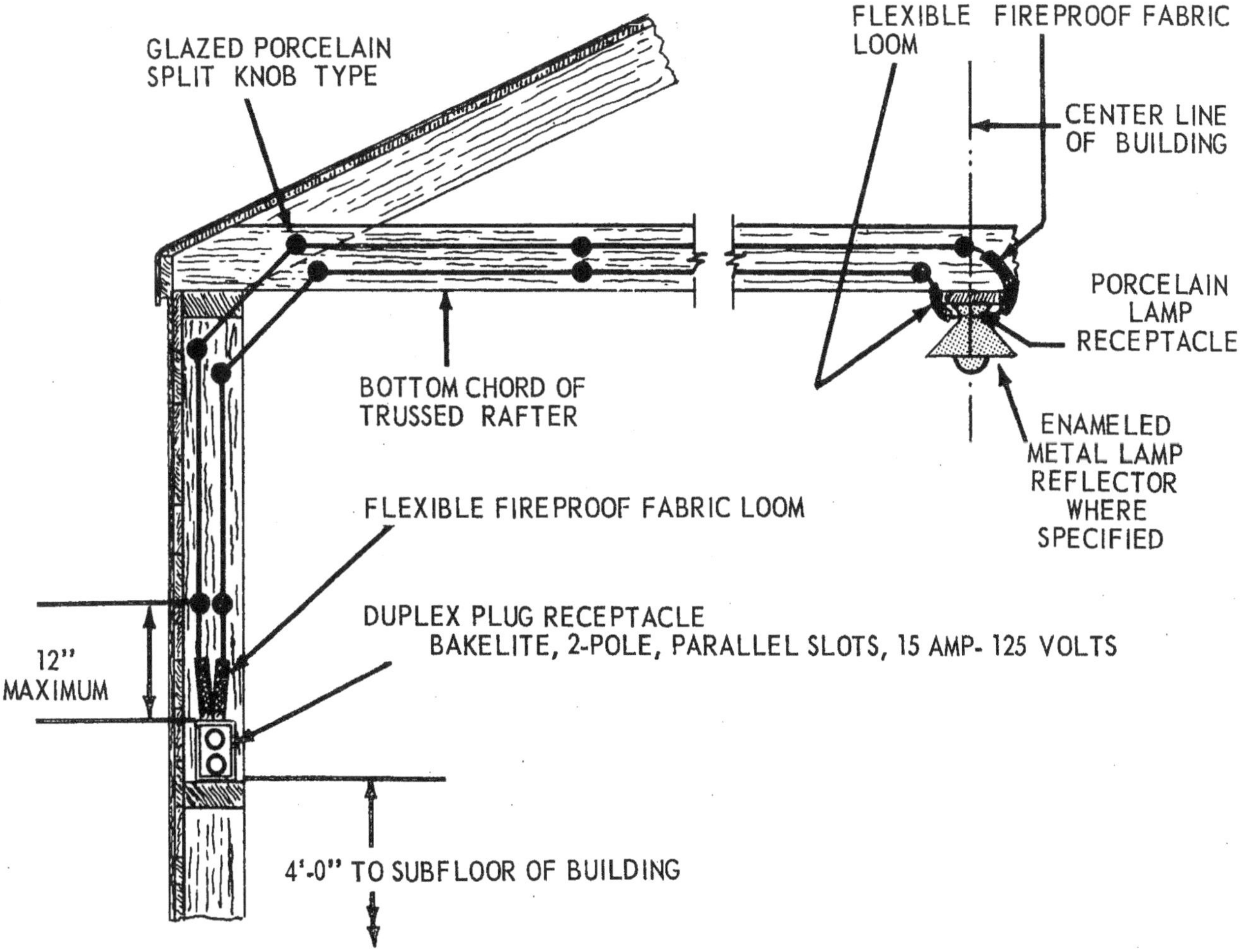

① BASE   ② WIRE CONNECTION   ③ COVER ATTACHED

Figure 69. Typical duplex receptacle installation.

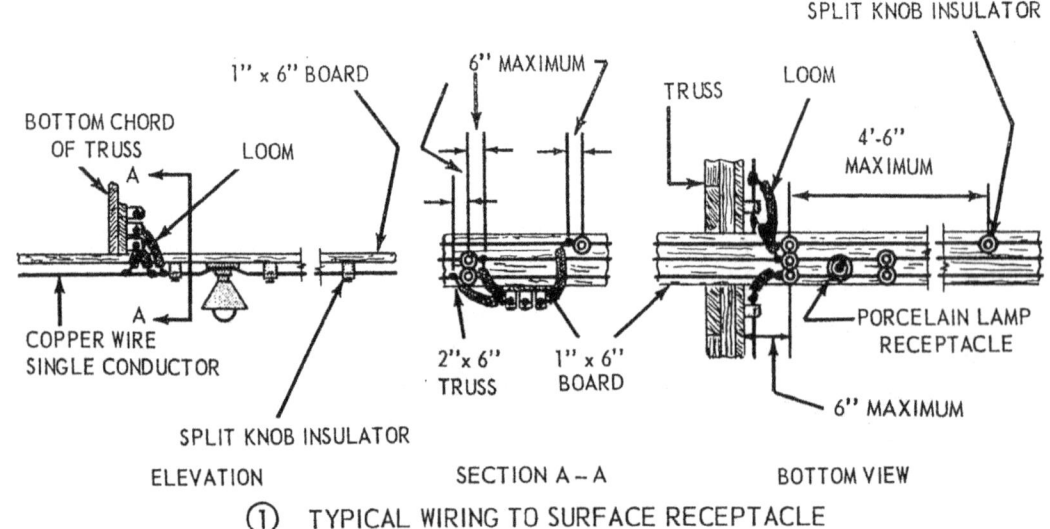
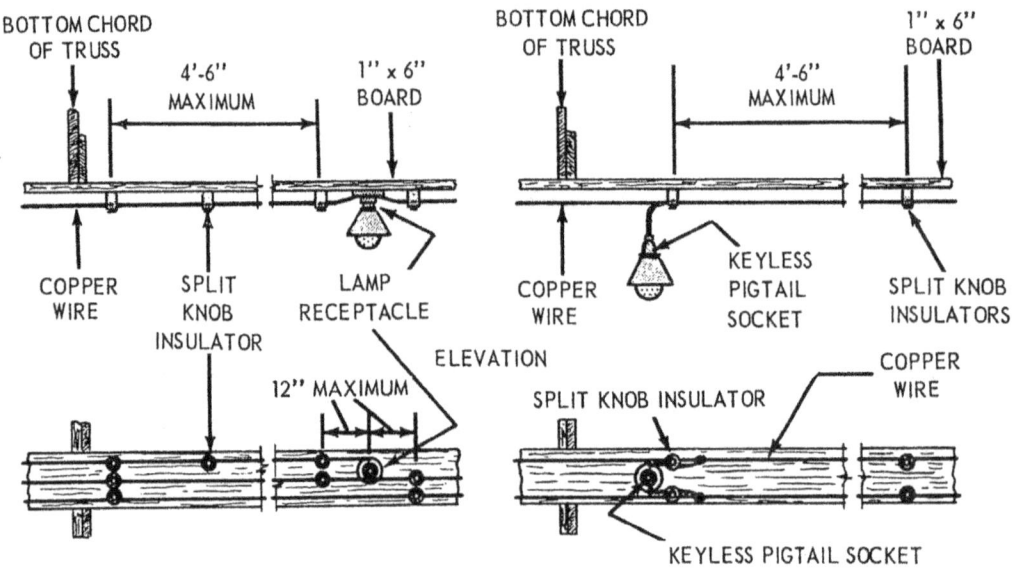
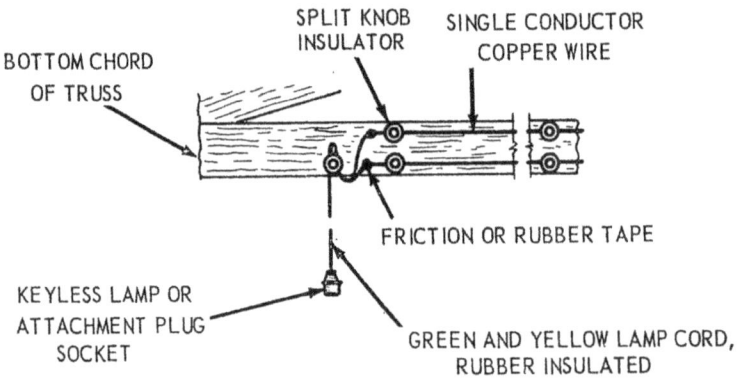

Figure 70. Lampholder installations.

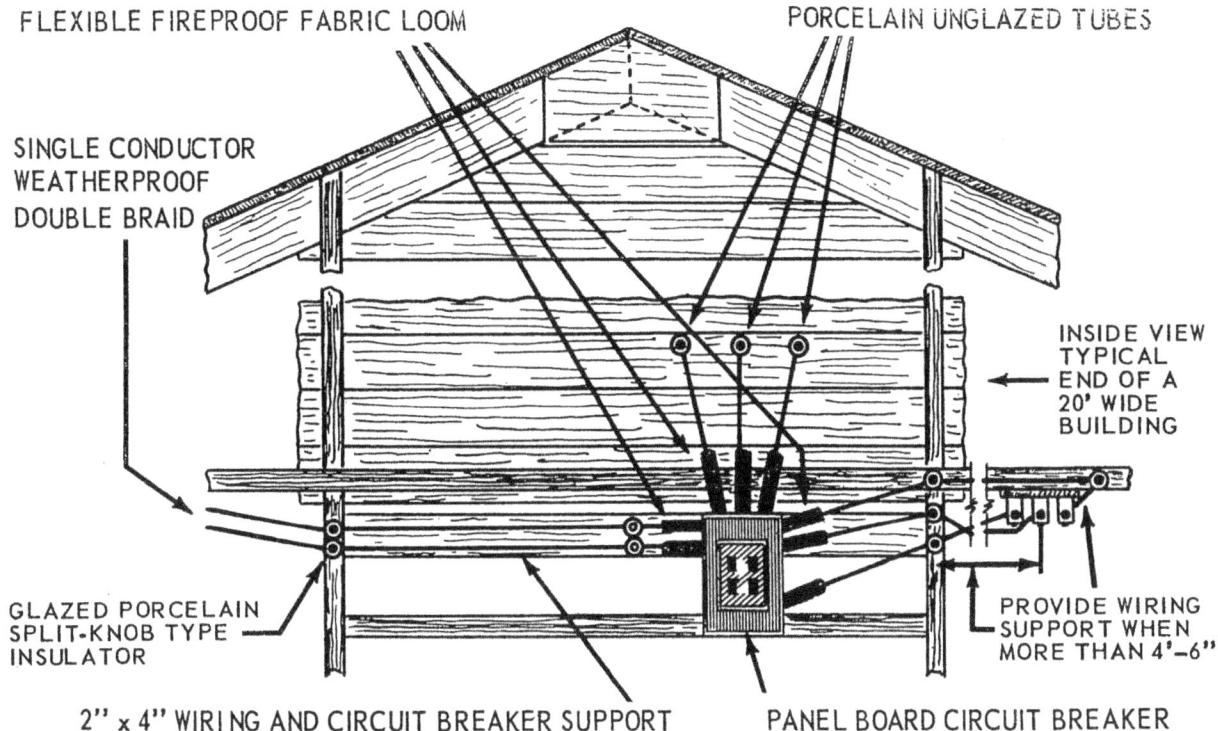

Figure 71. Typical main circuit breaker installation.

72. Additions to Existing Wiring

a. Circuiting. Additions to existing circuits require analysis to determine whether additional circuit capacity is needed to handle the new load. These considerations are the same as those required for other types of installations and are outlined in paragraph 55.

b. Wire Connection.

(1) *Where to connect.* An open wiring system has a distinct advantage over the other wiring methods in that wires for new or additional outlets can be attached to the circuit runs by merely making tap splices in the wire runs, or by extending the circuit from an outlet box. However, the electrician in planning these additional outlets in the existing circuits should be careful to have the shortest possible wire runs. This will result in attaining the lowest voltage drop.

(2) *How to connect.* First make sure the circuit is dead. This is a primary safety rule for all electricians working in existing wiring systems. This can be done by removing the fuse, tripping the circuit breaker to the OFF position, or pulling the service-entrance switch and disconnecting the entire building from power before commencing work. A voltage tester or test lamp is also used to doublecheck the circuit upon which work is to be done. The wires must then be connected and supported in the same manner as outlined for an original building installation.

c. Connections to Other Types of Wiring. Conduit and cable wiring cannot be installed with splices in the conduit or cable runs. Consequently, all splicing and connections must be made within the confines of an outlet, junction, or fuse box. Therefore, when open wiring is combined with one of the other wiring systems the transition from one system to another must be made in one of these boxes. Since standard outlet, junction, or fuse boxes are used, open wiring must be encased in loom at the box entry. An example combining knob-and-tube wiring and conduit wiring is illustrated in figure 74.

Section II. EXPEDIENT WIRING

73. Use

There are many applications where electrical wiring installations are needed for temporary use. One example is a forward area installation. A complete installation including knobs, tubes, cleats, and damage protection would require too much time and would be impractical. Consequently, expedient wir-

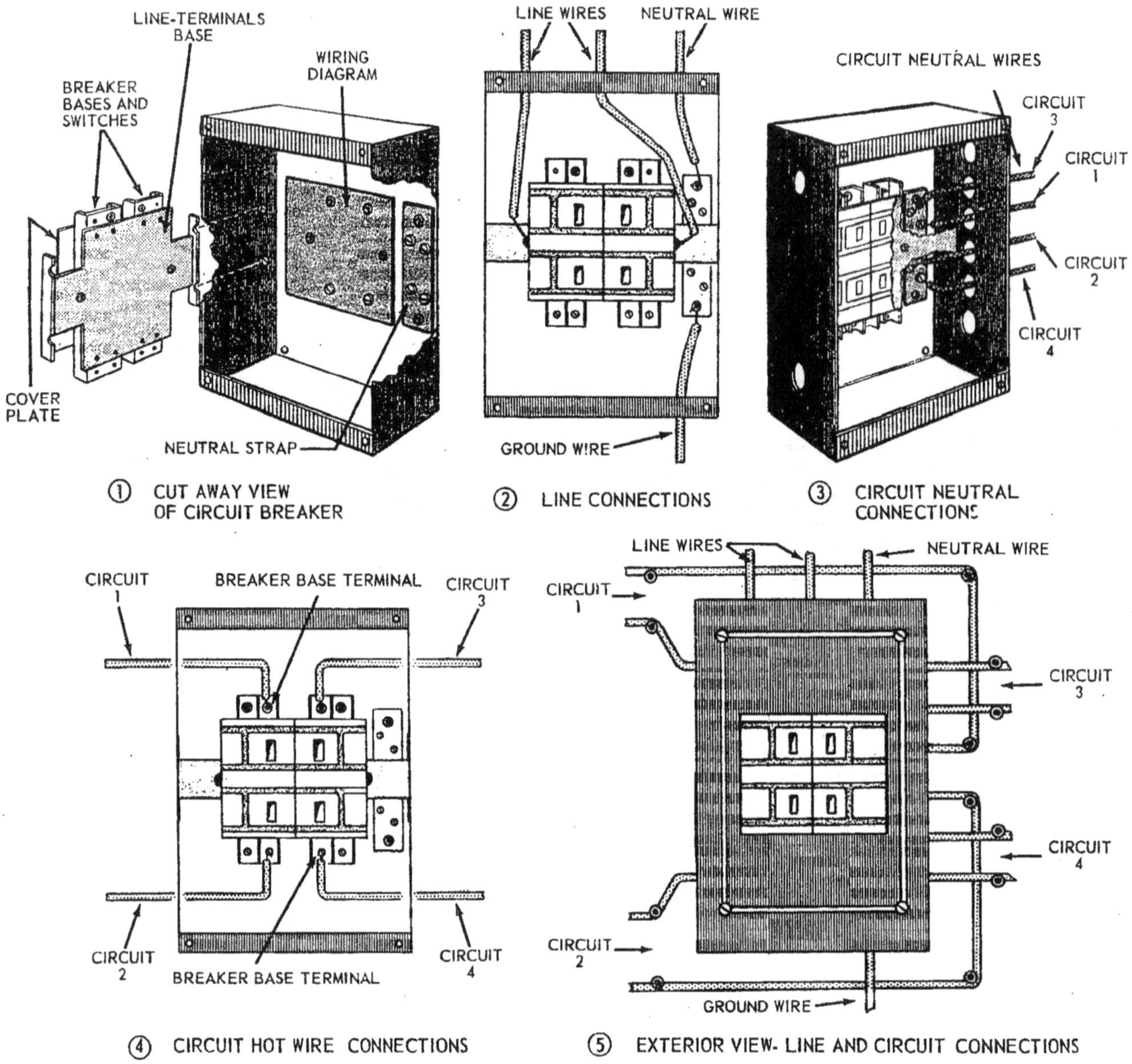

Figure 72. Typical circuit breaker wiring.

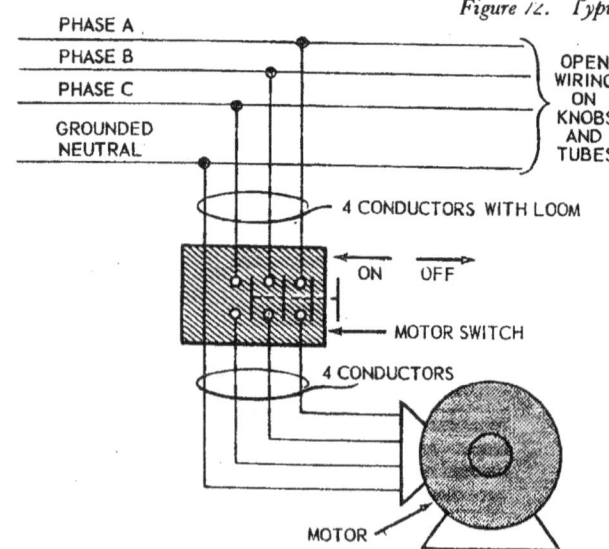

Figure 73. Motor connection.

ing used for temporary buildings and forward areas does not require the mounting and protective devices described in paragraphs 66 through 72. Generally the wires are attached to building members with nails, and pigtail sockets are used for outlets.

74. Installation

a. Wire.

(1) *Supports.* The wire sizes should be selected in accordance with normal installations. The wires should be laid over ceiling joists and fastened by nails driven into the joists and then bent over the wire as shown in figure 75. The nails should exert enough force to firmly grip the wire without injuring the insulation. If loom is available, it

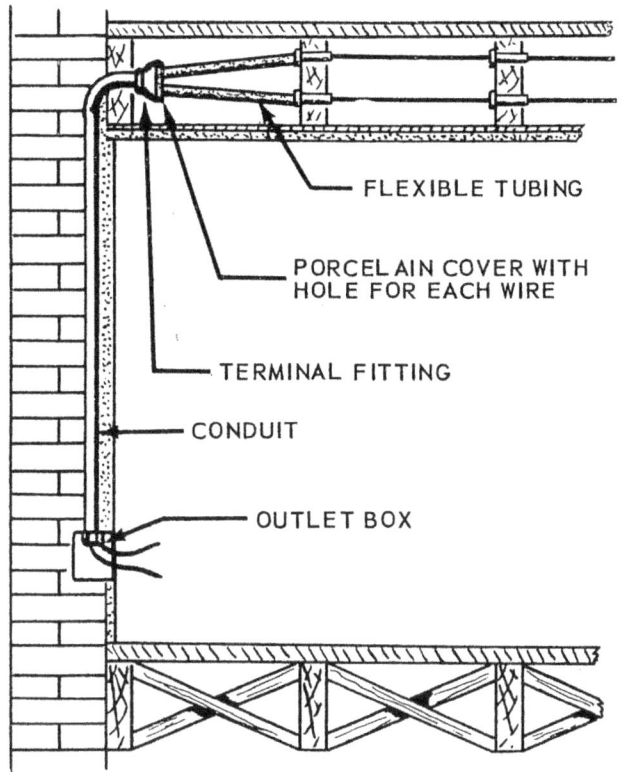

Figure 74. Changing from knob-and-tube to conduit wiring.

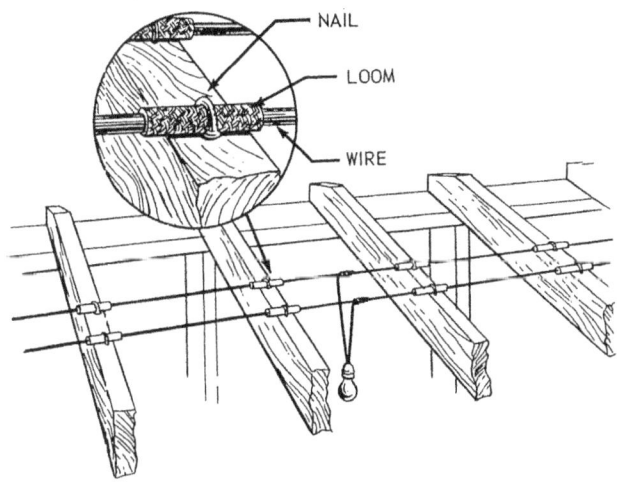

Figure 75. Expedient wiring.

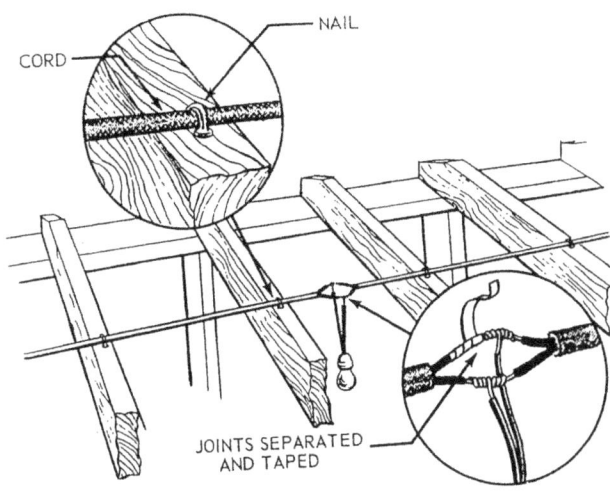

Figure 76. Expedient-wiring cord installation.

should be installed to protect the wire at the nail support. This is particularly essential if the wooden joists are wet. If possible, expedient wiring installations should be fastened to joists or studs at a distance of at least 7 feet above the floor. This will prevent accidental injury to the system or personnel which might result from the absence of damage protection.

(2) *Spacing.* The spacing of wires should be the same as that outlined for exposed knob and tube wiring.

(3) *Joints, splices, and taps.* Joints, splices, taps, and connections are made as outlined in paragraphs 60 through 65 with the exception of the procedures outlined for soldering and taping. In expedient wiring, soldering is omitted and only friction tape is used as a protective covering on the connections.

(4) *Fixture drops.* Fixture drops, preferable pigtail sockets, are installed by tapping their leads to wires, as shown in figure 75, and then taping the taps. The sockets are supported by the tap wires.

b. *Cord.* Figure 76 illustrates the application of a two-conductor cord in an expedient-wiring installation. The cord used should always be of the rubber-covered type and fastened securely to prevent the possibility of short circuits. The outer rubber sheathing should be removed at the point of fixture attachment and the fixture leads tapped into the conductor, purposely maintaining the separation between taps as shown. Each tap then should be individually taped.

Section III. BELL WIRING

75. Installation

Signal equipment may occasionally be supplied for 110-volt operation, in which case it must be installed in the same manner as outlets and sockets operating on this voltage. Most bells and buzzers are rated to operate on 8, 12, 18, or 24 volts ac or dc. These operating voltages are known as low-voltage or low-energy circuits. They can be installed with minimum consideration for circuit insulation since there is no danger of shock to personnel or fire due to short circuits. The wire commonly used is insulated with several layers of paraffin impregnated cotton or with a thermoplastic covering. Upon installation, these wires are attached to building members with small insulating staples and are threaded through building construction members without insulators.

76. Battery Operation

Early installations of low-voltage signal systems were powered by 6-volt dry cells. For example, 2 of these batteries were installed in series to service a 12-volt system. If the systems involved a number of signals over a large area, 1 or more batteries were added in series to offset the voltage drop. Though this type of alarm or announcing system is still being used and installed in some areas, it is a poor method because the batteries used as a power source require periodic replacement.

77. Transformer Operation

The majority of our present-day buzzer and bell signal systems operate from a transformer power source. The transformers are equipped to be mounted on outlet boxes and are constructed so that the 110-volt primary-winding leads normally extend from the side of the transformer adjacent to box mounting. These leads are permanently attached to the 110-volt power circuits, and the low-voltage secondary-winding leads of the transformer are connected to the bell circuit in a manner similar to a switch-and-light combination. If more than 1 buzzer and push button is to be installed they are paralleled with the first signal installation. A typical wiring schematic diagram for this type of installation is shown in figure 77.

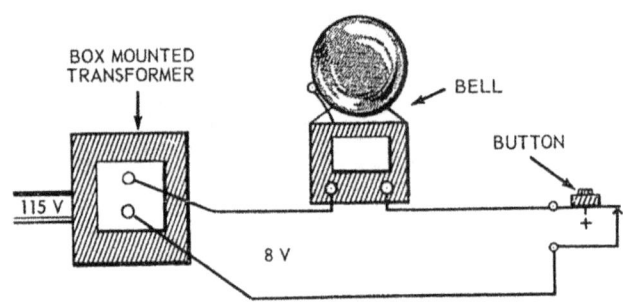

Figure 77. Bell and buzzer wiring.

www.ingramcontent.com/pod-product-compliance
Lightning Source LLC
Chambersburg PA
CBHW081821300426
44116CB00014B/2439